# Traveling Prehistoric Seas

*Dedicated to two Masters of Critical Thinking*

Joseph Needham and David Humiston Kelley

*Kelley on left, Needham on right*

# Traveling Prehistoric Seas

## Critical Thinking on Ancient Transoceanic Voyages

## Alice Beck Kehoe

 Routledge
Taylor & Francis Group

LONDON AND NEW YORK

First published 2016 by Left Coast Press, Inc.

Published 2016 by Routledge
2 Park Square, Milton Park, Abingdon, Oxon OX14 4RN
711 Third Avenue, New York, NY 10017, USA

*Routledge is an imprint of the Taylor & Francis Group, an informa business*

Library of Congress Cataloging-in-Publication Data
Names: Kehoe, Alice Beck, 1934-
Title: Traveling prehistoric seas : critical thinking on ancient transoceanic voyages / Alice Beck Kehoe.
Other titles: Critical thinking on ancient transoceanic voyages
Description: Walnut Creek, California : Left Coast Press, [2015] | Includes bibliographical references and index.
Identifiers: LCCN 2015030609| ISBN 9781629580661 (hardback : alk. paper) | ISBN 9781629580678 (pbk.          ) | ISBN 9781629580692 (consumer ebook)
Subjects: LCSH: America--Discovery and exploration--Polynesian. | America--Discovery and exploration--Pre-Columbian. | Discovery and exploration--History--To 1500. | Voyages and travel--History--To 1500. | Navigation--History--To 1500.
Classification: LCC E109.P65 K45 2015 | DDC 970.01--dc23
LC record available at http://lccn.loc.gov/2015030609


ISBN  978-1-62958-066-1 hardback
ISBN  978-1-62958-067-8 paperback

# Contents

## David B. Quinn on Samuel Eliot Morison

"The rejection of any pre-Columbian movement across the Atlantic apart from the Norse voyages leaves the ocean peculiarly empty for many centuries, but it is a justifiable reaction in an outstanding historian whose great merit is that he sees sharply in black-and-white terms and is therefore uniquely qualified to expound what is already known. He is perhaps too impatient to study the nuances of pre-Columbian enterprise." (Quinn, David B. 1974:22–23)

# Illustrations

## Figures

## Tables

# Preface

M y very first research project in archaeology was a paper for the high school Science Talent Search competition. My topic was pre-Columbian transpacific contacts. Reading Kroeber's massive 1948 textbook *Anthropology*, picked from the shelf in our public library, excited me with his demonstration of a Eurasian ecumene linked by spreads of all manner of things, from languages and crops to technologies and mythologies. I especially remember his discussion of depictions of the flying gallop, all four of a horse's feet in the air, untrue to actual gallop. Kroeber didn't think the pictures were merely visual illusions; he saw them to be evidence of diffusion of a pictorial convention. Decades later, Victor Mair (1988) published the diffusion of storyboards from India east to China and west to Europe. These were not world-shaking inventions, not like the spread of gunpowder that fascinated Joseph Needham (1986). These little devices clue us in to the almost infinite instances of person-to-person contacts across societies, most of them of little import, maybe assimilated. Ralph Linton gave us the mind-boggling accumulation of intersocietal borrowings that every ordinary American takes for granted as American (Linton 1931).

Quite to my surprise, I was among the forty finalists in that year's Science Talent Search; the Search wanted to broaden "science" beyond physics, chemistry, mathematics, and a little natural science. During our visit to Washington, D.C., for the final competition interviews, we were paired with practicing scientists in our fields of research. For me, it was Betty Meggers at the Smithsonian (because she was a woman, I think; she hadn't yet published on transpacific contacts). Dr. Meggers was kind, and it was exciting to go behind scenes at the Smithsonian;

that's all I recall from the visit. That summer, I landed a job typing catalogs in the Anthropology Department at the American Museum of Natural History in New York, commuting from my parents' home in a suburb. Once that task was completed, I still had three weeks before school started, and was given student-aide jobs helping curators. One of the curators was Gordon Ekholm.

For my Talent Search paper, I had used Ekholm and Heine-Geldern's publications. Their 1949 temporary exhibit in the American Museum was gone. I remember something like a catalog to it, but the Museum archivist couldn't find any catalog or working plan for the exhibit. Did I tell Dr. Ekholm about my prize paper, did we discuss transpacific contacts? No, I was too shy and respectful to initiate scholarly discussion with a curator. What I did gain from two summers' work and four years of student-aide volunteering while I was in college was solid respect for Dr. Ekholm. Several of the other curators in the department were strong personalities (Junius Bird, James Ford, Harry Tschopik, and of course, Margaret Mead); Ekholm was a hardworking, quiet man—a Minnesotan, he could have been from Lake Wobegon. One week, Robert Heine-Geldern visited, very much the European gentleman professor. From the student-aide's corner, I could see that these two men were earnest, highly trained and experienced professionals. Their work merited serious discussion.

Through the decades since, I remained interested in pre-Columbian contacts, continental as well as marine. Evidence for trade routes thousands of miles long was frequent, but we were taught to look at pre-contact societies as self-contained in their regions, "primitive" trade as barter for pretties and signs of high status, and means of traveling forbiddingly slow before European horses came in. Gradually, the more I came to know First Nations people—my dissertation was ethnographic, on orders from my Harvard professor concerned it might be assumed my husband wrote any archaeology I did—the more I became sensitized to the racism in the standard anthropological model. It's unwitting, that idea of American natives taught beginning in kindergarten—early socialization—and continuing in history and literature courses through college. My being a bright, active girl in a generation struggling against bias against women pushed me to suspect dominant models. My husband and I did plenty of straight archaeology in Montana and Saskatchewan, establishing our bona fides as field archaeologists; alongside our mainstream work, I continued thinking outside the box, facilitated by our friendship with David H. and Jane Holden Kelley in Calgary. I watched as Dave Kelley and the equally brilliant and modest

Floyd Lounsbury gained fame by breaking the Maya writing system. All our peers respected the mainstream archaeology performed by these scholars, as they had Ekholm's work. How, then, could their work on long-distance contacts be dismissed without consideration?

The answer, my friends, was blowing in the wind.[1] Euroamericans, moral people, want to feel secure and good in their American homes. From the beginning of massive European immigration, they legitimated conquest, displacement, and colonization by painting First Nations as semi-naked savages in wilderness. Right to replace them rested on the Doctrine of Discovery in international (European) law. If any other nations had discovered America, sixteenth-century contenders would have to cede rights (Lyman 1990). Anyone who questioned the reigning model and narrative has been counseled that they risked career, they might not be employed, their judgment would be considered faulty. Those few, rightly confident in their scholarly ability, who would not abandon such research were held to a double standard, their acceptable work praised while their long-distance contacts research was ignored.

Kelley, Lounsbury, Ekholm, Heine-Geldern, and Joseph Needham are no longer here to adduce their investigations and conclusions. The data have not died. Instead, with DNA research, their lines of reasoning have been much strengthened. When Mitch Allen urged me to write a text on pre-Columbian transoceanic contacts from the standpoint of Critical Thinking, that clicked. This book does not oppose mainstream archaeology. It calls up basic scientific logic and principles of evaluation to assess possibilities, plausibilities, and probabilities of a selection of the better-attested contacts. There are no frauds, myths, or mysteries, no fantastic archaeology in these pages. A good scientist looks at data.

## Acknowledgments

I am grateful to many colleagues who very generously shared papers and photos and seriously discussed issues. Above all, I am grateful to Mitch Allen for insisting that I write this text, and expertly critiquing the draft. Stephen Jett has been walking the walk, talking the talk, in the Sauer tradition, for years, always a good comrade. I feel insignificant as I write about Dave Kelley, Joseph Needham, Gordon Ekholm, Carl Sauer, Roger Green, not to mention some with whom I've talked recently, whom I'll refrain from specifying in this sentence. The best minds are intrigued by the conundrums of pre-Columbian transoceanic contacts. It's been a privilege to pursue the topic with such open-minded, intelligent scientists.

Alphabetically, my gratitude for help and discussion on research to: Mark Adams; David Anthony; Marshall Becker; Robert Bednarik; Roger Blench; Carole Crumley; Ruth Gruhn; Frederik Hallgren; Terry Jones; Annette Kolodny; Kristian Kristiansen; Victor Mair; Elizabeth Matisoo-Smith; Stuart Piggott (who belongs with the deceased scholars, but I didn't write about him in the book); Thomas Riley; Daniel Sandweiss; Alice Storey; Karine Taché; John Terrell; Robin Torrence; Jane Waldbaum; Marshall Weisler; Peter White; Diana Zaragoza. The usual disclaimer: Listing these good colleagues does not imply they agree with what I say in this text.

For support in production of the book, Ryan Harris and Lisa Devenish have been exemplary.

Last, and least only in size, Lacey napped on the printer by my desk, making sure I was safe, while Suzette purred on my lap, mitigating the stress of thinking critically.

## Chapter 1

# Critical Thinking Method

S cience, history, engineering, philosophy, medicine, law, and business all demand skill in Critical Thinking. Practitioners must look for empirical data, then reason logically from observing data to interpreting their significance. We must always be aware that "knowledge" accepted uncritically can undermine Critical Thinking. We realize that in matters of spiritual faith, people may choose to accept teachings from revered authority; in matters of science, authority and custom are not admissible. So we say, yet many examples exist of scientists rejecting valid data and reasonable interpretations because influential academics claim they can't be true. To think critically requires more than data and reason; it often requires resisting received dictates about what could be possible.

In his influential text, *The Structure of Scientific Revolutions* (1962), Thomas Kuhn described "normal science" as fitting observations into a standard paradigm, that is, a model. Over time, scientists would see data that appeared anomalous, unexpected, or contradictory to the paradigm. Scientists who insist on confronting colleagues with anomalies risk careers. A generation ago, the received notion that Pueblo communities in the United States Southwest were peaceful people caused observations of traumatic deaths associated with destroyed villages to be rejected as mistaken, and at least one graduate student who refused to delete these data from his dissertation was denied the doctoral degree. As Thomas Kuhn expected, thirty years of more and more such anomalous data shifted the paradigm to accommodate the fact that Pueblo communities suffered warfare, recounted in their histories to archaeologists who would listen. Kuhn's model of science was not steady progress toward verified knowledge, but a series of plateaus separated by jumps from one paradigm to another.

Peaceful Pueblos were part of the romantic myth of the noble savage, a way of criticizing the violence and greed in modern American life. The notion that America had been deeply different from the "Old World" of Eurasia and Africa supported European invaders' policies of eradicating native cultures in favor of imposing European practices and religion. American First Nations had failed to develop true civilizations, the conquering powers asserted, and this could be because they had been cut off from Old World religions, arts, and sciences. Their ancestors had walked over the Bering Strait when sea level was lower, in the Ice Age, then were isolated when the climate warmed and the Strait was flooded. Russian explorers' observations of Inuit traders in Siberia, and documentation of Chukchi and Inuit traveling by boat over the Strait, including intermarriage, was ignored. So have been data attesting to contacts between the Americas and the Old World farther south.

If Kuhn was correct about the power of anomalies to advance scientific understanding, these anomalous data relating to pre-Columbian transoceanic contacts ought to be critically examined. DNA tests are now presenting similarities that cannot be dismissed as subjective opinions. Charred sweet potatoes excavated by highly reputable professional archaeologists, dated to a thousand years ago and identified as a South American species, indisputably prove a round-trip voyage between Central Polynesia and northwestern South America (Green 2005:50, 61; Roullier et al. 2013). A new paradigm has been forced upon archaeology.

## The Paradigm of a pre-Columbian Global World

Critical thinking rests upon open-minded collection of data. A priori rejection of certain data because "everyone knows" something "is impossible" isn't scientific. Scientists should examine how data have been obtained, consider how they may fit known scenarios, and suggest an explanation that accounts for the data in a straightforward manner. In the historical sciences, data are literally given, not manipulated in a laboratory, and human behavior is observed in the widest range globally and historically. The critical thinker neither throws out babies with the dirty bathwater nor embraces every fantasy of extraterrestrials and spirits. What is usually most difficult for a person wishing to think critically is to be skeptical of what "everyone knows"—that which was learned in childhood or taught by authority figures.

In this book, we begin with the myth that Christopher Columbus discovered a hitherto unknown continent. The prevailing paradigm has been that only the development of fifteenth-century European ships enabled humans to cross oceans. That idea is disproved by histories of Asian ships, including the vaka—seagoing canoes from Oceana—that settled Polynesia. Once the feasibility of oceanic voyages before 1492 and by non-Europeans is accepted, on strong evidence, the possibilities of long-distance transmission of technologies, arts, and cosmologies are greatly increased. So, too, is demand for careful evaluation of sources of data. Then comparisons must be sought in archaeological and historical records, without preconceptions about "primitives" and "civilizations." Best fit can be presented, followed by discussion of its strengths and weaknesses. As is explained in chapter 4, historical sciences seek the more probable explanation, not absolute proof—actual history is infinitely vast and very imperfectly preserved, beyond the reach of human thinking. Scientific thinking in historical sciences begins with data recovered from archaeological, paleontological, and geological surveys and excavations, then proceeds to compare these data with historical texts and present day similar organisms, structures, or processes. The present day or historically documented best-fit comparison becomes the most tenable—most probable—explanation.

Although the new paradigm superficially appears to resemble nineteenth-century researches into diffusion of culture traits, it is significantly different (Storey and Jones 2011). In chapter 3 of this book, we adduce evidence for remarkable antiquity of ocean crossings and recognize several millennia-old major traditions of shipbuilding and navigation, particularly strong for marine travel in Asian seas. For Critical Thinking, this wealth of data on seafaring provides a secure foundation for the next step: historical documentation of long-distance maritime trips in the medieval and earlier eras, and archaeological evidence for transportation of material items to and from islands (chapter 4). This step supports the basic knowledge that ocean-going vessels were constructed and used for millennia, with concrete documentation of motives for travel. Chapter 5 introduces the definitive case: Polynesian voyaging, in which the means (seagoing ships), motive (cultural tradition of eastward exploring), and supporting data drawn from reputable excavations, radiocarbon dating of actual transported items, and DNA identities combine to make the case for high probability. Chapter 9 presents the other indubitable case, the Norse in northeastern North America from 1000 CE to mid-fifteenth century.

Subsequent chapters make the argument for cases less well supported than that for Polynesians, yet still probable. This book does not discuss low probability cases such as extraterrestrials, Templar knights looking for or carrying a Holy Grail, Egyptian religion, lost continents (Atlantis, Mu), lost tribes of Israel, exiled ancient Chinese kings, or

Christian hermits. While transoceanic trips would be possible for all but extraterrestrials, recent lost continents are geologically improbable, and the other cases impute motives not congruent with historical documentation of the groups suggested. In contrast to improbable cases, movements of valued cultivated plants have a higher degree of probability, as do transmission of useful technologies such as paper and the impressive architectural art styles known to have diffused throughout all of Asia and Island Southeast Asia, to the latter areas by seagoing ships (chapters 7 and 8).

## Diffusion

Ah, the D word! Dr. Phuddy H. Duddy, the famous American archaeologist, sits in the bar during a Society for American Archaeology meeting, speaking an Indo-European language originating in the Russian steppes and carried overseas to all the continents. He is drinking beer developed in the eastern Mediterranean, exchanging business cards of paper invented in China, wearing clothes of cotton domesticated in India and cut to a pattern from the Asian steppe. Mention the word *diffusion*, and he sneers. "That went out ages ago with Elliot Smith's nonsense about Egyptian pyramid builders being the Olmec," he tells his students.

Contrary to Phuddy Duddy's scorn, diffusion is not an outdated term. Sociologists and geographers have charted the diffusion of farm innovations in Iowa and Sweden, the diffusion of electric lighting in the United States, the diffusion of kindergartens, diffusion of automobiles, and on and on to the diffusion of smartphones and the Internet (Rogers 2003). In earlier eras, gunpowder and printing were diffused from Asia to Europe; earlier still, domesticated livestock, horse-riding, and wheeled transport (Hodgen 1964; Anthony 2007). Each of these cases is true diffusion: the introduced artifact or behavior spreading throughout a population, like molecules spreading throughout a gas. Or, like Starbucks coffee shops spreading to nearly every business corner in every city.

Pre-Columbian voyages did not necessarily lead to diffusion. In the case of sweet potatoes in Polynesia, the cultigen did diffuse through most of the islands, welcomed as a better root crop than its predecessor, Asian-derived taro. Other items, such as figurines mounted on wheel-and-axle platforms, appear in a limited area and in what seem to be ritual sites, not generally in households; technically, they did not diffuse through a population. Contacts with foreigners can lead to stimulus diffusion: an unfamiliar object or technology sparking invention of a similar but modified object (Kroeber 1952). Stimulus diffusion has led to proliferation of social media applications. An unfamiliar example is Catholic Reformation adoption of Aztec realistic pictures of human hearts, seen by missionaries at temples in Mexico and then pictured in Jesus' chest in European paintings meant to humanize the deity (Kehoe 1979). This case illustrates how meaning can change while a picture does not—the Aztec heart representing human sacrifices to nourish the power of the sun, and the Catholic heart representing a deity's love for devotees. When assessing probability of contact, the differences between diffusion of an introduced item, limited acceptance of it, or stimulus diffusion should be kept in mind.

## Independent Invention

Stimulus diffusion leads into the large space between contact introductions and independent inventions. The case for frequent independent inventions rests upon our species' common genetics, brain structure, and biological needs. Everyone needs to eat, drink, sleep, and be sheltered from damaging weather, plus most humans want to reproduce—obviously, only those who did passed on their genes. Finding that tropical forest residents shelter themselves from rain by placing large leaves over a light pole frame doesn't mean the idea was invented once and diffused throughout the tropics, because it is obvious and easy. On the other hand, it is unlikely that people who had no draft animals or wheeled vehicles would invent wheels with axles to propel animal figurines, especially when the occurrence of these mobile figurines is very limited in time and space in Mesoamerica, and nowhere else in the Americas.

To claim independent invention, we would need to show that the two apparent inventions are far apart in time as well as in space, for space can be traversed but time cannot. Most claims endeavor to show precursor inventions that could lead to the item in question; for example, wood block printing leading to the printing of books. In that large space between certain borrowings and independent invention, we see that wood block printing of pictures in Europe made it easy for Gutenberg and others to see how alphabet letters could be formed and used to print books; they had learned from travelers that this was being done in China with Chinese writing characters. Also in that large space are similarities in flint- and chert-knapped tools, given the crystalline structure of this class of rock and common purposes of cutting meat and scraping hides, activities developed many thousands of years ago and diffused with the spread of humans across the continents. Roughed-out chunks of flint or chert in a quarry often look like very ancient Paleolithic hand axes. Found in a prehistoric quarry in a Washington, D.C. park, such chunks were thought to indicate great antiquity for humans in North America, until careful comparisons of many chunks, and comparisons with village trash from relatively large First Nations communities, showed that the park site is a quarry and the chunks had simply not been removed for further working (Holmes 1897). This pioneer archaeological investigation is a landmark in scientific method in a historical science, with its emphasis on unbiased collection of data and broad but detailed comparisons.

Independence in inventions is a very important subject today, not only in anthropology but in business. Thousands of attorneys earn their livings advising or litigating issues of whether patents infringe on other claimed independent inventions. Histories of science reveal that debates over independence, and over priorities, of inventions began with the discussion of whether Isaac Newton or Gottfried Leibniz invented calculus, and this continues to the present day (Merton 1973:287–288). Our modern Western culture believes individuals possess capabilities to deploy for personal advancement or failure, so that success in society is a sign of an individual's superior qualities, while conversely, ordinariness signals limited abilities or laziness. Political philosopher C. B. Macpherson (1962) termed this ideology "possessive individualism," linking it to modern Western culture's emphasis on private property, including workers' property in themselves to sell their labor. Money and fame link, as do poverty and ignominy. Hence, "independent invention" is emotionally loaded in our society. "Possessive individualism" may seem far removed from archaeological debates, but societal values are deeply inculcated and can subconsciously influence judgment even in science, as sociologist Robert Merton described for many instances.

Inventions are usually cumulative. A better can opener cannot be invented until tin and aluminum cans are invented, and commercial canning and marketing through neighborhood food stores is developed. These processes depend upon rapid transport of large cargoes, and technology related to railroads, highways, and airplanes. All these are the result of multiple processes of extracting, refining, and distributing metals and other materials; and on this chain continues. Truly independent inventions are extremely rare. When considering the issue of transmission versus independent invention, probability lies on the side of transmission. Independent invention in a particular case needs to be supported by evidence of precedent conditions for each example. The case for transmission of wheel-and-axle mounted animal figurines in Mesoamerica rests upon the absence of any precedent conditions, neither wheels and axles, nor wagons associated with domesticated animals. Dramatically, no follow-up took place, either—no inventions of wheeled transport devices or domestication of animals for transport in Mesoamerica (not even importation of llamas from South America). Cumulative antecedents historically are precondition for inventions.

## Historical Contingencies

Franz Boas, the immigrant German scientist who struggled to combat racist ideas prevalent in American anthropology in the late nineteenth and twentieth centuries, insisted on the principle of historical particularism: every society has its own history combining population movements and encounters with adaptation to its environment. Unique events occur, whether natural disasters, trade markets, wars, alliances, charismatic persons, gifted artists, philosophers, or leaders. No universal line of cultural development exists and no end stage exists, but always, dynamic adjustments to local possibilities and setbacks can be found. Boas's view did not sit well with American propaganda about the White Man's Manifest Destiny. In the next chapter, you will read about the myth of Columbus invoked to promote that ideology. Here, the point is that historical particularism supports the picture of antecedent conditions important for inventions. It also provides, in hundreds of ethnographic-ethnohistorical studies, an abundance of examples of contacts between societies and resulting transmissions of art, technologies, stories, cultigens, and persons.

Archaeologist Peter Jordan carried out a detailed comparative analysis of constituents of cultural traditions in three societies, using both ethnographic observations and historical and archaeological data (Jordan 2015). His subjects were Siberian Eastern Khanty who combine winter hunting and trapping, summer fishing, and herding reindeer; Coast Salish in southern British Columbia, Canada, who lived by fishing, primarily for salmon; and northern California First Nations living by fishing, hunting, and harvesting acorns and other plants. The two American groups are termed hunter-gatherers although they cultivated root crops, maintained berry bushes, and the Californians planted acorn oak orchards. Trade was economically and socially important. Jordan found that societies' transmission of cultural behavior, including material items, down through generations tended to show sets that cohered, such as language, but also many customs and crafts that had different histories might change or drop out. Items with strong pragmatic use, such as hunting and fishing equipment, could be modified or replaced, often with discussion among the practitioners (Jordan 2015:200–201). Aesthetic elements, as on baskets in California, showed transmission across political and language communities (Jordan 2015:300). Above all, Jordan came to appreciate the effects of historical contingencies (Jordan 2015:312, 347).

Jordan's empirical study of culture transmissions counters the Western stereotype of other societies being enslaved to tradition and hostile to strangers and to innovation. Especially pertinent to this book is his choice of two Pacific coastal regions where ships from Asia might have made landfalls, carried on the Japan (Kuroshio) Current originating off Taiwan and the Philippines, flowing eastward past Japan. Both the Coast Salish region of British Columbia and northern California have temperate rain forests kept moist and warm by this strong current along their shores. Alternately, trading expeditions and shorter trading enterprises could have sailed around the North Pacific Rim to the Aleutians, southern Alaska, British Columbia, and on south. Iron for knives came to Northwest Coast communities as early as 1450 CE, possibly across the North Pacific (Acheson 2003:227; McMillan 1999:90–91, 157–158). For critical theory, Jordan's combination of firsthand ethnographic observation of Khanty life and practices, down to minutiae of ski bindings and sledge runners, along with direct discussion with them about why they do as they do, creates a firm database for his comparisons drawn from earlier ethnographies. His discovery of the importance of historical contingencies stands on this body of empirical data.

## The Argument of this Book

The purpose of this book is to demonstrate how Critical Thinking can be applied to data in the historical sciences. The essential point is that historical data cannot be manipulated in a laboratory to test hypotheses; instead, its probability is evaluated. To do this, the scientist is obliged to seek as much relevant data as can be discovered, testing probabilities of interpretations—a process known as IBE (inference to the best explanation). Claims for pre-Columbian contacts between the Americas and the "Old World" (Eurasia, Africa, and Oceania), have been controversial since Columbus's discovery was announced in 1492. Twenty-first-century archaeological and genetic researches have significantly changed probabilities in several classic cases for such voyages. They make the issues ripe for critical thinking today.

The following three chapters set the stage for presenting evidence for pre-Columbian transoceanic contacts. First is an explanation of the myth that Columbus discovered a New World completely isolated from the world known by Europeans before his 1492 voyage. Only by understanding the ideology of Manifest Destiny and European nations' efforts to legitimize their invasions, conquests, and dispossessions can we separate bias from evidence of pre-Columbian voyages. The subsequent two chapters present evidence for seaworthy boats and for long distance trips before 1492. It may surprise readers that the first people, women and men, in Australia, 50,000 years ago in the Ice Age, crossed open ocean, perhaps on rafts. Surprising also are the pilgrimages of medieval Icelandic and Greenland Norse from their far north homes, eastward across all of Europe to Jerusalem, with returns. Trade prospects stimulated merchants throughout Asia and the islands of the western Pacific to build large, stable ocean-going vessels and explore widely from the Indian Ocean to farthest Indonesia and the Philippines, and likely occasionally farther, since the time of the Egyptian pharaohs four thousand years ago.

A remarkable culture systematically exploring the Pacific began about that time in southeast Asia and Taiwan, moving into western Oceania (and also in the opposite direction to Madagascar and Africa). Always seeking unoccupied islands to colonize, these Austronesians gave rise to the Polynesians who discovered every island in the Pacific, even small, remote Rapa Nui (Easter Island) two thousand kilometers (1,600 miles) from their originating communities in the central Pacific. Chapter 5 presents the history of Polynesian seafaring, the high probability that its strong cultural tradition of voyaging to find new lands reached the Americas after the settling of Hawai'i and Rapa Nui, and the archaeological data from well-excavated, radiocarbon dated projects proving at least one return journey from South America to Central Polynesian islands, and landfalls on the Chilean coast in South America. Genetic analyses of sweet potato and chicken bones corroborate the archaeological inferences. Critical Thinking finds the amount, breadth, and quality of data for Polynesian trips to America to be highly probable.

The subsequent three chapters examine data adduced for carrying organisms, technologies, and art, architecture, and mythologies across the oceans—mostly across the Pacific—before the voyages of Columbus and of Magellan (1500 CE). Geographer Carl Sauer (1889–1975) argued that finding organisms on one continent that evolved on another, particularly organisms associated with humans such as cultigens or infections, is historically important evidence for otherwise undocumented relationships between societies. South American sweet potatoes in central Polynesia a thousand years ago are such historically significant evidence. Technologies developed through generations on one continent, suddenly appearing full blown on another, are similar evidence of contact. Examples include platforms on wheels revolving on axles, common in Eurasia for nearly six thousand years but appearing in the Americas only once, around 1100 CE, in a limited area along the Isthmus of Tehuantepec between the Pacific and the Atlantic in Mexico, and never extended to other uses of wheels and axles. Paper for books and for cut-outs of ritual figures, developed in China for two thousand years and present in Mesoamerica when the Spanish invaded in the early sixteenth century CE, is another likely candidate for transpacific transmission, because the process of making paper is complex, and known to have diffused from China to Europe in the thirteenth century CE. Asia has a very long history of felting fibers for cloth, with paper an end product of a series of steps similar to felting, while felting is not known to be indigenous in the Americas. Art, architecture, and mythologies include a number of similarities between Asia and the Americas, most of them themes rather than very specific close parallels. Arguments against transmission of art and myth motifs, such as "lion-dog" guardian statues of fearsome creatures that are doglike but feline too, or of serpent deities, insist that human experience of the natural world inspires artists to create threatening figures based on fierce dogs, big cats, and serpents. Even a serpent with feathers, in Mesoamerica and in Asia (the naga), is argued to be a natural combination of an earthbound power with a sky power. Critical thinking looks for clusters of parallel traits, that is to say, collocations, that are less likely to have been independently invented all at one time. The final chapter in this section of the book looks at transatlantic crossings, of which Norse use of northeastern America is historically documented in addition to providing archaeological data. Skepticism about Greenland Norse crossing to Canada for resources lacking in Greenland highlights the power of the Columbus myth to deny even these medieval Europeans a history, technology, and motive to utilize American assets.

Last in the book are two chapters recapitulating this chapter's exposition of Critical Thinking and its application to the cases at issue surrounding pre-Columbian transoceanic contact. Scientific logic is fundamental, as is the difference between historical sciences and the physical sciences more familiar to science students. While the book is aimed at undergraduate readers, these chapters challenge conventional ideas about science uncritically accepted by some archaeologists. Whether or not a reader is convinced that pre-Columbian transoceanic contacts between continents are feasible, or that they happened, is less the book's goal than is teaching Critical Thinking.

## Chapter 2

# The Myth of Columbus

"**I**n fourteen hundred and ninety-two, Columbus sailed the ocean blue." This is true. It is not true that he discovered a new world, and it is not even true that he was the first documented European to see the Americas. Bjarni Herjólfsson earned that notice when his ship was blown off course to Greenland in 986.

Bjarni, a merchant working between Norway and Iceland, was traveling to see his parents who had recently moved from Iceland to the new Norse settlement in Greenland. When storm and fog lifted, Bjarni and his crew saw a forested land they knew was not Greenland. Anxious to find his parents, Bjarni refused his crew's appeals to go ashore during the several days they coasted along Labrador. At the Greenland Norse settlement and then at the Norwegian royal court, Bjarni described the unknown land he had seen, inspiring Leif, son of the Greenland colony's leader, Eirik the Red. Leif organized a settler party to explore the Canadian coast west of Greenland, from northern Labrador to the Gulf of St. Lawrence. L'Anse aux Meadows, a Norse settlement on the northern end of Newfoundland that has been radiocarbon dated to around 1000 CE, may be Leif's short-lived colony (Kolodny 2012:51–57). Two Icelandic family epics, the *Grænlendinga saga* (Greenlanders' Saga) and *Eiríks saga rauða* (Saga of Erik the Red), describe these explorations and colonizing efforts.

How could textbooks generally ignore this credible, documented history of European colonization of the western side of the North Atlantic, Greenland, and its Norse farmers' use of the Canadian Maritimes? Why is the Italian mariner sailing five hundred years after Leif Eiriksson lauded as the discoverer of an unknown new world? Why, to delve deeper, is any European credited with discovering a new world teeming with the millions descended from real discoverers coming from Asia near the end of the Ice Age, fifteen thousand years ago? Racism? Propaganda? The politics of capitalist competition?

Columbus's "discovery of America" is a myth, the kind of myth that anthropologists have studied for more than a century. Bronislaw Malinowski, a prominent British-resident anthropologist, termed myths like the one crediting Columbus *social charters*. Such myths profess to tell, in the form of a story, the origin of a community or nation. Once upon a time, says the story, a hero (or heroine) transformed a people into the community we know. Because the hero was super intelligent or magically powerful, perhaps divine or divinely blessed, the community has prospered up to today. Moral of the story: What we do, and have done, is right. Like a charter for a school or business, a social charter myth prescribes a community's basic organization and operations.

Columbus, in the myth, "opened a New World" for exploitation by the major European powers of his day.[1] At that time, 1492, Scandinavian nations were not yet strong enough to contend with the more southern European nations. Greenland's climate had worsened for farmers and the Norse Greenlanders had abandoned their two settlements. The myth of Columbus is a story of an Italian working for Spain, dealing with Portuguese, and challenged by other Italians working for England. It is a story with a clear, exciting plot. The well-told story has no space for sidebars about Columbus's predecessors. They are relegated to "prehistory," thereby excluded from history. Critical thinking demands they be discussed.

## Roots of the Columbus Myth

Cristoforo Colombo, born 1451 in Genoa, Italy, died 1506, was an ambitious seaman determined to forge a place in the forefront of his peers in a time of fervid efforts to find seaways between Atlantic Europe and fabled riches of the Orient. Conquest of Constantinople (modern Istanbul, Turkey) by the Ottoman Turks in 1453 had chopped off Europe's accustomed source of Chinese silks, Southeast Asian spices, and other luxury goods from Asia. European entrepreneurs, often supported by their monarchs, searched for new shipping routes out of their Atlantic ports, sailing along western Africa and finding a route to the Indian Ocean around the Cape of Good Hope at the south end of Africa, or sailing into the Atlantic hoping to reach China and Japan by circling the globe westward. Colombo calculated this distance, using figures from the classical Greek scientist Aristotle. Because he didn't realize that Aristotle's "league" measurement wasn't the same as the

**Figure 2.1.** European depiction of heroic Columbus encountering New World savages; engraving by Theodor de Bry (1528–1598).Courtesy the Library of Congress, via Wikimedia Commons

"league" of medieval Europe, Colombo's result was much shorter than the correct distance.[2] He insisted to possible patrons, in Portugal and Spain, that he had skills and knowledge for a successful voyage, if they would give him ships and men.

At first denied, in part because a Spanish committee decided, correctly, that his projected sailing distance was erroneous, in 1492 Spain's king and queen decided to risk sponsoring him. Their conquest of Muslim-ruled Granada early in 1492 ended ten years' expense of war, bringing them new wealth that they augmented by decreeing that all Jews who refused to convert to Christianity must emigrate, forfeiting to the Crown the possessions they could not carry away. With the three ships the monarchs provided to him out of this confiscation, Colombo sailed into the Atlantic on the morning after the last of the ships laden with Jews left the Spanish port. Two-and-a-half months later, Colombo's ships encountered Caribbean island outliers of America.

Surprisingly, Columbus wasn't hailed as Discoverer of America until America, that is, the United States, was born. A patriotic young Princeton graduate, Philip Freneu, wrote an epic poem "The Pictures of Columbus" in 1774, published in 1788. His Columbus displays "every sentiment that sways the brave," seeking royal patrons who share his "daring aims and persevering soul" (Bauer 2011:15, 18). During the same period, shortly after the American Revolution, a second patriot, Joel Barlow, published in 1787 a poem tying the new nation to Biblical themes: Columbus is the new Moses traveling through "dreary wastes" to the Promised Land (Bauer 2011:28). The new nation that won its heroic struggles against nefarious King George across the ocean praised the non-British Genoese who claimed America for Britain's enemy, Spain. "It is not a conquered, but a discovered country. It came not to the king by descent, but was explored by the settlers," wrote John Adams, second president of the United States (Usner 2013:636). In 1791, dictionary maker Noah Webster, who had established an American English, also published "The Story of Columbus" in a reader for American children, praising the hero's "courage and coolness in the hour of danger" (Bauer 2011:23).

A generation later, in 1828, popular writer Washington Irving published a thick biography of the hero Columbus, enhancing it by embroidering what he found in archives. Founding Fathers Jefferson and John Adams had recently died, both on July 4, 1826. Populist General Andrew Jackson was elected president in 1828, forcibly cleansing the United States of its First Nations east of the Mississippi. Strong-willed, manly, vigorous Columbus matched Jackson's forceful personality and determination to seize the lands of the feckless natives. Soon after Pearl Harbor in 1941, Columbus was hailed a naval hero, with U. S. Admiral and Harvard historian Samuel Eliot Morison publishing in 1942 another popular biography, *Admiral of the Ocean Sea*. Scholars point out how cannily Christoforo Colombo composed his public letters to the Spanish rulers Ferdinand and Isabella, providing plenty of self-praise that easily rendered him the hero Americans sought.

For the fourth centenary of Columbus's discovery in 1892, the rapidly growing city of Chicago hosted an awesome exposition of America's glories and power. Building a "White City" at the shore of its inland sea, Lake Michigan, Chicago constructed imposing stone exhibition halls filled with scientific, technical, and luxury marvels. Outside, a midway stretched westward, offering fairgoers the sight of exotic "primitive" people in native costumes beside their huts, interspersed with hootchie-cootchie dancers and carnival games. At the lakefront, the SS *Christopher Columbus*, largest ship on the Great Lakes, provided excursion

**Figure 2.2.** Maliseet First Nation artist Bernard Perley depicts his people's views of several European discoveries. Bernard C. Perley, used with permission

sails to better view the magnificent vista. So ambitious it couldn't be completed in time for 1892, the World Columbian Exposition of 1893 epitomized Columbus opening the New World in the West. Columbus Day, October 12, was celebrated in towns and schools in the calendar of American civil religion, calling up patriotic exhortations to emulate the daring vision, the steadfast courage, of this first civilized man to broach the wilderness.

One century later, the fifth centenary provoked a radically opposite commemoration ("commemoration," many insisted, not "celebra-
tion"). America in 1992 had increasing First Nations[3] populations and
burgeoning Latin American and Asian numbers. The First Nations ob-
jected to initial expectations that this quincentenary would be marked
by parades honoring the heroic Genoese, with pretty White girls draped
and crowned as Columbia. Fourteen hundred and ninety-two marked,
for First Nations, inauguration of five hundred years of slaughter, hor-
rible new diseases, destruction of homes, seizure of lands, ethnocidal
denial of their heritages, imposed poverty, and tearing children from
parents' arms to incarcerate them in cold, distant boarding schools. October 12 was a day of mourning for them. Significantly, when a national Jubilee Commission was appointed in 1985, no American Indian
was included. Backlash from a range of First Nations leaders calling
attention to the devastation unleashed by Columbus's invasions of Caribbean islands upset the Commission's planning. The "Quincentenary
. . . had become a battleground for our entire view of Western culture"
(Summerhill and Williams 2000:119).

*Postcolonialism* is the label for this perspective on Western culture.
After five centuries of aggrandizement, European powers rocking
from the ravages of World War II decided that administering far-flung
colonies was too costly. Global companies undergirded by international banking could better exploit Third World countries. Although
economic independence was a chimera for most of the new nations,
their intelligentsia, freed of the colonizer's yoke, developed subaltern
literatures challenging foreign conquerors' versions of their histories
(Kolodny 2015). American First Nations' views were voiced by scholars and writers chronicling true American heroes, from Popé who led
the Pueblos' revolt against Spanish domination in 1680, through Te-
cumseh's alliance of Indian troops with Britain in the War of 1812, to
the 28 American Indian soldiers awarded the highest honor given by
the United States, the Congressional Medal of Honor. Civilian heroes,
too, are celebrated, including Pocahontas, whose diplomatic marriage to John Rolfe stabilized the Jamestown settlement; Sacajawea,
the captive young concubine bravely guiding Lewis and Clark; Hin-
maton-yalatkit (Chief Joseph), desperately seeking safety in Canada
for his Nimipu in 1877; and twentieth-century stalwarts like David
Sohappy, a Wanapum protecting his people's salmon fishery. From
a postcolonial standpoint, Columbus is the poster boy for European
imperialists' self-serving lies.

## The Myth of Columbus and the Myth of Progress

While the expanding United States was creating Columbus the model hero, it similarly beatified Progress. Pictured like a Greek goddess, Progress much resembled Columbia, both depicted treading in the air above American pioneers in covered wagon trains heading west. The goddess's outstretched right arm pointed to the farther sea. She might be labeled Destiny, referring to the popular slogan coined in 1845 to launch the Mexican War, *America's Manifest Destiny is to stretch from sea to sea.*

War-mongering for empire was justified by racism, alleging all darker-skinned people to be inferior to fair Northwest Europeans. Scales of progress to civilization were constructed, with American Indians and Africans on the bottom, China, Japan, and India in the middle, and the imperial European powers at the top. Lewis Henry Morgan, a lawyer in Rochester, New York, did fieldwork among Iroquois near his home and on month-long trips to see Indians along the Missouri River. Climaxing his studies, in 1877 he published *Ancient Society*, setting up three stages of human progress, from Savagery through Barbarism (simple agricultural villages) to Civilization. Accusing Cortés and the other Spanish conquistadors of exaggerating Mexican cities and pomp, he declared no native American nations had achieved Civilization, not even the Aztecs.

Morgan's scheme found favor with the founder of the Smithsonian's Bureau of American Ethnology, the intrepid explorer of the Colorado River, Major John Wesley Powell, and also with English aristocrat John Lubbock, whose own popular books, *Pre-historic Times* (1865) and *The Origin of Civilisation and the Primitive Condition of Man: Mental and Social Condition of Savages* (1870), illustrated the "lowest stage of savagery" with photos of South American Indians beggared by commercial seal hunters killing off their principal food. Morgan's and Lubbock's idea of native America goes back to John Locke's 1689 statement that "in the beginning all the World was America" (Locke 1689: Chapter 5, par. 49). This rendered native America the exemplar of the primitive stage beyond which Europeans developed their superior societies. Serving as spinmeister to the politician Earl of Shaftesbury, Locke persuasively justified his patron's taking of Carolina from its inhabitants (Kehoe 2009). Columbus's discovery of a New World becomes discovery of a benighted world separated from fulfilling God's command to improve the earth.

"Progress" may seem obvious. See how computers progressed from huge rooms of vacuum tubes in stacks, to the powerful little device that fits in a hand. See how aircraft progressed from flimsy one-man contraptions to airships carrying hundreds across oceans. Mechanization of work has certainly progressed to relieve men and women and children of backbreaking labor. "Progress" is often equated with technological development[4], belatedly acknowledging downsides in pollution and destruction. The nineteenth-century idea, promulgated by English popular philosopher Herbert Spencer, that there is a vital force propelling us in progress toward a perfect world, was blasted by the bestiality of World War I. That horror fit the medieval belief that, far from progressing toward utopia, the world was degenerating, damned by sin. Progress isn't obvious unless an observer is primed to see it and to ignore degeneration such as despoiling forests and waterways. It is a myth that "every day in every way we get better and better."[5]

Bolstering the idea of progress in the era of Western imperialism was the assumption that those technologically powerful nations had evolved farther from primate ancestors and savages, compared to the countries they conquered. Colonies were peopled by inferior, less evolved "races"—"living fossils" exemplifying stages in the evolution of civilization. It was "natural" that enlightened, literate, progressed White men should rule over darker-skinned natives, and over European peasants browned by laboring outdoors. Those enlightened, schooled White men expounded the social-charter myth of progress, legitimating their domination.

During the nineteenth century, technical progress in mechanizing work tied into professionalization of science in Western nations. Dropping the label "natural philosophy," the sciences as we know them were separated. Standards of research were formulated. A basic idea was that science consists in experiments that may be replicated to check whether their conclusions are valid. How can a geologist, a paleontologist, a biological taxonomist, or an archaeologist replicate nature's experiments that produced observed data? Nature's time scale can be enormous, far beyond human lifetimes. Scientists who cannot replicate an inferred process, as physicists and chemists might in a laboratory, look for "natural experiments"—situations that differ from each other in one, likely significant, factor. For example, was a drying climate the stimulus for developing agriculture? Compare the situations of early agricultural societies, and see whether or not most evidence a drying climate. (The answer here is that the hypothesis was rejected; data demonstrated agriculture and its early situations are extremely varied.)

**Figure 2.3.** Maliseet First Nation cartoon depicting opinion of Europeans. Bernard C. Perley, used with permission

The method of seeking natural experiments for what cannot be manipulated experimentally led archaeologists to seize the idea that the Americas were totally isolated from Eurasia and Africa until 1492; American cultural developments would show whether Progress, as Europeans knew it, is natural to human societies, or instead perhaps due to circumstances unique to the White race of Europe. America, isolated, was a natural experiment for the science of culture.

The myth of Columbus's discovery of a new world enabled the science-minded to put forth the Americas as a natural experiment, where the varied degrees of progress seen among American First Nations replicated similar differing stages of progress observed in Africa, Asia, Australia, and rural Europe. In Europe, Asia, and Africa, the natural experiment was compromised by millennia of intercourse between the more and the less evolved peoples. In isolated Australia, the experiment was incomplete because its natives apparently never evolved beyond "savagery." The Americas, then, by virtue of postulated complete isolation since the Ice Age and because they did show stages of progress up to "archaic" kingdoms, could serve as the scientific test of the validity of progressive cultural evolution inherent in human societies. America's capitulation to European White men proved that such men, indeed, were the most progressed, evolved to lead those others their superiority had colonized.

Postcolonial anthropology cannot accept either the myth of Columbus the discoverer of a hidden new world, nor the myth of progress. Both myths are social charters perpetrating injustice and exploitation. We don't deny that often "might makes right," yet, neither should we complacently accept its consequences. Critically examining premises and political outcomes of these two myths frees us, as citizens, to more intelligently deal with contemporary problems. Biological anthropology refutes the idea of less-evolved races of people, and cultural ecology shows how populations adapted to environments, often with sophisticated techniques that made deserts bloom and icy wastes produce food and shelter. In this book, we will look at the world before 1492, a world in which humans have always lived in global networks, moving and mixing. The myth of Columbus and the myth of progress came from an era of slavery, of the subjugation of women, of voting limited to men of property, of inhuman working conditions in mines and mills and plantations. They don't belong in today's world.

Critical Thinking can be discomforting. Demanding as many data as may be relevant, thoroughly checking their authenticity, alert for discrepancies and contradictions, critical thinkers come up to "popular knowledge" handed down by political parties to get votes and legislation serving their interests. Denying non-Western societies' achievements in seafaring to justify taking over their "newly discovered" territories, like denying their achievements in "civilization," has been part of the ideology of Manifest Destiny. In this book, we see how archaeology and genetics have amassed data that make untenable the notion that oceans cut the Americas out of the global world until 1492.

## Chapter 3

# The Question of Boats

**P**art of the folklore about Columbus is the notion that no one could have crossed oceans until the type of caravel ship he used was invented. The truth is that those caravels were an improvement upon earlier medieval Mediterranean ships—lighter, faster, more maneuverable, with lateen sails allowing tacking into the wind. Nevertheless, compared to ships of other maritime traditions, they were not remarkable. In this chapter we will look at boat building in a global perspective, at evidence of very ancient ocean voyaging, and evidence of ocean crossings in astoundingly small boats, vouched for by the Guinness World Records staff.

The question whether earlier transoceanic voyaging was *possible* is abundantly and conclusively answered, *yes*. This affirmation is a precondition for discussing the question of intersocietal contacts across oceans before 1492. Corollary to that question is the further one, of the significance of such contacts, if there is a probability of occurrences. From the basic question of evidence of boats, follows the profound question of what makes human societies change: "psychic unity" or stimulating contacts (Ford 1969)? Denying the possibility of transoceanic voyages by non-Europeans weighs the question against contacts. Providing evidence of a wide variety of seagoing boats, and of great antiquity, strengthens the probability of contacts (Simmons 2014).

At this point, let us clarify how archaeologists, as scientists, can approach such a question. The great handicap is that a boat's wake is ephemeral. Evidence for voyaging has to be sought at its ends, on land or in shipwrecks. We must begin with observations that we can record. These are our *empirical data*. "Data," the plural of *datum*, is Latin for

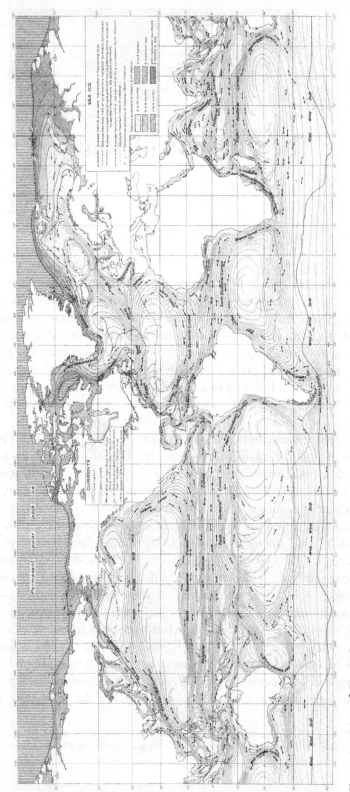

Figure 3.1. Map of Ocean Currents.

"that which is given;" "empirical" derives from the Latin and Greek for "trial." In other words, scientists make trials of that which is given by observation. In some fields of science, trials are carried out by experiments manipulating data under controlled conditions. To a limited extent, this is done in archaeology; for example, by practicing flintknapping or building a mound, measuring the time, labor, soil, and weather involved.

Most archaeology is not experimental. Instead, historical sciences, including paleontology, geology, and astronomy, as well as archaeology, depend heavily upon the given, what can be observed as it already exists. We cannot manipulate real living societies, much less those in the past, and our observations are handicapped by our being on the same scale of time and size and number as other humans, past and present; contrast us, as observers, with those who observe fruit flies' thousands of generations. Archaeologists as historical scientists proceed inductively from the given, data, toward IBE, inference to the best explanation (Cleland 2002:481, Kelley and Hanen 1988:252–256, Turner 2007:32–33, 73). Inductive logic recognizes *probability* rather than simple true-or-false, seeks to include all relevant data, and is especially concerned with the strength of links between data and conclusion (Hurley 2012:33).

## Earliest Boats

Australia is the strong evidence for human use of watercraft about 50,000 years ago, in the Middle Paleolithic cultural stage of humans in the Pleistocene (Ice Age).[1] Human skeletons of this age discovered in Australia could not have been there unless their people had crossed open ocean between the lands of Pleistocene Sunda (Island Southeast Asia, including Indonesia) and Sahul (Australia, Tasmania, and New Guinea) (Matisoo-Smith 2012). Sunda was part of the Eurasian continent, and Sahul a separate continent with different fauna and flora, noted by Darwin's colleague Alfred Russell Wallace, who identified the distinctions.

Scientist Robert Bednarik led a project using replicas of Middle Paleolithic tools to build a bamboo raft to sail this ocean strait. The *Nale Tasih 2* successfully carried five men, food and repair staples, and a box of sand for a cooking fire across 800 km (500 miles) between Kupang in West Timor and Australia's continental shelf (its coast 50,000 years ago) in six days (Bednarik 2000, 2014, personal communication June 27, 2015). Is this a scientific experiment in archaeology that proves such a craft enabled humans to reach Australia and the more easterly Western Pacific islands 50,000 years ago?

**Figure 3.2.** The *Lombok*—bamboo raft constructed with Paleolithic tools, testing voyaging between eastern Indonesian islands, 2008. For authenticity, three women are on board with the men, the minimum needed to start a colony. Robert Bednarik, used with permission

The *Nale Tasih* project used a deductive argument:

People crossed an ocean strait to Australia in the Middle Paleolithic.

A seaworthy raft constructed using Middle Paleolithic tools and raw materials crossed a strait to Australia.

Therefore, the first migrants to Australia likely used a raft such as the *Nale Tasih 2*.

Set out as logic, one can see that there is a stretch between the premises and the conclusion. Skeptics point out that the *Nale Tasih 2* carried steering oars and a sail, both of them relatively sophisticated inventions which are not evidenced in the Middle Paleolithic. Continuing his scientific experiments, Bednarik's succeeding *Nale Tasih 3* and *Nale Tasih 4*, *Rangki Papa*, and *Lombok* seagoing rafts did not carry either sail or steering oars, and three succeeded in reaching target islands, although demanded strenuous paddling to deal with powerful currents (Bednarik 2014:216–218). Like Thor Heyerdahl's balsa raft *Kon-Tiki*, sailed in 1947 from Peru to Central Polynesia, Bednarik's rafts demonstrated the *possibility* that such craft made the same voyages in antiquity, but experimental replication in these instances is not proof. Whatever the watercraft used 50,000 years ago, men and women did build something sufficiently seaworthy to carry them, men *and* women, on purposeful voyages to uninhabited lands. Human skeletons in Australia dated to 50,000 years old prove the crossing.

Early development of boats finds a connection with incentives to go upon seas and lakes. Drawn to lakes, rivers, and river mouths by the necessity of drinking water, humans would have found a diversity of resources because where land meets water is an ecotone, a zone with fauna and flora of both ecosystems. Just offshore they would have seen plants and fish they could harvest by getting on something that floats. Floating on the edge of near-shore, they would have seen enticing fish and sea mammals farther out. In temperate and tropical waters, flotation in which a person is in the water straddling the float, like paddling a surfboard, and rafts where water may safely wash over the surface, are feasible. In colder waters, a boat that keeps off water is necessary (McGrail 1997:81). Early humans who went overseas to the island of Timor caught deep sea fish, including tuna, 42,000 years ago, presumably from rafts (O'Connor, Ono, and Clarkson 2011).

The basic boat in northern North America was a shell of sewn hides or bark, into which a wooden framework was inserted. Hide shell boats were used in Asia by Mongols and northern Siberian peoples (Needham, Wang, and Lu 1971:386) and in Europe, in Ireland until relatively recently when the hide was replaced by waterproofed canvas. These hide or bark boats don't have keels, so they ride easily over waves. In warmer climates, where trees grow large trunks, hollowed out tree trunks were used to make logboats, commonly called dugouts. Logboats can be hollowed out by building small fires in the log and scraping out the burned wood, over and over until the desired space is achieved; stone adzes are adequate for this task.

Over thousands of years, boatwrights enlarged basic types. Inuit umiaks and Irish curraghs, shell boats using many hides over large frames, carried families and goods. The Roman period Irish curraghs transported cattle and commercial cargoes over the Irish Sea. Logboats were enlarged by lashing planks to make a higher freeboard, then by at least the third millennium BCE, these transformed into ships built of wooden planks fastened to frames. Empires invested in larger and larger ships for their navies, while merchants commissioned ships to economically carry cargoes. China excelled in constructing big, stable, flat-bottomed cargo ships called junks; Europe mastered faster keeled ships better suited to the relatively calm Mediterranean than the oceans. India, meeting place for both traditions and also African overseas trade, created its own versions of ships.[2] Out in the Pacific, a third great maritime technology developed as islanders stabilized logboats by attaching a second boat, parallel, or an outrigger float, and raising the freeboard with planks. All these types of boat—raft, logboat, hide or bark boat, flat-bottomed plank, keeled plank, and outrigger—could be built seaworthy and capable of carrying numbers of people and cargo.

Figure 3.3. Tlingit logboats (dugout canoes), southeastern Alaska, one for daily use (top) and one painted for formal visits to coastal communities (bottom). Photos by Alice Kehoe

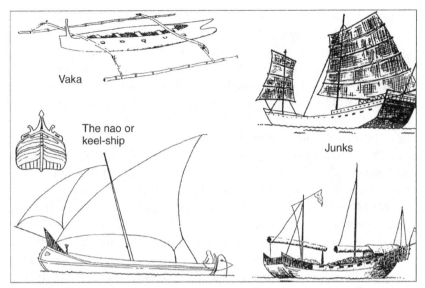

**Figure 3.4.** The three principal shipbuilding traditions: Polynesian outrigger or double canoes; Chinese flat-bottomed junks; and European keeled ships. Not shown is the curragh or the umiak (hide- or bark-covered frame boat). From Doran, 1973: Nao, Junk, and Vaka: Boats and Culture History

How people first reached Australia, New Guinea, and the islands of western Oceania points toward tropical zones where large bamboo and trees were readily available to lash to make rafts, or possibly large logboats, using controlled burning and stone chopping tools known in the Middle Paleolithic. Rafts and logboats could be paddled over the straits between islands and to Australia, the minimum voyages being at least 100 km (62 miles) over a full day and night. By daylight, travelers could steer away from high landmarks at the home port, then toward such landmarks appearing near the destination; by night, they probably steered by star movements (McGrail 2000:282, 287–288). Island Southeast Asia and Sahul people could have colonized during the last Pleistocene glacial period without venturing far out of sight of any land.

Drastic changes in sea level and coasts prevent us from re-enacting colonization voyages of around 50,000 BCE. Computer modeling based on data from seafloor mapping and coring, giving estimates of ancient coastlines and landmarks, shows virtual voyages on paddled rafts toward signs of new islands. Virtual voyaging can model explorers checking out landfalls, returning home, and loading families and basic goods to repeat the journey. Computer modeling, although affected by the amount of data available and selected, and by programing, is a safe and comfortable way to test hypotheses on feasible voyaging.

Migrating to America from northeastern Asia later, when that cold region had been colonized through technology to deal with the weather, calls for boats like the Inuit umiak. Rich productivity along the northwest American coast allows grizzly bears there to be twice as big as inland grizzlies, and ocean trout to grow faster than freshwater cousins (Erlandson et al. 2007:164). Underlying such productivity is the abundant seaweed kelp, growing like forests offshore and harboring shellfish and food for fish and mammals like sea lions and the extinct giant sea cow.

"Kelp forests" were even more abundant and productive in the Terminal Pleistocene (last portion of the Ice Age, 17,000–9,400 BCE), forming a nearly continuous zone from Japan, around the North Pacific Rim, down the west coast of America to Baja California, and after a tropical but also productive break, from Ecuador all the way south to the tip of South America (Erlandson et al. 2007:165, 168). Upper Paleolithic people with harpoons (actually found in many sites from this period) and nets and boats could have traveled along this zone from Manchuria to Chile, more easily and safely than land hunters trekking through the tundra of Beringia, the exposed land bridge between Siberia and Alaska, now underwater at the Bering Strait. We need not choose one versus the other route for humans migrating into the Americas; both are probable. Discovering these early camps is, for those on land, like looking for needles in a haystack. Discovering camps for the shore travelers is looking for needles buried in the muck of the ocean bottom, because rising sea level from the melting of the great continental glaciers flooded Terminal Pleistocene shores. This is a good example of the archaeological principle that lack of evidence is not necessarily a call to reject a hypothesis—absence of evidence cannot be assumed to be evidence of absence.

## Sea Travel

Most people today think that only a very brave or foolhardy person would paddle or sail in a small boat upon the open ocean. Those who do so in our time make headlines (Table 3.1). Any European ship of a thousand years ago would seem dangerously small to us. China's junks were bigger and more stable, boarding hundreds of passengers plus crew and cargo (Needham, Wang, and Lu 1971:379 ff. offer the most detailed discussion of Chinese boats).

Specialized ships, particularly warships, could be quite different from merchant vessels. During the Classical period in the Mediterranean, two thousand years ago, Greeks and their enemies built galleys for naval fighting that had as many as three banks of rowers pulling huge oars, up to eight men on each oar. In addition to 4,000 oarsmen, it was reported, the largest carried nearly 3,000 soldiers and a crew of hundreds, plus food, drinking water, and weapons (Paine 2013:112).

Contrasting with such super-specialized ships, commoners' boats for fishing and ferrying reflected local conditions such as shallow shelves or deep fjords. Their captains depended upon years of experience to handle the craft, responding not to instruments but to the feel of wind and waves. They steered by landmarks, the positions of sun and stars through the hours, currents, and regular wind directions (thus the term *trade winds* by which merchants planned their itineraries). Seamen's familiarity with the sea gave them confidence similar to the confidence an experienced coachman had driving distances over rutted dirt roads.

Familiarity with the sea lies behind the verified record-breakers listed in the Guinness Book of World Records. Table 3.1 presents a selection of ocean crossings in remarkably small craft. These lay to rest the idea that only European caravels with crews of a few dozen or more, and their bigger successors, could have crossed the Atlantic and Pacific.

Even more instructive is a look at Polynesian voyaging. Here, the serious purpose of finding a new country in which to live stimulated a long series of explorations beginning in the second millennium BCE from southern China and adjacent southeastern Asia. Boats experts Seán McGrail and Geoffrey Irwin suggest that when undeveloped land became scarce in Melanesia, ancestral Polynesians began voyaging into the prevailing easterly winds, on the strategy that if they did not encounter new islands before food and water on board were depleted to a certain level, the sailors would turn back, confident that the prevailing wind, now at their backs, would enable them to return home. They might even sight islands on the return leg. This strategy made exploring the vast Pacific less foolhardy (McGrail 2001:315–316; Irwin 2010:136, 138). Another factor in Polynesian voyaging is the speed and stability of their outrigger *vakas* (Polynesian boats), tested and improved over more than two thousand years on the Pacific. Exploratory voyages headed by ambitious men or, as oral histories tell, leaders and their warriors defeated in conflicts, would have taken light, fast boats, returning if successful to load colonists and supplies on larger boats.

Testing hypotheses regarding Polynesian migrations is difficult, given the immense distances and experimenters' inexperience with Polynesian boats. A large, double-hulled *vaka* with two masts bearing "claw" (Oceanic lateen) sails, built in 1976, known as the *Hokule'a,* was sailed up until 1999 to all the major islands of Eastern Polynesia, including distant Rapa Nui (Easter Island). Navigated by Polynesian masters of traditional sailing, based on winds, currents, cloud types, sun and stars, and memorized knowledge of island locations relevant to star positions, *Hokule'a* demonstrated that formidable distances could be traversed relatively quickly; for example, in 34 days from Maui in Hawai'i to Tahiti. Hawai'ian oral history of an invading Tahitian *kahuna* (priest) with his soldiers conquering earlier settlers on Maui is thus credible.

Useful and exciting as *Hokule'a* is, she is expensive, so instead of building and sailing more replications of *vakas*, computer simulations have tested hypotheses of Oceanic voyages (Irwin 2010:138–139). Computer models are secondhand observations, the quality of the results depending on the amount and reliability of input data. When experienced sailors advise on the simulations, more relevant data may be entered, increasing the probability that outcomes approach real-world events. Archaeological data can validate or invalidate computer simulations.

## Boat People

Numerous human societies have lived on the water, right above the beach, on platforms on piles in shallow water, or on houseboats. In warm climates, children start swimming as soon as they start walking. Warm or cold, kids ride in boats with their moms and dads the way American kids ride in cars, part of everyday life. Boys and girls paddle or row small boats to fetch wanted items, or to play. To be on the sea or river or lake is as natural as being on land (Feinberg 1993[1988]:119–122).

As populations increased during the Holocene (postglacial age), production for exchange developed, transport became a business, and water routes answered the need to deliver cargoes to markets. Great cities are often ports or lie at major river junctions. Sea routes facilitated piracy and war attacks, too. Feeling at home on water was an important component in human history.

Where will we find evidence of boat people? If they lived on the shore, storms, tsunamis, changes in sea level, and erosion destroy or deeply bury sites. If they lived on boats, only rarely discovered and excavated shipwrecks would testify to their way of life, and it could be interpreted as seaboard life between ports, rather than primarily living on the boats. If they lived on platforms over water, their remains most likely would be deep in muck—the famous excavated Neolithic Swiss Lake Dwellings were raised above a marshy foreshore, not actually over water.

The possibility of boat people and coastal dwellers constantly using boats comes from *analogy* with the frequency of such communities along shores and on rivers.[3] They are not hard to see today, whether sampans in Southeast Asia selling souvenirs to tourists at waterfront markets, narrowboats on England's Midlands canals, barges on French rivers, or houseboats in the Seattle harbor. Today, they are documented by photographs, censuses, and licenses required by harbor authorities. Historical documents refer to "sea people," for example, *hai chung* in Chinese books about astronomy and navigation written in the first and the sixth centuries CE (Needham, Wang and Lu 1971:560–562). For archaeologists, peaceful boat-dwelling families will not be visible.

Raiders from the seas do leave evidence. Best known are the infamous Sea Peoples of the late Bronze Age in the eastern Mediterranean, from the end of the thirteenth century BCE into the twelfth. All along the coasts, cities were brutally overrun by attackers coming in ships as well as overland. Written records give names to raiders, sometimes roughly matching ethnic groups, otherwise a puzzle. Why they erupted at this time is another puzzle: raids upon port towns were by no means a new phenomenon, but not on a scale so widespread and so destructive. Evidence exists of prolonged drought in the eastern Mediterranean during this time, from which may be inferred crop failures, food shortages, political unrest, and recourse to raiding and conquest (Drake 2012, Cline 2014).

"Sea Peoples" may be what these fleets of armed ships looked like to the hapless victims in port cities, but they probably weren't boat people who had no land base. They appear more to have been like the Vikings of Scandinavia, from the late eighth century CE to about 1050. Vikings were boatloads of Norse men sailing fast ships to raid towns and farmlands of Atlantic Europe, looting and capturing slaves, and not infrequently settling in the raided lands, marrying local women. Men of the Sea Peoples may have done the same, disappearing to archaeologists in households whose women and enslaved menfolk continued their own culture. Viking raids were opportunities for young men to prove their courage and hardihood and seize valuables that could be presented to parents of young women back home to persuade them to marriage— rather like historic Plains Indians youths going on horse raids to make their name and bring back horses for bride gifts. Seagoing Vikings ended when Scandinavian kings accepted Christianity, enabling their kingdoms to be integrated into the larger medieval European economy. Sea raiders, recorded along Southeast Asian and African coasts as well as European, were instruments of culture contacts in spite of the fear and sorrows they caused. They left genetic traces, too, the men's Y chromosomes persisting in descendants of the women they slept with.

## The Problem of Palimpsests

Palimpsests are places or things that show traces of earlier usage underneath later use. Palimpsests are what the forensic detective in a crime film picks up, a paper or surface revealing clues under misleading signs of later use. A palimpsest in archaeology is not the same as a series of occupations in stratigraphic succession; instead, it is what appears to be a single stratum that, upon careful analysis, is seen to be made up of thinner layers more or less melded together. Recognizing this problem, after World War II, French archaeologists, including François Bordes and André Leroi-Gourhan, worked very meticulously to discern slight changes in sediments and assess how closely artifacts and features were associated. Recording micro-stratigraphy or trying to determine whether little stone flakes fit onto core stones lying near is costly of time and so of funds supporting workers. Where there are large ruins, it may be more vital to uncover extensive constructions during a funded project. These, too, will likely be palimpsests of successive buildings, the scale of work differing from excavations of Paleolithic rock shelters that Bordes and Leroi-Gourham investigated.

Good harbors can be very challenging palimpsests for the archaeologist, on top of the questions of shore level changes, storm and erosion damage, and their opposite, the burying of sites. Around the Mediterranean and around the Indian Ocean, thousands of years of voyaging in every direction, for trade and for colonies, make port towns palimpsests that call upon linguists and biological anthropologists as well as archaeologists.

The large island of Madagascar, in the western part of the Indian Ocean, 400 km (250 miles) east of Mozambique in East Africa, is a good example of palimpsests of voyagers. During the time humans have been in Africa, Madagascar could only be reached by boat. Evidence for the earliest humans on the island is indirect: animal bones with cut-marks from butchering with stone tools, and otherwise unexplained disappearance of the largest animals on the island at the end of the first millennium BCE (two thousand years ago). Habitation sites of the hunters have not yet been discovered. An interesting clue to extinction of the large animals at this time is a decline in spores of a fungus that lives off large herbivore feces. A few centuries later, Mediterranean traders put in at Madagascar to pick up tortoises, according to a geographical treatise of the time; paleo-ecology studies show that the trading ships unwittingly disembarked European rats and mice that spread throughout the island, reducing populations of native rodents that couldn't compete.

Not recorded in existing texts, so far as is known, traders sailed to Madagascar and East Africa from the other direction, too—from Indonesia. They spoke Austronesian languages (Polynesian is one branch of Austronesian language) and in the tenth century CE, Arab books say, raided as well as traded. Malagasy, the language of Madagascar, is Austronesian, most closely similar to the language of Sumatra in Indonesia. It incorporates many words from Bantu languages spoken in Africa, apparently used by African slaves sold into Madagascar.

Complicating the history of Indonesian travelers noted by Arabs in the first millennium CE, several cultivated plants indicate much earlier voyaging between Indonesia and Africa. Bananas were carried to Africa by Island Southeast Asia boats three thousand years ago, on the evidence of phytoliths (tiny fossilized fragments of plants) identified in soil showing human disturbance. Coconut palms and taro, which like bananas are native to Island Southeast Asia, were perhaps later introductions from Indonesia. An African cultivated bean seems to have been taken the other way, to Indonesia. The picture of Madagascar history is a true palimpsest, from the possibility of occasional landings by Indonesian traders going to Africa three thousand years ago, then indirect but strong evidence of hunter-gatherers coming over from Mozambique a little more than two thousand years ago, to the Roman pottery and beads proving Mediterranean traders along the East African coast, and geography texts describing them taking tortoises from Madagascar. Then, during the first millennium CE, development is seen of very active Arab and Indian as well as Indonesian trade in the western Indian Ocean and the establishment of enough Indonesians on Madagascar to create the historic Malagasy-speaking kingdoms (Blench 2010). Archaeology alone could not construct this picture.

## Conclusion: Prehistoric Seafaring Floats

Using Critical Thinking to consider whether there could have been pre-Columbian contacts with the Americas across the oceans, the first and fundamental question has been whether oceangoing boats were available before Europeans developed the caravels Columbus used.

This crucial question is answered positively by several kinds of evidence. First and foremost are human remains in Australia dated around 50,000 years ago. Humans could not have evolved in Australia (it had no native primates, not even native mammals), nor have human remains older than that been discovered in Australia. To get to Australia in the later Ice Age, 50,000 years ago, people had to build some kind of boat to cross the open waters of the Torres Strait. Experiments and tools discovered of this age from the region make it probable that the first Australians built large rafts to cross over. Rafts were probably also used to reach the island of Timor in Indonesia at about this time.

A second line of evidence bearing on the question of feasibility of ocean crossings is the great variety of seagoing vessels known historically and ethnographically from around the world. Archaeology and historical documents covering the past 5,000 years, and experiments with replica vessels, show boats capable of carrying people on long voyages. Older boats—rafts, logboats, and shell-built boats—would be so perishable they are unlikely to be preserved. The few older logboats that have been found prove use of such craft at the end of the Pleistocene Ice Age; rafts and the wood parts of shell boat frames would be difficult to recognize in an ancient archaeological site, even if preserved.

Finally, the book *Guinness World Records* documents an extraordinary range of ocean crossings in small boats. It is true that pre-Columbian sailors could not have crossed the Pacific in a vessel floating on beer cans, nor likely that anyone crossed the Atlantic on a sailboard less than six feet long before the later twentieth century. These feats do prove that determined people can cross an ocean on anything that will float. Shipwreck survivors are another proof that months-long voyages have been accomplished. This chapter demonstrates that pre-Columbian transoceanic voyages were both *possible* and *probable*.

Table 3.1. Trans-Oceanic Crossings

## Noteworthy Experiments

| Year | Captain/Crew | Vessel | Origin | Destination | Duration |
|------|-------------|--------|--------|-------------|----------|
| 1947 | Thor Heyerdahl and crew | *Kon-Tiki* balsa raft | Callao, Peru | Raroia, Tuamoto Islands (eastern Polynesia) | 101 days |
| 1970 | Thor Heyerdahl and crew | *Ra II* reed-bundle boat | Safi, Morocco | Barbados in the Caribbean | 57 days |
| 1976– 1977 | Tim Severin and crew | *Brendan* | Ireland | Newfoundland | * |

* Overwintered in Iceland when three weeks of storms made it too late in autumn to attempt sailing to Newfoundland.

## Record Attempts

| Year | Voyage |
| --- | --- |
| 1866 | First recorded Atlantic crossing by a ship smaller than 60 ft., the 48-foot sloop *Alice* carried owner T. C. Appleton, Captain Clarn, three seamen, and a cook. It sailed from Boston to the Isle of Wight in 19 days. |
| 1868 | *Nonpareil* was a vessel with three rubber cigar-shaped floats, each 26 feet long, and a light planking deck, two masts, and a portable pump to reinflate the floats. Crewed by John Mikes, George Miller, and Jerry Mallene, it sailed from New York to Southampton in 43 days. |
| 1870 | John C. Buckley and Nicolas Primoraz sailed on *City of Ragusa*, a 20-foot ship's lifeboat (whaleboat type), yawl-rigged, from Queenstown, Ireland to Boston in 85 days. |
| 1876 | Alfred Johnson, a New England halibut fisherman, sailed *Centennial*, a 20-foot fishing dory with four sails on one mast, from Gloucester, NJ (the vicinity of Philadelphia's Centennial World's Fair) to Nova Scotia, then to Abercastel, Wales in 46 days, then continued to Liverpool. |
| 1889 | J. W. Lawlor and two seamen voyaged from Boston to Le Havre on 40-foot *Neversink* in 49 days. |
| Pre-1891 | Two brothers with the surname Andrews set out from Boston and reached Cornwall in 48 days on a centerboard boat of 18-inch draft with one lateen sail, such as those used on Swiss lakes. Merrien lists this event merely as "after 1877." |
| 1891 | Lawlor, alone, in *Sea Serpent*, a 15-foot craft with spritsail, traveled from Boston to Cornwall in 45 days. |
| 1894 | George Harbo and Frank Samuelson, Norwegian-born naturalized American dory fishermen out of Sandy Hook, NJ, voyaged on 17-foot, 8-inch *Police Gazette*, a clinker-built whaleboat (sponsored by Police Gazette newspaper). It had no sail, but was equipped with air tanks at each end, and was rowed from New York to the Scilly Isles in 55 days. |
| 1899 | Howard Blackburn voyaged from Gloucester, MA, to Gloucester, England in 61 days on *Great Western*, a 30-ft. sloop. In 1901, Blackburn sailed from Gloucester, MA, to Cape Espièhel at the mouth of the Tagus, Portugal, on 24-foot, 8-inch *Great Republic* in 38 days. On the 39th day, he sailed into Lisbon. Blackburn was a Nova Scotia-born halibut fisherman on the Newfoundland Banks, out of Gloucester, MA. In 1883, he lost his fingers, toes, and half his right foot to frostbite when his dory was caught in a snowstorm and he lost sight of his ship. |
| 1923 | Alain Gerbault, on the 36-ft. cutter *Fire Crest*, sailed from Gibraltar to New York in 101 days. |

1928    Captain Franz Romer voyaged from Cape St. Vincent, Portugal, to St. Thomas, Virgin Islands, in *Deutscher Sport*, a kayak made of waterproof fabric over a wooden frame, in 90 days.

1950    Frederick Benjamin Carlin, an Australian mining engineer, with his wife, voyaged in a World War II amphibious jeep that he refitted, with one fuel tank under the jeep and another towed. They motored from Halifax to Flores, Azores, on to Madeira, the Canaries, and Morocco, and finally drove into Paris on June 1, 1951. Carlin drove on to the Pacific, crossing to Japan and then Tokyo and finally to Anchorage, Alaska, in 1957.

1952    Dr. Alain Bombard voyaged in a 15-foot rubber dinghy *l'Hérétique*, living entirely off caught fish, taking 65 days to depart Casablanca and travel via Las Palmas to Barbados.

1952–53 Ann Davison, an Englishwoman, sailed the 21-ft., 6-in. sloop *Felicity Ann* from the Canaries to Dominica, West Indies. Mrs. Davison and her husband had intended to cross the Atlantic on the *Reliance* but both boat and husband were lost at sea a few miles out. She then sailed alone on the *Felicity Ann*.

## Around the World, Solo

1895–98 John Slocum, sea captain, sailed out of Gloucester, MA, on the 36-ft., 9-in. *Spray*.

1901–04 J. C. (John Claus) Voss, a naturalized Canadian, voyaged in the 50-ft. red cedar Indian canoe *Tilikum*, fit with three masts. For portions of the sail, Voss had a second man on board.

1942–43 Vito Dumas, of Argentina, sailed the 32-ft. ketch *Legh II*, for 13 months, 2 weeks—the fastest circumnavigation up to Merrien's publication date of 1954.

## Later Small Boat Crossings, Atlantic

1980    Gerard d'Aboville, a Breton, rowed an 18-foot boat from Cape Cod to Ouessant, France, a distance of 3,320 miles. His journey took 72 days, and was the first documented solo crossing from mainland to mainland.

1982    Bill Dunlop sailed a 9-foot boat from Maine to Falmouth, England, in 78 days.

1983    Wayne Dickinson sailed from Florida to northwestern Ireland in an 8-ft., 11-in. sailboat in 142 days.

1985    Two Frenchmen crossed the Atlantic on a surfboard with a 20-inch-high hold for sleeping (one at a time). The trip took 39 days.

1986   Alain Pichavant and Stephane Peyron sailed a 31-foot sailboard from Senegal to Guadeloupe in 24 days, whence they continued to New York. Peyron then sailed, in 1987, on a 25-foot sailboard from New York to La Rochelle, France, in 46 days.

1988   Rüdiger Nehberg pedaled from Senegal to Sao Luis, northern Brazil, in a small Fiberglas pedal-boat; the trip lasted 74 days.

1991   British sailor Tom McNally sailed from Portugal to San Juan, Puerto Rico, in a boat measuring 5 feet, 4-1/2 inches.

1993   Hugo Vihlen set out in the boat *Father's Day*, measuring 5 feet, 4 inches, from St. John's, Newfoundland, to Southern England. The voyage took 106 days and set the record for the smallest boat to cross the Atlantic. In 1968, he had sailed *The April Fool*, measuring 5 feet, 11-7/8 inches, from Casablanca to Fort Lauderdale, Florida, in 85 days (Boehm, ed. 1983:352).

1999   Tori Murden (female, age 36) rowed a 23-ft. boat, *American Pearl*, 3,000 miles from the Canary Islands westward to Fort-du-Bas, Guadeloupe, in 81 days. She was the first American and first woman to row alone across the Atlantic. Murden was also the first American and first woman to ski to the South Pole.

## Later Small Boat Crossings, Pacific

1882   Bernard Gilboy, an American, sailed the 19-ft. schooner *Pacific* from San Francisco to 40 miles NE of Sandy Cape, Australia, (6,500 miles) in 162 days. He lost sail and rudder, so a schooner took him to land.

1972   John Fairfax and Sylvia Cook rowed 8,000 miles in a 35-foot boat from San Francisco, following the coast to Mexico before crossing to Hayman Island on the central Australian coast. Fairfax rowed from the Canary Islands to Florida in 180 days in 1969.

1978   Webb Chiles left San Diego to circumnavigate the world in an 18-foot open boat; two years later, he sailed into Cairns Harbor, 1,250 miles north of Sydney, Australia, having stopped on several islands.

1980   On November 30, six Japanese researchers arrived in Chile. Six-and-a-half months earlier, they left Shimoda, Japan, in a 43-foot catamaran, the *Yasei-Go*. They took the Kuroshio Current east to the Northern Pacific Current, following that to San Francisco, then sailing down the coast to Chile (Milwaukee *Journal Sentinel* 12/1/80).

1981   Gerry Spiess made a 7,800-mile Pacific crossing to Sydney in five months in a 10-foot sailboat; he had previously crossed the Atlantic in the boat.

1982–8 Peter Bird rowed from San Francisco nearly to Australia's Great Barrier Reef.

1984   Arnaud de Rosnay disappeared at sea from a sailboard going from China to Taiwan. Earlier, his longest of seven open-water crossings was a thousand kilometers from the Marquesas to Ahé in the Tuamotus.

1987   Ed Gillet paddled a kayak from Monterey Bay to Maui, Hawai'i, in 63 days.

1991   Gerard d'Aboville rowed a 26-foot boat from Japan to Ilwaco, Wash., in 134 days.

1999   Kenichi Horie (age 60), traveled from San Francisco to western Japan in 103 days on a sailboat made of 528 empty stainless steel beer kegs with sails made of recycled plastic bottles. In 1996, Horie crossed on a solar-powered "yacht" made of melted-down aluminum beer cans. In 1962, Horie, age 23, crossed on a 19-ft yacht. All were solo crossings; the 1999 crossing was 6,800 miles. (Milwaukee *Journal Sentinel* 7/9/99)

2001   Jim Shekhdar (age 54), a British computer salesman, rowed alone from Peru to Brisbane, Queensland, Australia, in 274 days (June 2000 to March 30, 2001), a distance of 8,060 miles. This set the record for the fastest Pacific crossing. (Milwaukee *Journal Sentinel* 3/31/01)

2003   Raphaela Le Gouvello windsurfed from Lima, Peru to Tahiti in 89 days.

REFERENCES

Boehm, David A., Stephen Topping, and Cyd Smith, eds., Guinness World Records 1983, New York: Sterling.

Merrien, Jean (real name, René Marie de la Poix de Fréminville) 1954 Lonely Voyagers [Les Navigateurs Solitaires], English translation 1954, by J. H. Watkins. New York: G. P. Putnam's Sons.

Chapter 4

# Peripatetic People

The argument that no boats were capable of crossing oceans before the time of Columbus has been rebutted in the previous chapter. Another argument raised is that no one would have deliberately set out on a long open-sea journey before the European Age of Discovery. This argument, too, can be rejected by an abundance of data. People, most often men, traversed seas to obtain raw materials, to sell and to obtain manufactured goods and foodstuffs, and to see more of the world, for education or adventure. People crossed seas on pilgrimages to holy places. People fled in boats from wars and persecution. Poverty and crop failures drove people to take ships to distant places. It's still happening (Crawford and Campbell, ed. 2012).

Historical sciences use the principle that observations of present-day processes are key to interpreting the past. George Gaylord Simpson (1902–1984), doyen of paleontologists in the mid-twentieth century, summed up the method:

1. Obtaining and studying the historical data.
2. Determination of present processes.
3. Confrontation of 1. and 2. with a view toward ordering, filling in, and explaining the history (Simpson 1970:81, 84-85)

In the same essay, Simpson roundly denounced the notion that to be scientific, a researcher should begin with a hypothesis and then collect data that might support the hypothesis, or might show it cannot be supported. If a conclusion follows logically from premises of the hypothesis, then the argument is technically valid. "Valid" does not mean "true"; it applies only to the logic of the argument (Hurley 2012:44–47). The problem with this hypothetico-deductive procedure is the source of the initial hypothesis. As anthropologists, we know how culture-bound we humans tend to be. The myth of Columbus is a good example of how we absorb what is taught to us when we are young children, particularly when early teaching is reinforced as we grow up. The hypothesis that dinosaurs became extinct because Noah didn't take them into his ark looks like it can be validated because plesiosaurs and similar extinct reptiles are found in marine sediment deposits. Several million people who were taught this explanation as children will insist the conclusion is *true* as well as a valid argument. Such an example provoked Simpson, the paleontologist, to insist that "obtaining and studying the historical data" comes *first*, with *comparison to presently observable processes* the second step in research. Archaeologists term this step "ethnographic analogy."

Crucial to the questions of pre-Columbian transoceanic contacts is the use of this *inductive* form of argument. Inductive arguments are not either valid or invalid, as deductive arguments must be. Inductive arguments conclude with assessments of *probability* (Hurley 2012:49–50). We needed to begin with finding out whether seagoing boats were available before 1492 (Simpson's step 1), with the evidence that they were widely used for millennia setting the ground for a strong argument that at least some apparent evidence for such contacts may be valid. This chapter looks at the "present processes"—Simpson's step 2—to see what analogies there may be that seem to fit the apparent evidence.

## Polynesians Again

Remote Oceania (see chapter 5). The historical data is incontrovertible: Polynesians lived on nearly every habitable island in the eastern Pacific when European exploration began in 1520. Europeans frequently observed Polynesians purposefully sailing on the open ocean far from land, using large, stable boats well designed for tropical climate voyaging. On all the islands, Polynesians told histories of their ancestors coming by sea to their islands. Most island histories told of repeated arrivals. Since all the islands were already settled by 1520—and archaeology has confirmed centuries of settlements—Europeans did not observe the process of colonization; this is known from the Polynesians' own historical knowledge. Europeans did observe, for five centuries, Polynesians voyaging to obtain raw materials directly from other islands, to trade with others, to raise their social status by managing challenging voyages, or to find havens when exiled by war or devastated by severe storms or drought. Add these observations to the fact that the easternmost islands, Hawai'i and Rapa Nui (Easter Island) were colonized at least three centuries before 1520, and the conclusion that Polynesians did find the American continents on one or more eastward voyages of discovery becomes probable. How could those expert explorers pushing ever eastward fail to discover a huge continent blocking the eastern Pacific?

That rhetorical question asks about probability. Archaeologist David Hurst Thomas tells us, in the textbook he wrote on statistics for archaeology, "the theory of statistics is grounded almost entirely upon probablistic thinking" (Thomas 1986:95). Taking into account winds and ocean currents, eastward exploring Polynesians sailing from the Marquesas in central Polynesia could have sailed south to Tahiti and on to about latitude 35° south, turning east with the strong westerly winds, and finally making landfall in central Chile (Finney 1994).

This is where the El Arenal site lies, with chicken bones radiocarbon dated to the fourteenth century CE, plus in this coastal area, artifacts resembling Polynesian types have been found. The El Arenal dates, only slightly later than the colonization of Hawai'i and Rapa Nui, suggest continued eastward explorations ending only with landfalls on the well-populated American continents. In other words, Polynesian cultures' valorization of explorations for colonization did not end abruptly and inexplicably with Hawai'i and Rapa Nui, but with voyages that found no more uninhabited islands, instead discovering millions of people on a continent. Thus the *probability* of South America having been visited by exploring Polynesians after the settlements on Central Polynesia and Rapa Nui is reasonably strong.

"The more we know, the more we know we don't know"—or in fancy words, "recursive ignorance"—is very true of archaeology. Every new excavation, new bit of historical knowledge, new understanding of ecology, biology, and genetics adds to our database. Sometimes an accepted interpretation can be seen to no longer be inference to the best explanation (IBE). Or, a generally rejected explanation may become better validated. Sometimes, new data argued to support one explanation crack open a gulf between opposing scientists. Replacement of one paradigm by another can take a generation or more, taking hold only as opposing scientists die off. When an ideological principle such as Manifest Destiny lies like a worm inside a popular intellectual position, the better paradigm can encounter strongly embedded opposition.

## Trade Voyaging

Journeying to trade is ubiquitous among human societies, and may be as old as our species. About the time that "anatomically modern humans," as biological anthropologists term our species, began expanding out of Africa around 100,000 years ago (Relethford 2008), archaeological sites in southern Africa show stone for tools, ochre for painting, and shells within sites at distances far enough to suggest trade rather than trekking from the sources. Some of these sites are inland from the sea, where additional archaeology indicates exploitation of coastal resources (Ziegler et al. 2013). Upper Paleolithic sites in Europe contain a variety of small, pretty shells perforated to be strung, or possibly also sewn on clothing. Many of the sites are several days' walk from the seacoast, but as with superior stone for knapping tools, we can't tell whether valued materials were traded, were obtained on journeys to the sources, or during regular trips to harvest seasonal foods. Several sites in Greece dated to 9000 BCE have cutting tools made of obsidian, a volcanic glass, taken from the island of Melos in the Aegean section of the Mediterranean (Laskaris et al. 2011)[1]. Considering the sea voyage to Melos, the procurers may have brought the obsidian to trade, saving their customers the time and effort of personal journeys.

Voyaging to trade can involve professional mariners working with merchants who customarily travel with them or consign cargoes to them, or it can involve trading settlements where foreign merchants create enclaves linked by ships (Curtin 1984:2–3). A great deal of trade is carried on by vessels small enough to put in to fishing villages and local towns lacking deep harbors, and such boats can carry bulk cargoes and livestock. Medieval Atlantic Europe's cogs and the Indian Ocean's dhows are examples of these practical means of maintaining regional markets.

For long distances, linking states and aristocracies, more commodious ships were wanted, and because they were costly to build, to man, and at sea for months, they needed to earn good profits. Hence, long distance trade was built on the transport of valuables, with displays at foreign ports serving the political function of impressing viewers with the originating kingdom's wealth and power, in addition to enriching its merchants. Not infrequently, a prince was welcomed aboard a great ship, only to find it sailing away to its home where the unlucky prince was forced to become the ruler's vassal. The sea can be a processional way for a dominating empire, its armed fleets parading like Roman legions or battalions of Nazi storm troopers.

**Figure 4.1.** Medieval trade brought goods from many sources to consumers. Permission Master and Fellows of Trinity College, Cambridge University

We think of Egypt as a valley in a desert. Its own people depend on its great Nile River for transport through its land and on to its sea, the Mediterranean, while at its back, as it were, a canal or portage route gives access to the Indian Ocean and East Africa. So central are boats to Egypt that its pharaohs were buried with actual boats to sail them into the afterlife. Next to the largest of the Giza pyramids, that of Pharaoh Khufu, is his 44 meter (144 feet) ship of cedar planks hewn from trees imported, by ship, from Lebanon on the Mediterranean. Sleek and graceful in spite of its length, Khufu's funeral ship is as impressive in its technology as the pyramid beside it. It makes credible the Egyptian texts describing diplomatic missions and lucrative cargoes of gold, precious stones, incense herbs, spices, exotic animals and slaves, and ivory from Africa and Indian Ocean countries. These were as necessary for the political economy, symbolized by the richly costumed pharaoh surrounded by every luxury and sign of power, as were the bushels of grain, livestock, and building materials carried by barges and papyrus-bundle boats on the Nile. Supporting evidence for substantial Egyptian maritime operations from about 2200 to 1300 BCE comes from its harbor on the Red Sea at Wadi Gawasis, the end of the shortest overland route from the Nile Valley to the Red Sea. Everything needed for sea trade voyages, including food and water, boxes of trade goods, ships' tack, and disassembled boats 21 meters (70 feet) long, was carried overland through the desert to this port, to be reassembled and launched to sail to Punt in East Africa (Bard and Fattovich 2009).

Instead of the usual history map with the Mediterranean Sea in the middle, a map with the Indian Ocean in the middle better represents the historical human world about two thousand years ago. Europe, dominated by the Roman empire, is in the northwest; northern Africa, with Egypt and the eastern Mediterranean, are in the west; eastern Africa in the southwest; Persia and India are in the center; Farther India (Indochina, Malaysia, Indonesia) is in the eastern south; and China is in the east. Australia is off the beaten path, with limited trade with neighboring Sulawesi in Indonesia (how ancient this trade may be is not known) (Clarke and Frederick 2006).

East of New Guinea, Lapita traders were sailing out into the central Pacific. In the Americas, large canoes and sailing rafts carried traders along the Pacific coasts of the North, Mexico to northern South America, and Chile and Peru to Ecuador, while Maya expanded around the Gulf of Mexico and traded into the Caribbean islands. Commercial trade has been integral to populous nations. Seas have been its highways.

Trade is more than exchange of designated goods. Foreign merchants' clothing, accoutrements, formal behavior, and languages inform local people of a wider world rich in novel ideas. Merchants may entice the adventurous to join them in journeys or strike out independently, and they hire seamen and servants or buy slaves. Trading enclaves generally bring in local women as wives, concubines, and household workers, creating creole communities of mixed heritage. No one place can supply all the things people need, so we have trade. And we have gifts: gift-giving is a form of trade, creating exchange, smoothing relations, acknowledging respect, provoking desire. While much that was given or traded was perishable, it is always *plausible* that people engaged in trade.

## Pilgrimages

Nikulás Berggson, a Benedictine monk in Iceland, in the early 1150s made pilgrimage from his far northern monastery to the holy city of Jerusalem (Hill 1983). On the outbound journey, he visited Rome and monasteries and shrines in Italy, Venice, Albania, Corfu, Greece, Constantinople, Cyprus, Acre in Israel, and finally inland from that harbor to Jerusalem. Traveling in Italy, he used Roman roads; from Venice eastward, he mostly took ships. Returning, Nikulás went directly to Denmark in fifteen weeks, across to Norway, and at last to Iceland, a week's sail from Norway. Probably wintering at friendly monasteries in Europe, Nikulás would have taken two or three years to complete his pilgrimage to the Holy Land. Direct from Iceland to Jerusalem is

Figure 4.2. Figurine of medieval Norse abbott, perhaps Nikulás Berggson, the Benedictine monk who made pilgrimage from Iceland to Jerusalem in the 1150s CE. Metropolitan Museum of Art, New York

nearly 5,000 km (over 3,000 miles), though much farther via the roads and coastal shipping routes Nikulás took. His pilgrimage earned him the title "Jórsalafari"—Jerusalem (Jórsalaland)-wayfarer, adding to his prestige that gained him the position of abbot of his monastery.

Nikulás was not the only medieval Icelander or even Norse Greenlander to successfully complete this arduous roundtrip journey by sea and land. Björn Einarsson and his wife Solveig were two other Jórsalafari, from even farther west, Greenland, about 1385 (Seaver 1996:149). Besides pious men and women pilgrims, the Crusades pulled thousands of men out of every region of Europe toward the Holy Land, with at least part of their trips by sea. Venice embarked so many Crusader soldiers and pilgrims naïve about ships that the city in 1392 appointed officials to inspect and certify their seaworthiness, forbidding unsafe vessels from sailing (Tomasi 2002:6). Complementing Christian pilgrimages to Jerusalem, Muslims ideally make pilgrimage (*hajj*) to Mecca in Saudi Arabia, the final residence of the prophet Mohammed. Approached through the Indian Ocean as Jerusalem is approached through Mediterranean voyages, the hajj to Mecca has been integrated into shipping for more than a thousand years. Hindu and Buddhist

**Figure 4.3.** Medieval pilgrims, engraving c. 1490.
http://spartacus-educational.com/NORpilgrimage.htm

shrines similarly have drawn pilgrims from as far as China and Japan, like Nikulás, taking ships for some segments of their journeys, land routes for other segments. Asian monks often spent a few years studying at destination temples before returning to teach in their homelands.

Major pilgrimage centers such as Jerusalem, Rome, Lourdes, Mecca, Varanasi in India, or Guadalupe in Mexico mix hundreds of thousands of people, even a million or more, especially on significant holy days. Massed together in worship, they may downplay wealth and ethnic differences, for example, by wearing simple white clothing and eating communally in dining halls provided by monks. At the same time, part of the emotional experience of pilgrimage is feeling the diversity of persons under the common purpose. Pilgrims come home with souvenirs and stories of a variety of buildings and cultures, and with foreign diseases, too (Bhardwaj 1997:6). Traveling for a sanctified reason, pilgrims are respected both along the journey and at home. Those who travel to historic places sanctified in civil religion, such as Gettysburg Battlefield or the Capitol and Washington's other gleaming white public monuments, likewise are respected. Pilgrimage seems nearly as ubiquitous as trade among human societies, and nearly as strong a mechanism for spreading knowledge, technology, and arts.

## Sanctifying Places

Certain places become sites that bestow legitimacy upon leaders. Rome is one, where leaders of the Catholic Church are publicly invested at the Vatican. Cholula in Mexico was another of these places, the site of a huge conical pyramid looming over great plazas and a major international market for several centuries before the 1519 attack by Cortés and his Indian allies. On the pyramid was the principal shrine to Quetzalcoatl, the deity who sacrificed himself to revitalize humankind after a cataclysmic destruction. From all over eastern Mexico, newly inheriting or elected lords made pilgrimage to Cholula to be legitimized by the two high priests of the shrine, conferring a nose ornament signifying highest office. Today, the shrine, now in the shape of a Catholic cathedral, draws 350,000 people to its religious festival (Evans and Webster 2001:149).

Capital cities, being seats of government, attract officials and civil servants, envoys, and tourists from other countries as well as their own. London, Paris, Moscow, Beijing, New Delhi, Mexico City, Buenos Aires, and Washington, D.C. carry an international flavor from the hundreds of thousands of foreign businesspeople and tourists on their streets every day. Except for London, a river port, none of these cities are themselves ports; before airplanes, visitors would travel by road from ports to these cities. From the standpoint of trade, the standpoint of civil religion landmarks for their citizens, and the standpoint of legitimating officials and official business, capital cities cast wide nets, bringing together people from most of the globe. They showcase their nations' monuments and art treasures, producing souvenir images carried back by visitors. The Pantheon, built in Rome two thousand years ago as a civic temple for "all the gods" (*pan-theon*), still standing intact, has been the model for thousands of civic buildings and churches during these two millennia—compare the original with, for example, the Foster County courthouse in Carrington, North Dakota. The icon's columned entrance, pediment, and dome over a rotunda symbolize a seat of sanctifying power even when its neighbors are wheat silos.

## Migration

Migration has been a potent mover in global histories (Crawford and Campbell 2012). Astoundingly, in four centuries, an entire continent was overrun by migrants, its several hundred nations and languages sunk beneath the invaders' language and culture imported from overseas. Most of America's First Nations survived, though barely, the tsunami of European migration. Conventionally, post-Columbian migrations are supposed to be fundamentally different from Old World population movements: The myth of Columbus claims the "empty" New World offered freedom and economic opportunities denied in Europe. Aside from the several million Africans forcibly transported across the Atlantic to be slaves in America, there were hundreds of thousands of Europeans driven from peasant farms by aristocratic landlords' decisions to go into agribusiness, thousands more assisted to go because no work could be provided for them, and millions recruited by entrepreneurs to supply labor, skills, or homestead on the frontier. All of these factors operated within Eurasia-Africa before 1492.

Archaeologist David Anthony studied historical migrations going back to Julius Caesar, describing the migration of the Helvetii out of Switzerland to fight for more and better land (Anthony 1990:898–899). Anthony emphasizes that the conventional notion of "folk-wandering" without a determined route or goal is improbable. Instead, agents precede family migrations. Agents may be scouts, often younger men, explicitly sent out to find settlement locations, or they may be traders, soldiers, craftspeople, or elite persons married out to create alliances. These "outliers" return or send information back, enabling families to plan a route and obtain assistance settling in the new home. From a distance of time, it may look as if a "people" moved en masse, whether the Angles and Saxons moving across the Channel into England over a couple of centuries, or their descendants a millennium later crossing the Atlantic to America. In fact, both examples were the piecemeal moves of families and small groups of friends following scouts' feedback.

Looking at migration as David Anthony does, one realizes migration can happen at any scale, from the highly visible like the European takeover of America, to the hardly detectable, archaeologically. The critical point is that human migrations are very different from seasonal migrations of birds or caribou or wildebeest where thousands of massed animals move wavelike across a landscape. Human migrations are aggregates of individual and small group movements, perhaps propelled out by ethnic cleansing projects or a regional natural disaster, but as a rule, traveling to kin or contacts in the new land.

One characteristic Anthony observed that makes it difficult for archaeologists to be confident migration occurred is that migrants "leapfrog" over settlements between their point of departure and their goal (Anthony 1990:902–903). Particularly if travel is by sea, there may be no trace of the movement between origin and new residence. Conversely, trade may distribute imports over diverse nations, with no direct contact between the manufacturers and the customers who obtained their products. A more-or-less continuous distribution of, say, fine ceramics preferred for drinking imported wine, is not a sign of migration of the potters, only of trade agents. Put in contemporary terms, Coca-Cola signs and Golden Arches are not evidence of post-Columbian migration from America to the rest of the world. They are, rather, signs of outreach by individuals from the originating society, successful efforts to link with entrepreneurs in other nations.

## Summary

Simpson's procedure for the historical sciences requires three steps:

1. Obtaining and studying the historical data.
2. Determination of present processes.
3. Confrontation of 1. and 2. with a view toward ordering, filling in, and explaining the history (Simpson 1970:81, 84–85).

In this chapter, we looked at step 2, determining present processes of long distance travel. Trade, both of raw materials and of manufactures, comes most readily to notice. Trade evidenced by materials or manufactures originating in one location and archaeologically recovered in another is firmly documented in our earliest texts, from Egypt and Mesopotamia, as well as highly probable in Upper Paleolithic and Neolithic sites before writing. Pilgrimage may be less familiar today compared to medieval times (Chaucer's *Canterbury Tales* are told to each other by a party of pilgrims), although it remains a powerful incentive to travel, whether to Rome or Mecca or Jerusalem, to saints' relics in hope of healing, to temples where one can gain spiritual merit, or to heritage and historic events sites. Migrating for better economic opportunities or to fulfill a calling, as missionaries do, bring people to live with foreigners in societies quite different from that of the homeland.

Present and historically documented (as with Abbott Nikulás) traveling shows a process of moving very great numbers of individuals across long distances, often by sea. The seas would be "peculiarly empty," to use historian David Quinn's phrase, if this were not true for humankind before 1492 CE. The next chapters look at data that appear to evidence contacts across oceans before the voyages of Columbus and Magellan, in 1492 and 1520.

# Chapter 5

# Polynesian Voyaging: Landfall in the Americas

One case of pre-Columbian transoceanic voyaging is indubitable: the colonization of the eastern Pacific by Polynesians. At first post-Columbian contact by European explorers, nearly every island and atoll in the vast central and eastern Pacific was inhabited by people speaking Polynesian languages and sharing many cultural traits. No land bridges had ever connected the islands; the people had arrived on the islands in distinctive sailing canoes. Their presence proved the oceangoing capability of the boats and their navigators. Their motive seemed clear: finding new lands to accommodate growing populations.

It used to be thought that Polynesia was colonized in a simple west-to-east series of movements, marked archaeologically by finds of a red, decorated pottery called Lapita. It appears in Near Oceania (Melanesia) around 1500 BCE and then spreads into Central Polynesia (Samoa and Tonga) within about five hundred years. Then, after some six hundred years, it ceases to be made. Polynesian colonization was believed to be a series of hops: a straightforward movement eastward into the larger islands of Central Polynesia, followed by a standstill while those populations expanded to the islands' carrying limits, then another push eastward to Hawai'i and Rapa Nui.

Much more archaeology on the islands, coupled with genetic analyses, reveals voyages in every direction within the huge Polynesian triangle from the Solomon Islands through Samoa and Tonga, out to Hawai'i and New Zealand and Rapa Nui, and touching the American coasts at least in Chile, Ecuador, and southern California, where strong currents would carry boats. Proof that the great exploratory voyages

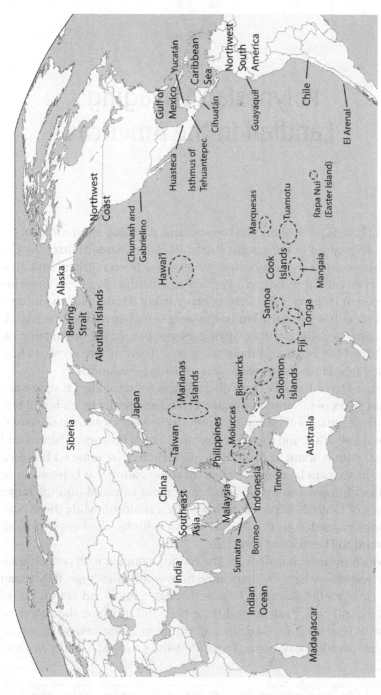

**Figure 5.1.** Map of Polynesia /Island Southeast Asia.

around one thousand years ago did significantly find America lies in archaeological discoveries of sweet potatoes (*Ipomoea batata*) from South America cultivated in the Central Polynesian islands in the thirteenth century CE (Roullier et al. 2013).

John Terrell is an archaeologist who has worked in both New Guinea and Melanesia, and in Polynesia on Oceanic history. At the western side, New Guinea hosts an amazing number of independent native languages, contrasting with the amazing broad expanse of the single language group, Polynesian. This fits the long history of Pleistocene (Ice Age) Sahul, of which New Guinea is the northeastern sector, giving fifty thousand or more years of human habitation, versus the three thousand or fewer years of humans in the Polynesian islands. Having himself personally observed New Guinea communities engaged in elaborate visiting and trading rare shells and ornamental feathers (classically described in Bronislaw Malinowski's 1922 ethnography, *Argonauts of the Western Pacific*), Terrell argues that a plausible interpretation of Lapita is not a few canoes hellbent to colonize Oceania, carrying their precious ancestral pottery with them. Rather, he proposes two sets of conditions: first, that stabilization of sea level in the mid-Holocene, after around 3000 BCE, encouraged New Guinea and Bismarck Archipelago peoples to develop more seaside settlements and marine technologies, and as populations grew, to venture upon ocean explorations and colonizations (Terrell 2014).

Second, coming from societies that valued trade in beautiful rarities, Bismarck people created handsome red-slipped, sometimes highly decorated pots, called Lapita by archaeologists. Welcomed in the newer-settled islands, their wares were carried here and there among the islands until, many generations later, Lapita pots seemed so old-fashioned and unexciting that they lost trading value. Polynesia is unusual in that its communities once made pottery and then gave up ceramics.

The *probability* of this two-part interpretation rests upon its good fit with radiocarbon-dated archaeological discoveries, Melanesian and Polynesian human genetic[1], sea-level changes and related landforms, and observed cultural behavior in Melanesian and Polynesian communities. Conforming to so many independent data including ethnographically described cultural values in the two regions, Terrell's interpretation is highly probable. He expands upon the issue of probability by emphasizing that first, a researcher should consider *plausibility.* "It is sensible," he says, "to constrain the range of possible interpretations to those that are plausible given a reasonable set of likely prior probabilities," or limiting conditions (Terrell and Cochrane 2014). As an anthropological archaeologist doing science, Terrell looks to environmental and social histories and ethnography to select plausible inferences for the region. Probability of interpretive hypotheses is evaluated for best fit within the limiting conditions.

## Origins and Development of Polynesians

Patrick Kirch and Roger Green (2001:60, 77), two long-experienced, leading archaeologists working in Oceania, identify Western Polynesia as the homeland of Polynesians. Polynesian and the islands of its speakers are the easternmost of Austronesian languages (Kirch and Green 2001:55–56). Austronesian, the overarching language stock, includes languages in Southeast Asia and Island Southeast Asia, including languages spoken on Taiwan and the Philippines. Its westernmost language is Malagasy, the language of Madagascar in the Indian Ocean off the coast of Africa; Malagasy is related to Indonesian languages, especially to those spoken in Borneo. Austronesians were sailors traversing immense open-water distances by 2000 BCE (Blench 2014b:6). Their forebears on Taiwan and the mainland were rice farmers by 3500 BCE. As their descendants traveled, they perforce depended on fish and crops suited to smaller islands, including taro, sago palm, and breadfruit (Terrell et al. 2003:334–336).

Polynesian origins need to take into account the presence of speakers of a great variety of other languages in Western Oceania, says linguist Roger Blench (2014c). He emphasizes that New Guinea and Melanesia have been inhabited as long as Australia (Blench 2014d:2), and that these peoples, living along coasts and on islands, traversed the seas. The area of the China Sea, Island Southeast Asia, and Western Oceania is a very large region characterized for millennia by constant movement of people and goods between communities for a range of purposes and of varying duration and distance without necessarily involving permanent residential relocations. Such mobility is widely documented across the ISEA-New Guinea-Archipelago region in historical times, creating and maintaining social networks between individuals and communities across long distances on a regular, intermittent, or unpredictable basis, irrespective of duration, frequency, or intensity. These networks are conduits for transfers of goods and raw materials, beliefs and rituals, songs and dances, languages, people, and genes (Sprecht et al. 2014:92).

This sea-oriented, fragmented cultural pattern, called Nusantao by archaeologist Wilhelm Solheim (2006), contrasts with our familiar picture of migrations of Neolithic farmers, then Indo-European warrior groups, then Christianity moving wavelike westward over Europe.

Austronesian speakers seem likely to have introduced Lapita pottery, and somewhat later, pigs, chickens, dogs, and the Pacific rat (rats may have sneaked aboard large canoes, or been taken, since they were eaten in Polynesia) (Sprecht et al. 2014:113–116). Terrell, Blench, and other Oceanic archaeologists emphasize that this handsome, distinctive pottery flourished in the Bismarck Archipelago off northeastern New Guinea around 1350 BCE. Lapita's roots appear to lie in the Philippines and the Marianas islands (Guam, Saipan, Tinian, Rota) 2,000 km (1,250 miles) east of the Philippines; that is to say, colonization of uninhabited Marianas islands at 1500 BCE is the first instance of long-distance colonization of Oceanic islands.

Pottery painted red before firing developed in Taiwan around 3500 BCE; the technology was taken to the Philippines about 2000 BCE, where decorative motifs were applied; then to the Marianas; and finally to the Bismarcks where decorations were elaborated, although the majority of pots were left red but undecorated (Carson et al. 2013:22). Red-slipped pottery went also westward to Indonesia at 1500 BCE (Carson et al. 2013:21). The dentate-stamped designs, made with a toothed instrument, resembles tattooing, which historically was common among Polynesians. Lapita pots were carried by the first colonizers of Remote Oceania in the central Pacific; the colonizers were only a very few of the thousands making and trading Lapita pots in the Bismarcks and Solomon islands of Melanesia.

Then, centuries later, one or a few Austronesian-speaking communities in the Bismarcks set off in sophisticated sailing canoes to find islands to colonize, settling in Tonga about 840 BCE (Wilmshurst et al. 2011:1818:Terrell 2015:13. The islands of Fiji, northwest of Tonga, had been settled a couple centuries earlier, and those of Samoa, northeast of Fiji and Tonga, soon after. Fiji is 2,133 km (1,325 miles) from the Solomon Islands at the eastern tip of the Bismarck archipelago. The Society and Cook Islands in the center of Remote Oceania (that is, Polynesia), were settled between 1025 and 1121 CE, and the Marquesas, Tuamotu, and Mangareva a thousand miles east of the Societies and Cook, *and* the easternmost islands Hawai'i and Rapa Nui (Easter Island), settled between 1200 and 1290 CE (Wilmshurst, Hunt, Lipo and Anderson 2011:1816).

Out in Remote Oceania, the picture changes. Now, on islands that had no human inhabitants before the landings, Austronesian-based

**Figure 5.2.** The *Hōkūle'a*, a full-size replica of a Polynesian Hawai'ian *wa'a kaulua* voyaging canoe. Photo by Hong Kong Huey, 2009

**Figure 5.3.** A Tonga voyaging canoe encountered by Dutch explorers, 1616. About twenty-five passengers were on its deck. Courtesy Ben Finney

**Table 5.1.** Ocean Distances

| Origin | Destination | Distance |
| --- | --- | --- |
| Bismarcks/Solomon Islands | Fiji | 1,325 mi./2,133 km |
| Fiji | Tonga | 500 mi./805 km |
| Fiji | Samoa | 709 mi./1,141 km |
| Tonga | Samoa | 552 mi./889 km |
| Samoa | Society and Cook Islands | 1,250 mi./2,000 km |
| Society Islands | Marquesas | 1,000 mi./1,600 km |
| Marquesas | Hawai'i | 2,000 mi./3,220 km |
| Marquesas | Rapa Nui | 2,275 mi./3,661 km |
| Hawai'i | Southern California | 2,400 mi./3,877 km |
| Rapa Nui | Araucanian area, Chile | 2,261 mi./3,838 km |

Polynesian became the only language, and the culture they carried became Polynesian culture. Pottery making was dropped after the colonization of Tonga and Samoa. Those islands apparently accommodated the Polynesians for nearly two thousand years. Suddenly, in the eleventh century CE, exploring expeditions went out in large, fast double canoes, first directly eastward, discovering and colonizing the Societies and Cook Islands. Fanning out from these a century later, their descendants found New Zealand in the far south, Hawai'i in the far northeast, and Rapa Nui in the far southeast.

A final landfall, on the coast of Chile in the fourteenth century, completed Polynesians' traverse of the Pacific (Storey, Quiroz, and Matisoo-Smith 2011:168). What impelled such extraordinary voyages over a vast, nearly empty ocean isn't obvious, although a peak of El Niño wind patterns, facilitating eastward sailing, did coincide with the century of last colonizations (Wilmshurst, Hunt, Lipo, and Anderson 2011:1818).

This picture of a burst of late, rapid colonization includes return journeys from the first discoveries. Discoverers likely sailed back to home bases to load people and supplies for a settlement—it's implausible that they would be carrying women, breeding pairs of pigs and chickens and maybe deliberately, Pacific rats, enough plants for agriculture, and tools on a voyage exploring unknown waters (Storey, Clarke,

**Figure 5.4.** Rapa Nui's famous giant statues. Permission and source, Easter Island Project, courtesy Jo Anne Tilburg.

and Matisoo-Smith 2011). On at least one return, sailors carried South American sweet potatoes to Mangaia in the Cook Islands (Wilmshurst, Hunt, Lipo, and Anderson 2011:1818). That sweet potatoes could have been brought west to Polynesia by South American Indians on a large sailing raft like Heyerdahl's *Kon-Tiki* is possible but less probable than a round trip by highly experienced Polynesians in their superb fast ships.

## El Arenal

Before the recent compendium of carefully analyzed radiocarbon dates from Polynesia that shows the first colonizations of Fiji, Tonga, and Samoa, then a long hiatus before extensive explorations a thousand years ago, archaeologists assumed Polynesians had advanced slowly and steadily across the Pacific over two or perhaps three millennia. Seeing how maritime their communities are, how much prestige is enjoyed by master sailors and navigators, researchers inferred that long-distance exploratory voyaging is a basic part of Polynesian culture. Steady chugging across the

Pacific might have brought Polynesians to the Americas, it was admitted, yet without any smoking guns of Polynesian manufacture there, most American archaeologists denied they had advanced that far before European contacts (1520 CE, Magellan's voyage). Oceanic archaeologists, with plenty of firsthand experience on islands, did generally assume at least a landfall or two, particularly after Kirch and Hather's finds of sweet potato in Mangaia, directly dated to nearly a thousand years ago.

In 2007, an interdisciplinary team of scientists published a report on a site, El Arenal 1, near the coast of Chile, where an acceptable professional excavation had discovered chicken bones directly radiocarbon dated to before European invasions (Spaniards, 1537–1541 CE). El Arenal is an area of sand dunes on an estuary in Arauco Province in southern Chile, the homeland of the Mapuche First Nation. Due to dune movement, artifacts were eroding out of the site, El Arenal 1. Excavations between 2002 and 2008, to an average depth of one meter, yielded ceramic sherds, stone tool blades, and animal bones from a series of occupations in the Late Prehistoric period beginning around 1000 CE. The site appeared to have been abandoned before 1500 CE.

From an occupation dated both by radiocarbon on organic materials and by thermoluminescence on the sherds (a technique measuring accumulated radiation in crystalline minerals in pottery clay) to around 1400 CE, eighty-three chicken bones were recovered, along with butchered bones of the local guanaco, nutria (like a large muskrat), and ducks. A pre-Columbian date for the chickens is confirmed by radiocarbon dating several of them. Chickens are native to Asia and have been a common Polynesian domesticate. El Arenal's chickens are genetically the same as Polynesian chickens (if you've been to Hawai'i, you've seen these chickens roaming all over). A minimum of five chickens were eaten at the El Arenal 1 site.

Several geographers, including Carl Sauer (chapter 6), noted over the years that the earliest Spanish invaders and explorers in South America noticed chickens in Indian villages. Several unusual breeds were mentioned, and that the birds were prized for their gorgeous feathers as well as for meat and eggs. Polynesians also valued rooster feathers for feather cloaks and headdresses. Cock-fighting was seen, as well.[2]

American archaeologists generally dismissed these observations, supposing that undocumented Spanish incursions, perhaps deserters from invading armies, had introduced the birds. Now, El Arenal 1 scientifically validated the geographers' identification of chickens in Indian villages before Spanish contact. The validation involved experts on chicken genetics, skeleton morphology, radiocarbon, and Polynesian archaeology, in

**Figure 5.5.** A Polynesian chicken in Hawai'i. Photo by Alice Kehoe

addition to the careful work by Chilean archaeologists (Storey, Quiróz, and Matisoo-Smith 2011; Matisoo-Smith 2014:5–6).

After the identification of chickens in coastal Chile at the time of the final Polynesian colonizations of Remote Oceania, Oceanic biological anthropologist Elizabeth Matisoo-Smith joined Chilean archaeologist José Miguel Ramírez-Aliaga, who had worked on Rapa Nui, to search museum collections for more evidence. On Mocha Island off the coast of Chile, 100 km (62 miles ) from El Arenal, they recognized Polynesian characteristics in human skeletons in the local Concepcion Museum's collections (Matisoo-Smith 2011, 2014:6). Some artifacts from Mocha Island and mainland Chilean Mapuche territory resemble Polynesian types, and, like the name *kumara* for sweet potato, bear the same name. Among these are polished stone axes or adzes called *toki* in both Mapuche and Polynesia, including the Chatham Islands southeast of New Zealand. Curved, polished stone hand clubs, some resembling stylized bird heads, called *clavas* by Mapuche and *wahaikas* by Maori in New Zealand, are very similar in Chile, New Zealand, and the Chathams (Ramírez-Aliaga 2011:99–103). Most striking are canoes with lashed planks along the sides to raise freeboard (height above the waterline), a standard boat technology in Polynesia that is found in the Americas only in two localities, Chumash territory in coastal Southern California, and Mapuche territory in southern Chile (Ramírez-Aliaga 2011:107–108). Mapuche called this type of canoe *dalca*.

## Ecuador and California Landfalls

Two other areas in the Americas have evidence of Polynesian contacts: the Gulf of Guayaquil in Ecuador, and southern California. Like southern Chile, Guayaquil and the southern California coast are points to which prevailing westerlies and ocean currents would carry sailing vessels. Ecuador's Gulf of Guayaquil is an excellent harbor that was frequented by pre-Columbian Peruvian and Mexican traders exchanging wares in this intermediate area. Apparently without lashed-plank canoes, its traders did use large sailing rafts, the triangular (lateen) sails resembling those of Polynesians (and the Indian Ocean). Because sweet potatoes were in Central Polynesia at the time of initial settlement, about a century before the last great eastward explorations, it seems probable that they had been obtained from landfalls in the Gulf of Guayaquil during the early phase of that second exploration period (Scaglion and Cordero 2011).

Boats were important to California Chumash, who frequently paddled the Santa Barbara Channel between the mainland and the Channel Islands. Besides logboats and boats made of bundles of tule reeds, they made a lashed-plank canoe of the same Polynesian type as Mapuche *dalca*, the Chumash calling these boats *tomol* (Jones 2011:81–87). Seemingly foreign to the Chumash language, the word could be derived from Hawai'ian Eastern Polynesian *tumu rakau*, "wooden canoe." Neighboring the Chumash are the Gabrieliño First Nation, speaking an unrelated language; they too made lashed-plank boats, calling theirs *taraina*. Compare Eastern Polynesian *talai*, "carve" or "hew" wood (with Gabrieliño adding suffix *-na*), and Gabrieliño *ti'at* "sew," with Eastern Polynesian *tia* "sew" (Klar 2011:195–197). Similarly, to a linguist, Chumash *kalui* or *qalui*, "harpoon," seems derived from Polynesian *tala hui* "sharp-pointed bone" (harpoon point) (Klar 2011:198–200). Harpoons were commonly used by Chumash and coastal Chileans, and also in the Marquesas, Mangareva, and New Zealand (Jones 2011:91). Chumash began using two-part barbed and single-piece barbed bone fishhooks, both types very similar to Polynesian types, about the same time as they began building lashed-plank boats; previously, for several thousand years, they had used simpler fishhooks like those of other California native nations (Jones 2011:72–81).

## Summary

The weight of data from professionally excavated archaeological sites throughout Oceania and coastal America, along with ethnohistoric documentations, make the case for Polynesian landfalls in the Americas. The

**Figure 5.6.** A Chumash tomolo (lashed-plank canoe), California. Black Gold Cooperative Library System

site of El Arenal 1 in Chile is most persuasive, with eighty-three chicken bones from birds like those kept by Polynesians, directly dated to the time of final Polynesian eastward explorations more than a century before European invasions in South America. Equally compelling is the dating of sweet potatoes in Central Polynesia to the early part of the final voyagings, the potatoes genetically affiliated with those cultivated at that time in northwestern South America. Once this framework of well-dated pre-Columbian exchanges of biological species was established, the cases of lashed-plank canoes, fish and harpoon hooks, and Chilean finds of Polynesian-type skeletons become more credible. That there appear to be no Polynesian colonies in the Americas fits the cultural background of Polynesian explorations, seeking uninhabited islands for settlement. Those sections of the Americas where winds and currents would have brought Polynesians had already been populated for millennia.

## Chapter 6

# The Strongest Evidence:
# Plants and Animals

Carl O. Sauer (1889–1975), professor of geography at the University of Michigan from 1915 to 1923 and the University of California-Berkeley from 1923 to 1957, developed the field of cultural geography, focusing on how people use and affect the land. Tramping the fields and woods of the Ozark plateau in Missouri as a boy, Sauer deeply experienced the ecological interplay of land forms, water, plants, animals, and people. Convinced that geographers needed to know histories of exploration, invasions, and colonizations, Sauer framed his field research against such knowledge. That produced anomalies—plants and other living things noted by early explorers on continents that they had not evolved on. Had they been brought by voyagers crossing oceans before 1492?

Anomalies are the touchstone of scientific research progress. Thomas Kuhn, in his pathbreaking *Structure of Scientific Revolutions*, explained:

> Normal science does not aim at novelties of fact or theory and, when successful, finds none. New and unsuspected phenomena are, however, repeatedly uncovered by scientific research. . . . Produced inadvertently by a game played under one set of rules, their assimilation requires the elaboration of another set. . . . Discovery commences with the awareness of anomaly. . . . It then continues with a more or less extended exploration of the area of anomaly. And it closes only when the paradigm[1] theory has been adjusted so that the anomalous has become the expected (Kuhn 1970:52–53).

The paradigm for conventional archaeological research in America has been drawn from John Locke's 1689 treatise stating that before his century's English invasions, America was the model of primitive uncivilized life, its savages failing to invest labor in improvements. Their lack of money or written title to landed property—his criteria for civilized society—showed that they had been cut off from intercourse with "higher" nations. Locke, an employee of the lords proprietors of Carolina Colony, was writing a legal argument to justify his employers' takeover of Indian nations' land. Like the myth of Columbus, Locke's doctrine that American First Nations were all savages in wilderness was embraced by generations of European and European-descended settlers blind to the injustices they imposed.

If the Americas had been completely isolated from the rest of the world until 1492, and its population was descended from Pleistocene hunters moving eastward through Arctic Beringia, then no American plants could have gotten to other continents before 1492. Carl Sauer and his geography students found evidence to the contrary, that the sweet potato was taken to Central Polynesia, maize to India and perhaps independently to China, and peanuts to China. Sauer emphasized fieldwork, surveying and recording plants and their ecological contexts, coupled with research in archives to discover first documentations of plants and subsequent distributions. Watching and talking with local farmers were important, too. The Sauer method of historical cultural geography produced dozens of anomalies to the reigning paradigm of Americas isolation.

Historical plant geography demands expertise in genetics and ancient texts as well as identification and mapping of plant distributions. Depictions of plants in sculpture and paintings are another line of research requiring both fieldwork and archives. Geographers in the Sauer tradition work with laboratory scientists, art historians, and scholars expert in reading Sanskrit, Chinese, and many other languages. Their paradigm accommodates a huge range of data, accepting the probability of voyages over the past 50,000 years (attested by humans in Australia that long ago) and becoming more frequent during the modern Holocene era as populations increased and trade, explorations, and pilgrimage expanded. Biological remains become proxy clues for voyages and intersocietal contacts; Elizabeth Matisoo-Smith maps Polynesian presence by dating Pacific rat bones, brought by humans, in tropical island sites where most results of human activities have decayed away. That American archaeologists have not adjusted their paradigm to take account of the geographers' work shows the power of intense socialization into the myth of Columbus. Carl Sauer, from boyhood, recognized another power: that of direct field observation and comparisons–the method of historical sciences outlined by George Gaylord Simpson.

## Distributions of Plants and Animals as Evidence of pre-Columbian Contacts

Carl Johannessen, retired professor of geography at the University of Oregon, is the last surviving student of Carl Sauer. Collaborating with John Sorenson of Brigham Young University, who for years has been building a bibliography on pre-Columbian transoceanic contacts, Johannessen organized reports on plants and animals discovered on continents to which they are not native. For each, he evaluated its data for the questions of pre-Columbian occurrence and, if probable, possibility that it moved independent of human agency. His results are presented in a set of tables: Flora, Microfauna, and Other Fauna, Decisive Evidence; then the same categories showing Significant But Not Decisive Evidence; and a third set Needing Further Research. Evaluations are supported by several hundred pages of detailed data and references, using the IBE method, inference to the best explanation.

Unpleasant though they are, tropical parasitic worms exclusively infesting humans are perhaps the strongest evidence for pre-Columbian voyaging between Southeast Asia-Oceania and South America. Eurasian hookworms, roundworms, pinworms, and whipworms have been found inside Peruvian and Bolivian mummies and in dried human feces in Peru dated to 2700 BCE, in Brazil dated to 5000 BCE, and the American Southwest. These creatures evolved to live inside human hosts, plus part of their life cycle has to be in warm soil. They could not have survived migrations through the Arctic (Beringia). Therefore, confronting the data of pre-Columbian occurrences in America with present processes of the animals' life cycle leads to high probability of Holocene carriage within humans voyaging across the Pacific from southern Asia or Oceania, where the parasites are endemic (Sorenson and Johannessen 2013:260–294, including other disease vectors).

Chickens now are a Eurasian domesticate attested in pre-Columbian America, after years of scientific debate (Chapter 5). Carl Sauer recounted his surprise, on a field trip to Chile in 1942, when an inn served him boiled chicken eggs that were blue or olive green. "We saw them in Araucanian village after village," he noted (Sauer 1952:59). Twenty years earlier, Swedish anthropologist Erland Nordenskiöld had recorded distributions throughout South America of unusual breeds of chickens, usually in Indian villages, with Indian-languages words for the fowl. Sauer's students, George Carter and Carl Johannessen, continued field recording Indian breeds of chickens in South America, agreeing with Sauer that both the many instances of earliest Spanish explorers in the sixteenth century obtaining chickens from Indians, and the differences between these chickens, and their descendants, from European chickens suggest pre-Columbian importation from Asia or Oceania. One breed has black meat (quite edible) and black bones as well as black feathers. Discovery of bones of at least five chickens in El Arenal I, on the Araucanian coast of Chile, radiocarbon dated to the fourteenth century CE, confirmed Sauer's inference that the unusual chickens he ate there likely descended from pre-Columbian imports from the Pacific (Storey et al. 2007).

Among Eurasian populations, tuberculosis is one of several diseases endemic to and found in Near Eastern and European skeletons from as early as the Neolithic, around 6000 BCE (Roberts and Buikstra 2003:182–183). It has been recognized in pre-Columbian America in three areas: western South America, the American Southwest, and eastern North America (Roberts and Buikstra 2003:195–200). No recognized finds of tuberculosis have been made in pre-Columbian Mesoamerica. The South American cases, from Chile, Peru, and Colombia, include the tuberculosis bacillus in a couple of mummies dated 700 CE, the oldest cases.[2] Where cases occurred in cemetery populations, more males than females were affected. Tuberculosis has been identified on a number of pre-contact skeletons in Hawai'i (Roberts and Buikstra 2003:180–182), raising the possibility that the South American cases derived from Polynesian landings.

The North American cases begin around 1000 CE. This is when the Norse find America, as detailed in two medieval histories, the *Saga of Eirik the Red* and *The Greenlanders' Saga* (for detailed summaries, see Kolodny 2012:48–93). Archaeological excavation at L'Anse aux Meadows in northern Newfoundland revealed a cluster of Norse buildings and locally smelted bog iron, a Norse technology, radiocarbon dated 1000 CE, precisely fitting the dates in the sagas for colonization efforts in "Vinland" by Eirik the Red's family (see Chapter 9). While the meaning of "Vinland" is debated, it could refer to pasture land desired for cattle, obviously available at L'Anse aux Meadows. A butternut shell recovered in the excavation proves Norse there had sailed on at least to the southern reaches of the Gulf of St. Lawrence, where there was a major native trade location, Tadoussac. If some Norse carrying endemic tuberculosis had visited in Indian homes, especially the tightly insulated winter wigwams (Dickason 1984:241, 325 n. 45), the tuberculosis bacillus could easily have been transmitted by breath droplets to Indians, then traveled along the active extensive trade routes inland, Indian to Indian.[3]

Most unexpected was discovery of American psychotropic plants in Eurasia as early as three thousand years ago. Svetlana Balabanova, a prominent forensic chemist in Germany, in 1992 tested nine Egyptian mummies from the University of Munich and others from the Egyptian Museum in Berlin and the Historical Museum in Vienna. To her surprise, she found evidence in some of the mummies, dating from 1000 BCE to 400 CE, for cocaine and nicotine as well as hashish and marijuana. While the latter two are from Eurasian plants, cocaine and nicotine are from American cultivated plants. Balabanova's identifications raised a flurry of efforts to challenge the obvious interpretation that wealthy Egyptians had obtained the ritually important American plants from voyagers across the Pacific. Ingested cocaine leaves a complex unique metabolite that experienced biochemists consider unmistakable. All contemporary cocaine is processed from the South American coca, *Erythroxylon coca*. Chewing coca leaves, the custom in South America, is like chewing tea leaves, mildly relaxing, not mind-altering.[4] Another *Erythroxylon* species grows in northern Madagascar, where it was used as a folk medicine.

A number of species of *Nicotiana*, tobacco, are found in the Americas, the South Pacific including Australia, and southwest Africa— the American species *Nicotiana tabacum* being the variety raised for smoking. Although this seems not to have been discussed, it is possible that the wild tobaccos in Africa and Australia are feral, not native. Tobacco leaves have pesticide properties. Chopped tobacco leaves were stuffed into the abdomen of the mummy of Pharoah Ramses II (1213 BCE), perhaps as pesticide, perhaps for the aroma, as it was customary to stuff mixtures of incense and perfume substances into this cavity in Egyptian mummies.

Discussions over Balabanova's findings have focused on whether the many mummies she examined may have been contaminated after excavation by people smoking while handling them, a question that ignores that what Balabanova reported are metabolites—that is, consumed and internally metabolized tobacco and cocaine. In any case, it isn't likely that people handling the many mummies were dropping cocaine on them. What seems a reasonable, if at first startling, hypothesis suggests that wealthy Egyptians purchased elixirs mixed by alchemists in hopes of prolonging or resurrecting life. If they did obtain coca leaves, they would have chewed them as people chew in the Andes, or brewed them as a tea (Counsell 2008:215). Documents from the first millennium BCE, the earliest medical treatment documents, record Chinese and Indian doctors' formulations of many plant extracts. Over and over, continuing to the twentieth century CE, "alchemical philosophers" experimented with bio-chemistry, hoping to find the mixture that would produce longevity or, ideally, immortality: the elixir of life (Needham and Lu 1983).

Egyptians imported quantities of luxury items from India and Southeast Asia, including incense, perfumes, and spices; it is prob-able that purported elixirs of life were among the imports. If this is the explanation, then coca and tobacco were imported across the Pa-cific from South America to Farther India, thence to India and, in processed form, to Egyptian aristocrats. Alternately, or also, coca and tobacco, highly prized in the Americas, were shipped to China, pro-cessed, and carried overland on the Silk Road to Egyptian markets. We can't prove the path of these ephemeral products. Placing the foren-sic discovery of metabolites of these American psychotropic plants in Egyptians of the first millennium BCE in the context of widely traded Asian alchemical elixirs seems an inference to the best explanation. It fits the cultural context of widespread trade in and through the Indi-an Ocean diffusing religious and medical ideas along with precious materials (Curtin 1984:101–103).

Very long distance contacts within the Old World include transport of bananas from New Guinea to West Africa (Perrier et al. 2011). Edi-ble bananas come from ancient hybrids created by human cultivators, with their earliest archaeological evidence in Kuk Swamp in highland New Guinea, approximately 5000 BCE. These edible fruits don't pro-duce viable seeds, so must be propagated by farmers (and identified in archaeological sites through phytoliths, tiny silica deposits in plant tissues that remain in soil after plants decay). Bananas have been found in western Oceania sites after 1500 BCE, in Pakistan at 2000 BCE, and in Cameroon in West Africa approximately 500 BCE. Genet-ics and linguistics, analyzed by a large multidisciplinary team, indicate cultivated bananas spread eastward from western Melanesia through Remote Oceania, spread northward to the Philippines, and westward to Indonesia and on to the Indian Ocean and to Cameroon in West Africa (whether by sea around Africa, or from East Africa overland, isn't known; no evidence of bananas in East Africa is recognized [De Langhe 2007:367, Blench 2009:375]). Perrier's team (2011:11317), and Roger Blench, who has researched both banana terms (Blench 2009) and mu-sical instruments in Africa, tracing complex patterns of long distance movement over millennia between East Africa, the Indian Ocean, and Indonesia (Blench 2014a), highlight how little is formally documented on contacts and transfers outside imperial state affairs.

## Disputed Identifications

Carl Sauer's work with plant geography entailed reading early books on botany. That science was one of the first of the "moderns," in the "battle of ancients and moderns" between traditional reliance on Classical Greek and Roman authorities versus reliance on direct observation and experimentation. Beginning in 1530, "Great Herbals" were published showing drawings of plants accompanied by detailed descriptions. A few years later, still in the 1530s, Great Herbals from southern Germany included woodcuts and descriptions of maize (that is, American corn). Sauer noted that not until 1570 did a great herbal publication say that maize originated in America; before then, botanists attributed it to Asia Minor. Thus maize and the imported American fowl were "Turkish corn" and "turkey," brought to Venice from its eastern Mediterranean ports and established in Italy's Po Valley, where *polenta*, cornmeal, is a staple food. An Italian, Peter Martyr, who was tutor to the princess of Spain, wrote in 1493 that he saw Columbus's presentation to the Spanish court, including the display of a grain the same as his Italian correspondents knew, as he did, from its cultivation in Italy. Martyr's description of the grain is clearly maize, so different from Eurasian grains in having large kernels on cobs growing on tall, tasseled plants. Sauer (1969) concluded that maize came to Italy and southern Germany *before Columbus*, from West Africa and/or Asia Minor.[5] How it arrived to these areas, he could not say.

Sauer's student, Carl Johannessen, pursued the question. Johannessen traveled widely in India and bordering regions of the Himalayas, Nepal, Sikkim, Bhutan, Assam, and Myanmar (Burma). He found peasant farmers in these rugged hills raising strange varieties of maize, including a popcorn with seven to nine ears high on the stalk, another popcorn that has leaves and tassels different from known American varieties, and a winter flint maize with short, fat, conical ears that look very much like fruits carried by female figures carved on the medieval Hoysala Dynasty Halebid temple, Somnathpur, Karnataka Pradish, India (Sorenson and Johannessen 2013:250, 255, 258, 335; Johannessen and Parker 1989). Shown with husks peeled halfway back, exposing cobs with ripe kernels (like sweet corn sold in grocery stores), these bas-reliefs dated to the eleventh and twelfth centuries CE are startlingly similar to familiar maize. Johannessen showed his photographs of carvings from this and other temples in India predating 1492 to a group of experts on maize breeds at the Ohio Agricultural Research and Development Center, Ohio State University, Wooster, and they concurred with his identification of the sculpted fruits as maize (Nault et al., 1995; Sorenson and Johannesen 2013:250). Other possible evidence of pre-Columbian maize in Asia that Johannessen discusses is more equivocal: "waxy" maize similar to rice (in being glutinous) that was raised in the Philippines, Korea, and across China to Myanmar results from a not-uncommon mutation that could have spread so widely from a sixteenth-century introduction by Spanish or Portuguese ships, and words for a grain in Sanskrit and in pre-1500 written Chinese documents might refer to another grain before being applied to maize historically.

Maize is a remarkable plant cultivated from a mutant teosinte. Because its seeds do not loosen upon ripening, maize cannot scatter its seeds like normal grains. Easy to harvest, the mutant was husked and its kernels separated for planting by Mexicans more than 5500 years ago (Blake 2006:57; see also Iltis 2006). Totally dependent on human assistance in reproducing, maize mutates frequently and its farmers can breed for qualities they desire. "Primitive"-looking types of popcorns in Himalayan regions could have been developed and spread within a few centuries after Spanish traffic from Mexico to the Indian Ocean. This is why the pictorial record of medieval temple bas-reliefs is stronger evidence of pre-Columbian contact than assuming it took more than 500 years to breed strange varieties presently cultivated in remote areas. Maize phytoliths recovered from pre-Columbian levels in professionally, soundly excavated sites would be the strongest evidence. They may turn up, with a probability slightly greater than finding the proverbial needle in a haystack.

Peanuts, custard apple (annona), and maize are reported, without comment, by British archaeologist Ian Glover in occupations in a cave he excavated in Timor, Indonesia, dated to 800 and 1000 CE (Glover 1977:43). Glover was young when he conducted that excavation and he seems to have failed to distinguish pre-Columbian occupations from those a few centuries later. Peanuts are native to the Andes and were cultivated in South America for several millennia. Chinese archaeologist K.C. Chang, who earned a PhD in archaeology at Harvard and taught at Yale, mentioned peanuts in a couple of Neolithic sites in China (Chang 1977:167, 181), and stronger identification has been reported for twenty peanuts found, along with quantities of other foods for the deceased, during a 1980s excavation of a Yangling imperial mausoleum near X'ian (China Heritage Project 2007). These date to the Han empire, two thousand years ago.[6] Beans, chili pepper, squashes, and marigolds are American cultigens that have been identified in medieval India around 1000 CE (Sorenson and Johannessen 2013:21–24)[7]. Marigolds are used in both the Andes and in India in quantities to adorn temples and celebrants in rituals.

To consider animals, small hairless dogs were raised in pre-Columbian Mexico and Peru, and in China, for ritual feast eating. The argument against transpacific carriage is that a single mutation produces the hairless feature (Drögemuller et al., 2008). On the other hand, in both China and Peru, the dogs are very small and look alike (crested hairless), and the Mexican variety is similar though without the crest (Jett 2008–2010). Dogs were raised for ritual feasts by Plains Indians of North America, where there were two breeds: a large type used to carry packs and pull travois (tied poles on which loads were fastened) and a smaller, fatter dog for eating. Plains feast dogs are ordinary, furry animals, smaller only compared to the big pack dogs. American and Chinese hairless feast dogs are unusually small and look to be the same highly bred type. Modeled and painted in artwork in Mexico from early in first millennium CE, they are not unequivocally evidenced in China until after Spanish imports from Mexico began (Jett 2008–2010), therefore, the Chinese breed may represent post-Columbian introduction.

Nautical archaeologist Richard Steffy recognized agave leaves on a ship dated to the fourth century BCE, the ship being of Greek design and discovered on the seabed of the Mediterranean north of Cyprus. Tough agave leaves and pine pitch were used to seal a lead covering onto the bottom of this ship, presumably to reduce toredo worm damage (Steffy 1985:84, 98). Agave is an American plant that is supposed to have been taken to Europe after 1492. In personal communication (to John L. Sorenson, April 18, 2001), Steffy stated that other archaeologists have discovered ships of Classical Greek, Phoenician, and Roman design close to the European and African coasts, similarly caulked with the agave fiber/pitch mixture. He told Sorenson that he believed archaeologists were unwilling to publish these data for fear of rejection by the archaeological community. Many Eurasian species, however, are similar to American agave in the plant's family (Asparagaceae), most with large fibrous leaves suitable for packing, so the probability is that the botanist whom Steffy consulted did not distinguish between American and Mediterranean agaves.

## Assessing Plants and Animals as Evidence of pre-Columbian Contacts

It is indubitable that finding a cultivated plant or domesticated animal native to the Western hemisphere in the Eastern, or vice versa, is evidence of human carriers across the oceans. Very few plants will propagate after immersion in sea water; very few birds could swallow seeds, fly thousands of miles over an ocean, then disgorge seeds that would grow in the new land. When the plant or animal is valued by its culti-vators, the probability that it would be carried for trade or to be used in voyagers' homelands is high.

Recall that historical sciences proceed inductively to assess proba-bility. Absolute proof is unlikely. For organisms recovered archaeolog-ically, the first question is the reliability of excavation. More recent ex-cavations are more probable to have proceeded with professional care for details, assisted by advanced technologies such as laser recording of stratigraphy. Tiny items such as peanuts and maize kernels easily slip down rodent burrows or are shifted by soil perturbations. Twenty peanuts in a Yangling tomb carry a higher probability of correct dating than two peanuts in a Neolithic village site. Similarly, sweet potato in Central Polynesia is attested by relatively recent excavations by profes-sional archaeologists who publish detailed stratigraphic and radiocar-bon data on the occurrences (Hather and Kirch 1991), with compara-bly detailed description on the cultigen in fourteenth-century Hawai'i (Ladefoged et al., 2005). Details demonstrate scientific procedures and the chain of logic leading to inference to the best explanation.

Written sources such as the Great Herbals cited by Sauer are less sure. Sauer emphasized that the ones he used illustrate the plants, with attention to defining characters. Earlier documents in Asia and Europe may have only verbal descriptions, or simply list a name that historical-ly is used for an American plant or animal. Referents for names change through time, and over distances. An obvious example of the pitfall of uncritically accepting a name is the word "corn" for maize. "Corn" was an English general term for grain; gradually, after European colo-nizations in North America, "Indian corn" (maize) was shortened to "corn." The English Corn Laws of 1815 were about the price of wheat. Scientific taxonomy for organisms using the Linnean system of genus and species can be definitive, especially if the citation includes refer-ence to type specimens in museums such as Kew in England, but Linné introduced his system in the eighteenth century, and over more than two centuries, many taxa have been renamed or the definitions rewrit-ten, so even these terms in earlier work need to be checked.

Parasites and microorganisms inside mummies are strong evidence, so long as their pre-Columbian homelands are known, and the mum-mified bodies have not been carelessly handled. Archaeologists worry that carelessness allows contamination from the present day to be de-posited on mummies' skin or in cuts. Svetlana Balabanova analyzed *metabolized* cocaine and nicotine *within* mummies' hair and bone to be confident that a smoker or cocaine user working in the laboratory had not contaminated the specimens. Until very recently, it wasn't routine that archaeologists and laboratory workers cover their hair to guard against not only insects that might fall upon the mummy, but also to prevent one of the workers' hairs from being picked up along with the mummy's, so multiple specimens are tested. Evidence on skeletons of disease ravages, as in the case of tubercular lesions, may be open to disagreement among specialists on whether the postulated disease is the only one that would leave such signs, or whether a related microorganism might be native to the region.

An assumption exists that a wide variety of species or breeds indicates a long evolution. "Gradualism" is a principle that won out over "catastrophism" among the early nineteenth century geologists—that tiny incremental changes over long periods produced what we see, not sudden volcanic eruptions. By the late twentieth century, so much evidence accumulated for relatively quick changes—for example, fluctuations in the warming trend ending the Pleistocene Ice Age—that "gradualism" could no longer be assumed. Cultivated plants and animals can be selectively bred, and the new varieties spread quickly because peasants as well as scientists know how to choose traits they want. Charles Darwin acquired his understanding of natural selection by quizzing farmers and breeders on their methods, realizing that circumstances in nature can act like breeders to favor certain characteristics. The assumption should be that useful new organisms, whether introduced from a distant place or bred, will rapidly spread. Like smartphones and pizza.

**Figure 6.1.** A Chinese hairless dog, "crested" variety, courtesy Animalia Life.

## Chapter 7

# Technologies

J oseph Needham (1900–1995) was a polymath. Trained in chemistry at Cambridge University, he, together with his wife, Dorothy Moyle Needham, developed major research in biochemistry at their alma mater. Both were interested in the history of science. In 1937, they accepted three Chinese advanced graduate students into their laboratories, among them Lu Gwei-Djen, daughter of an apothecary (pharmacist) in Nanking. Talking with these bright, curious young scientists just arrived from China, Joseph Needham was intrigued by how alike their minds were to his. If China produces such talented scientists, he wondered, why had its science not flowered into a Scientific Revolution like that of Europe in the early modern period?

Needham set himself to learning to speak and read Chinese, to research his question. Lu, educated by her father in classical Chinese medicine as well as schooled in Western biochemistry and public health, guided his quest into Chinese books and the philosophies behind them.

During World War II, Joseph and Dorothy Needham, who had become a close friend of Lu, served the war effort by moving to the Chinese Nationalist headquarters in Chungking (Chongqing) as liaison between Chinese and British scientists, an opportunity to visit monasteries, libraries, and workshops to familiarize themselves with the history and practices of science there. Meanwhile, Lu was in the United States working in the biochemistry of nutrition; she was instrumental in the U.S. campaign to eliminate the nutritional deficiency disease pellagra that was devastating Southern communities.[1] After the war, Joseph Needham accepted a position implementing the United Nations' new program UNESCO–United Nations Educational, Scientific, and Cultural Organization–specializing in the Scientific branch of the program. Lu, who had returned to China to teach nutritional science, was recruited by Needham to head UNESCO's office coordinating field sciences cooperation. She remained in this position, in Paris, for nine years before rejoining the Needhams in Cambridge, where they had returned in 1948.

That year, Joseph Needham conceived a plan for a series of books, to be published by Cambridge University Press, on the history of science and technology in China, with background material on the intellectual and spiritual traditions that encompassed them. Years were spent exploring the literature and technologies until a grand outline of topics was prepared, Needham himself undertaking to research and write certain ones (assisted by collaborators on specialties, as suitable), and other topics assigned to authors who would write independently in consultation with Needham, or come to the East Asian History of Science Institute he founded in Cambridge (now the Needham Research Institute). Retiring from teaching and his laboratory in biochemistry in 1966, he launched his second career: the *Science and Civilisation in China* project. Lu was his partner in the project, listed as co-author or collaborator for eight volumes; she died in 1991. Needham survived to 1995, writing nearly to the day of his death.

Volume 4, part III, of the *Science and Civilisation in China* series, issued in 1971, devotes 320 pages to "Nautics," including ships, navigation, means of propulsion, steering, docks, diving, and warships. In 1409, the climax of Chinese shipbuilding and marine travel came with the launching of the imperial Grand Fleet of Treasure Ships, captained by Admiral Zheng He. With awesome ships of over 1,500 tons carrying thousands of crewmen, Zheng He sailed around southern Asia into the Indian Ocean, calling upon local rulers to bow to his master, the Imperial Emperor. Engraved stone stelae, some in more than one language, were set up in the foreign ports to memorialize the Emperor's outreach. Zheng He lavishly gifted the local rulers with silks, bottles of perfumed oils, bronze, gilded and lacquered incense burners and lamps, and gold and silver coins (Needham 1971:509, 523). The last of seven voyages ended in 1435, with Zheng He coming home to a political reversal damning the enormous expenses of these massive displays of wealth and power. Did Zheng He sail as far as America? Neither Chinese nor Western scholars, including Needham, believe that he did; although the politicians who reversed the policy of display burned records of the voyages, enough documentation survives, including the stelae in foreign ports, to map out the Treasure Fleets' routes as those of the great routes active for more than a thousand years between East Africa, India, Southeast Asia and Island Southeast Asia, and China. In contrast to his Portuguese contemporaries, Zheng He and his Emperor were not out to find new sources of wealth, and certainly not to evangelize their religion; their purpose was to bind the known world of trade to China's court (Needham 1971:529).

On page 542 of the 1971 volume, Needham describes feeling *déjà vu* during a two-month visit to Mexico in late 1947, part of his duties with UNESCO. Barely two years after living in China, paying close attention to its technologies, architecture, and arts, he saw similarities between Chinese and pre-Columbian Mesoamerican buildings' strong horizontal lines of terraces, monumental stairs, and extended rather than high palaces and halls on the terraces[2]; the "omnipresent sky-dragons"— *naga* in India, *lung* in China, Feathered Serpent (*quetzalcoatl*) in Mesoamerica; double-headed cosmic serpents; *teponatzli* (carved log slit-drums similar to Chinese *mu-yü*); *li*-type tripod ceramic vessels, often with covers with a small effigy knob; frescoes and lacquers; and double-permutation calendar systems with similar day names and lunar mansions (Needham 1971:543–545). Home in Cambridge, Needham found Chinese chronicles from the Qin (Ch'in) (221–206 BCE) and Han (206 BCE–220 CE) periods describing several expeditions sent out to obtain drugs from three fabled islands, Phêng-Lai, Fang-Chang, and Ying-Chou. On these islands, it was said, live immortals who know the elixir of longevity. Ships transported young men and women and workmen to found colonies, not just to buy drugs (or in one account, sell the men and women to the immortals to pay for the drugs). The chronicles agree that none of the expeditions were known to have returned (Needham 1971:550–553).

Reading of Needham's perception of similarities, his efforts to learn more about the American examples from noted authorities in Mexico and standard works by archaeologists, I thought that perhaps a focused conference in Mexico might help evaluate the similarities. Joseph Needham had, by the 1970s, an unparalleled knowledge and understanding of Chinese sciences and technologies based on science. If he could see, firsthand, the sites and objects, and at that time quiz the archaeologists who had discovered or studied them, would that not make more precise the similarities and the differences? Reveal significant details and elucidate variations?

I telephoned David H. Kelley in Calgary, a Mayan expert actively interested in transoceanic contacts, particularly calendars and astrologies. Kelley agreed, and offered to contact scholars he knew, if I would work

on conference arrangements. Together we wrote to Needham, who replied quickly that he would very much like to be in such a conference,
to see Mexico again and its sites with experienced archaeologists. Of
course we would invite Dr. Lu as well.

Kelley and I drew up a plan for a two-week conference, submitted
it to the Wenner-Gren Foundation, a small philanthropy that supports
anthropological conferences and research, and when Wenner-Gren's
research director favored the plan, through the grants support officer
at my university, applied to the Ford Foundation for additional funds.
Money approved, we set an itinerary for two weeks in June, 1977, with
four scholars we thought favored transpacific contacts before 1492, and
four with orthodox denial. Mexican archaeologists were invited to meet
with the group as it moved from one area to another.

An interesting experience was had by all. The archaeologists who denied contacts repeatedly asserted that ships could not, or would not,
have crossed the Pacific before the European Age of Discovery. Polynesian voyaging was dismissed because, at that time, no definitive Polynesian artifacts had been found in the Americas. Kelley's doctoral dissertation at Harvard, on myth elements and linguistic similarities between
Polynesian and Uto-Aztecan,[3] had not (and still hasn't) been published.
Joseph Needham informed the nay-sayers that China had large seagoing
transport vessels by the first millennium BCE, without this knowledge
seeming to affect their certainty. "Pro" archaeologists included, besides
myself and Kelley, Paul Tolstoy and Gordon Ekholm, whose work will
be described later in this book. We had planned that each of the full-con-
ference participants would afterward prepare papers to be published; we
hoped to thus give a range and balance of arguments and data. Not one
of the deniers sent a word, no matter how often politely reminded of
the agreed-upon plan, so in the end, our goal of a thorough scholarly
hashing-out of the issues failed. Aside from my report to Wenner-Gren
(Kehoe 1978), only one publication resulted: Needham and Lu's 1985
*Trans-Pacific Echoes and Resonances: Listening Once Again*.

During the conference, and the friendship that continued afterward,
Joseph Needham impressed me with two qualities remarkably paired:
a keenly observant, razor-sharp, analytical mind; and a sincerely hum-
ble respect for other people. He insisted that everyone, even the two
eleven-year-olds who came along with their parents, address him by
his Christian name, Joseph, no title. One morning, he left the circle of
PhDs he was conversing with to go sit beside my boy, whom he noticed
reading the novel *The Andromeda Strain*, to discuss at length the biochemistry in the plot.

Gwei-Djen, as we addressed her, let Joseph take the lead in asking about contexts of artifacts in question, transoceanic contacts being his topic, while listening closely and in discussions, clarifying issues and offering her insights. Like Joseph, she was genuinely interested in people and how they came to have their ideas. Neither had any illusions that their researches would save the world. They spoke out for social justice, against stereotypes, saw their great project to be a bridge between Western and Asian civilizations as well as making important corrections to each area's ethnocentric histories of intellectual achievements.

Is it relevant to Critical Thinking to mention the personal qualities of the scientist-scholars Needham and Lu? Yes, because their strong love for humankind, coupled with enjoyment of challenging intellectual puzzles, were the impetus for the awesome research in *Science and Civilisation in China*, a massive breakthrough in the history of science. Needham's masterly laboratory work in the biochemistry of morphogenesis (embryology) earned him scientific renown, while his second-career research in Chinese science proved his exceptional originality and power to think through complex questions. His publications are copiously and meticulously footnoted, for every reader to evaluate for themselves (You don't read Chinese? Well, go learn to do so—he did). The considered evaluations of such a highly reputable scientist-scholar on possible pre-Columbian transpacific contacts should not be dismissed lightly.

## Technologies to Consider

*Technology* is a very common word today. The word was invented in the early modern European period, early seventeenth century, out of the Greek roots *tekhnologia* (*craft* plus *words*). From the Renaissance on, European intelligentsia boasted of their new mechanical devices (regardless of so many having diffused from Asia) (Boruchoff 2012), and a "technological culture" (Bijker 2009:608), attributing its successes and glories to material, especially mechanical, innovations. Reflecting this bias in our cultural tradition, we tend to give greater weight to similarities in technology as possible evidence of borrowings. Near the end of his life, almost half a century after he had conceived *Science and Civilisation in China*, Needham listed some 250 Chinese technological inventions and a list of 35 transmitted from China to the West (Needham 2004:217–224, 214). The same confidence in strength of evidence from technology oriented his examinations of similarities between Chinese and Mesoamerican artifacts. The more complex an artifact, the less likely it would have been independently invented in societies not in contact with each other.

## Patolli-Pachisi

Probability of borrowing, or of stimulus through contact (stimulus diffusion), is raised if similarities cluster, are specific in details, are complex, or are elements in a larger pattern that is similar in both cultures. Needham called these criteria the "collocation principle" (Needham and Lu 1985:10–13), citing also an 1896 statement by earlier anthropologist Edward Tylor: "The probability of contact increases in ratio to the number of arbitrary similar elements in any two trait-complexes" (Needham and Lu 1985:9). Tylor was writing of the striking congruence between the India game of pachisi and the pre-contact Mexican game called patolli. Many readers will have played this board game, sometimes spelled parcheesi: it has a board with a cross with circle in the middle; the arms of the cross are divided into squares seen as steps in a path around the board to "home" in the middle; players move game pieces along the path according to throws of dice; one player's piece overtaking another's in a square "captures" the first, making it go back steps; some squares are marked as "forts," where no penalty occurs. We know that our game we call pachisi, or parcheesi, diffused from India centuries ago to Europe and thence to America; the collocation principle suggests that the game with its identical board, pieces, casting dice to move, "forts," "capture," "home," called by the similar name "patolli," was copied by Mexicans from a visitor familiar with it from India—or could it have gone the other way?

Something so trivial as a game may be a clue to contacts between civilizations? You could say, why not a game? It's non-threatening, it's "cool," and with its board design and "men," easy to demonstrate even without a common language. That board design is actually the way Mesoamericans and other American Indians within their broad sphere of influence represent the world: an equal-armed cross (the four directions) with a middle. In India, it's a variant mandala.

Anthropologist Charles Erasmus published in 1950 a much-cited paper arguing against patolli deriving from pachisi. Erasmus invoked probability, referring to Tylor's use of the collocation principle to count up the number of elements in the game that were shared by India and Mexico. "Tylor's argument sounds very convincing," Erasmus wrote. "It has stalemated the question for over fifty years" (Erasmus 1950:370). Erasmus takes each of the elements, such as the dice and the board, and lists similar (in his opinion) instances not tied into the patolli set, in a variety of American First Nations games. Every kind of counter and tally stick (e.g., for bets in the Plains stick game), and games with a row of pits, not a cross-shaped pathway, are mentioned as variants and equivalents to the patolli game elements. There are limited possibilities in constructing a game with counters, dice, and a path, he asserts, citing Alexander Goldenweiser's 1913 essay *The Principle of Limited Possibilities in the Development of Culture.*

A few years after Tylor, the American anthropologist Stewart Culin compiled a study of indigenous American games, concluding in regard to patolli that it "seems" to have been invented in the American Southwest and spread therefrom into Mexico, becoming more complex as it developed there (Erasmus 1950:371). This diffusion Erasmus accepts as plausible, showing the Southwest game to be a circle of small stones (stations) interrupted at the cardinal directions with spaces ("gates"); the only similarity to pachisi-patolli is that players move their counters along a marked pathway. He thinks the Southwest simple circle could have developed into the Mexican cross-spaced pathway, then questions whether the patolli board cross is "really the same design?" as the pachisi cross (Erasmus 1950:381). But if the limitation of possibilities is to be considered, pathways could be spirals, mazes, squares, triangles, snakes-and-ladders, outlines of humans or animals or plants . . . "limitation of possibilities" is a weak argument for pathway form. Bottom line for Erasmus's essay is his unstated premise that diffusion of a board game from the American Southwest into Mexico *is* reasonably plausible, in spite of alleged limitation of possibilities.

A sociologist who had studied Chinese immigration into nineteenth-century America, Stanford Lyman, delved deep into the patolli-pachisi issue in a 1985 essay, unsurprisingly neglected considering it was published in Kyoto in a volume titled *Japanese Americans.* Lyman republished the essay in the United States with others of his in a 1990 collection, *Civilization: Contents, Discontents, Malcontents and Other Essays in Social Theory.* His discussion is framed broadly, laying out the sixteenth-century controversy over whether American Indians were descended from Adam and Eve.

Joseph de Acosta, in 1579, carefully argued that they were, and therefore their ancestors must have emigrated from Asia. Countering de Acosta, in 1655, Isaac de La Peyrere proposed that the Bible was the history of Jews, not of all humankind, this proposition allowing independent origins for other human races. De Acosta's view prevailed, setting up "a seemingly unbridgeable gulf" between America's "pre-history" and post-contact history (Lyman 1990:46).[4] The center of Lyman's essay is the pioneer American anthropologist Daniel Brinton (1837–1899), whose Wikipedia entry highlights his advocacy of "scientific racism" denying "the atmosphere of modern enlightenment" to "less-endowed races" (read, Africans and their descendants). Lyman's sociological point of view and research on Asian immigrants to Brinton's America prompted him to link Brinton's racism and his denial of Asian contacts, with the isolationist point of view on pre-Columbian America—the United States excluded Asians from citizenry in the nineteenth century, and U.S. historians excluded possible pre-Columbian contacts with Asia from American history.

Here we have an unexpected but logical entry into the transoceanic contacts debate. Stanford Lyman's linking illustrates the significance of a researcher's standpoint, that both the culture one grows up in *and* one's experiences are sources of knowledge and of evaluation (Wylie 2013:11; see also Wylie 2012). Daniel Brinton spelled out unequivocally, in 1893 at the International Congress of Anthropology meeting at the Columbus quadricentennial World Columbian Exposition, that no one had shown anything "in use at the time of the discovery, which had been previously imported from Asia, or from any other continent of the Old World" (quoted in Lyman 1990:57). Stewart Culin, a contemporary of Brinton, more than disagreed; he argued that Asians and American Indians share "the *same* culture," including patolli-pachisi, never mind the ocean between (Lyman 1990:69, Culin's italic). Culin, like Lyman, became interested in Chinese culture through studying Chinese immigrants to America, in his case, especially their gambling games and divination. That led to comparisons with American Indian games, collaboration with ethnographer Frank Hamilton Cushing, who was working in Zuni Pueblo, and finally the classic *Games of North American Indians*, published in 1907 by the Smithsonian's Bureau of American Ethnology. Erasmus used Culin's book in selecting games for his argument on limited possibilities, while denying Culin's interpretation.

Several accounts by sixteenth century Spanish observers in Mexico describe patolli, a relatively elaborate game collocating a distinctive mandalalike cross-shaped pathway with safe squares, counters, dice, and rules including capturing opponents. It was definitely played in Mexico at the time of Cortés' invasion (1519), described from the 1540s (Parlett 1999:51–52), and found archaeologically as the game board incised on flat rocks (Mountjoy 1985), on the floor of a building in Chichén Itzá (with evidence of snacking around the game boards) (Zimmerman et al. 2015), and perhaps also existed in the form of the pecked crosses at Teotihuacán and other sites (Kelley and Milone 2011:410). Pachisi became popular in India late in the same century. So far as actual evidence goes, *pachisi is definitively attested in India only from the later sixteenth century,* played on a grand scale by Mughal emperor Akbar the Great (1542–1605) (Parlett 1999:43).[5] Pachisi *could* have been patolli brought over from Mexico by Spaniards after their conquest of Mexico. The most plausible interpretation of the similarities is post-Columbian importation from Mexico to India; no one denies transpacific crossings in the mid-sixteenth century CE.

## Wheel-Mounted Animals

A striking difference between Eurasian and American societies was the lack of wheels in the Americas. How could so essential a technology, so readily diffused throughout Eurasia (Anthony 2007), not have spread throughout the Americas if the two continents had been in contact? What is really startling is that in fact, wheeled vehicles were made in Mesoamerica, only in one area at one limited time: small animal figurines mounted with axles through their feet, and wheels on the axles. They are similar to animal figurines in Chinese tombs, and to Chinese wheeled toys called bird-chariots. The Han-period tomb, dated 100 CE, of Wang Tê-Yuan, at Sui-tê near Yenan, has carving on its wall depicting a child pushing a wheeled object at the end of a stick (Needham and Wang 1965:257).

Figurines were essential in royal and nobles' tombs from the Han (206 BCE–220 CE) period through the Ming (1368–1644 CE) dynasties (Paludan 1994:32, 38, 55–57). During the Song (960–1279 CE) dynasty, paper effigies came into use, with ceramic figurines becoming somewhat less important. Ming revived earlier styles, especially those of the Tang (618–907 CE). Aboveground on the formal road to the tomb were erected large sculpted stone figures of officials, soldiers, and animals to guard the approach, warding off evil spirits. Underground in the tombs, figurines were ceramic, representing all the officials, concubines, entertainers, servants, buildings, foods, and animals needed for a high-ranked household. Wheeled carts and chariots with their oxen or horses would be included, although the animals would not be fitted with wheels themselves. Asia, both China and India, thus had figurines mounted on wheels or wheeled platforms, and in India, deities were represented this way, but in this variety, there seems no exact parallel to the wheeled animals in Early Postclassic Mesoamerican sites.

The American wheeled figurines have been found in sites on the northern side of the Isthmus of Tehuantepec, the narrowest section of Mexico, with the Atlantic off Veracruz on the north and the Pacific off Oaxaca on the south. They also were in the cities of Tula and Teotihuacán

**Figure 7.1.** Wheel-mounted dog, El Salvador, (left) and photo of wheeled toy from India, (right) selected by Gordon Ekholm to compare to Mesoamerican wheeled animals. Wheeled dog: FUNDAR (Fundación Nacional de Arqueología, El Salvador), courtesy Paul Amaroli; Wheeled toy: Natural History 59(8):350, courtesy American Museum of Natural History, New York

in east-central Mexico, and far to the south, in Cihuatán, near the Pacific in El Salvador (Diehl and Mandeville 1987, Fowler 1991). Cihuatán was said by the early Spanish explorers to have been a Postclassic outpost or settlement of Nahua (Aztec or related nations) from central Mexico. Nearly all the wheeled animals can be dated to the Early Postclassic, c. 900–1300 CE, when indigenous history books record many wars between Gulf Coast nations and those to the west and south.

Mesoamerican archaeologists have assumed the little wheeled animals were invented *ex nihilo*, from nothing pre-existing. Their excavators, including the first to publish on them, Gordon Ekholm (1946), are at pains to explain the vast difference between the wheels-and-axle for pushing a mounted object versus a spindle whorl used to spin twisting fibers; it is implausible that thread spinners invented paired wheels on axles to make figurines mobile. Commentators have felt compelled to point out that without large draft animals and in mountainous country, Mesoamericans could not have used wagons, and canoes and human porters were quite adequate for transportation. So, inventing wheels would not have led to widespread use of wagons, as in Eurasia. That leaves open the question of specifically the small wheeled animal figurines, limited in distribution in space and in time. Note that they are not a "style"—they are a complex technology of molded ceramic animal figurines, perforated legs in which axle rods are pushed, and flat clay wheels (unlike convex spindle whorls) mounted on the axles. Within

**Figure 7.2.** Guardian figure, Cihuatán, El Salvador, (left) and Asian fu "lion-dog" temple guardian figure (right). Note both animals wear a collar with small bells. Cihuatán excavated figure: FUNDAR (Fundación Nacional de Arqueología, El Salvador), courtesy Paul Amaroli; Fu dog: courtesy Shakespeare's Garden, Brookfield, CT

sites, they are found both in ceremonial precincts and in household debris; therefore, neither obviously ritual objects nor obviously toys. They could be made for rituals held in homes as well as in temples.

Gordon Ekholm, the archaeologist with extensive firsthand experience in field situations where wheeled animal figurines were found in Mesoamerica, changed his mind from initial assumption of independent invention to final IBE, inference that Early Postclassic Mesoamericanists more likely had copied wheeled tomb figurines or toys from India or Chinese originals (Ekholm 1950:350). This probability is enhanced by finds, in what appear to be temple precincts, of large feline figures at Cihuatán and at Tula that look much like the popular Chinese "lion-dog" temple guardians (Ekholm 1953:84; Bruhns 2015 and personal communication January 2013). In terms of Critical

Thinking, the uniqueness, for the Americas, of the Early Postclassic Meso-american wheeled animal figurines, contrasted to their wide occurrence in both India and China for two thousand years, in ritual and for play, plus their occurrence in Mesoamerica at the time of medieval Asian eastward explorations for the spice trade, weigh the probability that the figurines in Mesoamerica were inspired by Asian wheeled animal figurines, via transpacific voyages.

## Paper

Paper was invented in China about two thousand years ago, in the Han period. An entire volume in the *Science and Civilisation in China* series is devoted to paper and printing (Tsien 1985). It defines paper as "a felted sheet of fibres formed from a water suspension process using a sieve-like screen. When the water escapes and dries, the layer of intertwined fibres becomes a thin matted sheet which is called paper" (Tsien 1985:1). Felting—beating soaked fibers into a mat—is older than paper, and is the principal type of cloth for the pastoral nations of the Asian steppes, who used felt for their tents (yurts), clothing, blankets, and saddle cloths. Mongol emperors sat on a white felt sheet during their coronation ritual (Laufer 1930:14). Chinese learned felting from their northern neighbors; paper is basically a thin felt made from bast, cotton, hemp, flax, or other plant fibers instead of the wool used by the pastoralists.

Paper mulberry (*Broussonetia papyrifera*) is a tree native to China. Chinese histories attribute use of its inner bark for papermaking to an inventor of the second century CE (Tsien 1985:4). Abundance of this plant, easily cultivated, promoted use of paper for clothing and armor (combined with cotton cloth padding) in southern China, as well as for writing, paper currency, painting and calligraphy, screens, kites, umbrellas, hats, flags, toys, and cut-out effigies throughout China (Tsien 1985:361, 115–116). Especially popular has been the use of paper versions of ritual gifts and sacrifices in ceremonies, funerals, and tombs. What a happy substitute for killing animals and slaves! Paper substitutes also discouraged grave robbers, keeping tombs sacrosanct (Tsien 1985:104).

Paper was made in the first millennium CE in one other region besides China: Mesoamerica. Stone beaters have been found in the great Classic city of Teotihuacán, dated to the sixth century CE (Sandstrom and Sandstrom 1986:7, 14). At the time of the Spanish invasions, beginning 1519, paper was manufactured in a number of towns named for this industry (Sandstrom and Sandstrom 1986:15), primarily from mulberry inner bark, or from maguey (agave) fiber, and was used for books, legal documents, tribute lists, maps, banners, ritual clothing, and above all, cut-out effigies of deities. Spanish conquerors systematically destroyed all these paper artifacts, labeling native books and images works of the devil. In the steep, jungle-covered mountains of northeast Mexico, paper-making and the art of paper cutting has survived among Nahua, Otomí, and Tepehua villages. Priests and healers in these villages train to be expert at cutting out images of a variety of nonhuman beings and ancestors who are lured to decorated paper altars. Evil spirits are swept off sick people and off village officials, then their cut-outs violently ripped up to destroy them; good spirits' cut-outs are kept, wrapped in bundles, in village and household shrines (Sandstrom and Sandstrom 1986).

Contemporary rituals with cut-outs described in detail by ethnographers Alan and Pamela Sandstrom are similar enough to sixteenth-century Spanish invaders' descriptions of Mexican rituals using paper that we may infer survival from pre-contact customs, even though actual specimens have not survived five centuries (as have some paper cuttings from China, dated to the sixth century CE). The art process of paper cutting practiced by Nahua, Otomí, and Tepehua Indian priests today is astonishingly similar to the practice of China's National Treasure paper-cutting artists: the Indian spirit-beings images are different from Chinese deities images, but the difficult technique is the same, and in both countries, the artists also produce elaborate, delicate geometric designs (He 2005). In China, paper cutting is considered a folk art and its religious connotations downplayed by the government; in Mexico, paper cutting was little known outside the northeast mountain villages but is now fostered, along with painting on native-made paper, to sell to tourists. While paper cutting art is widespread at present, that its practice spread out of China through Eurasia isn't questioned (Tsien 1985:361).

Paul Tolstoy, an archaeologist with years of fieldwork in central Mexico and Ecuador, took up a research question put to him by Gordon Ekholm, curator of Mesoamerican archaeology at the American Museum of Natural History in New York—of whom, more in the next chapter. How should we account for the strong similarities between bark beaters of Mesoamerica and Indonesia? Bark beaters aren't trivial; they are used in making paper as well as bark cloth (*tapa* in Polynesia). Tolstoy analyzed bark cloth and paper making into discrete steps and equipment, compiling a table of more than four hundred components shared between Indonesia and Mesoamerica (Tolstoy 1963). He and Ekholm were surprised that the closest similarities were between Celebes (now called Sulawesi) and elsewhere in Indonesia, and Mesoamerica, not between China or mainland southeast Asia and Mesoamerica. This, he suggests, indicates the route was the historic Manila galleons' route between Acapulco, Mexico, the Philippines, and China, bypassing Hawai'i, a route advantageously using the Japan (Kuroshio) Current (Tolstoy 1991). Although logically, the bark cloth/paper complex might be traced through the central Pacific to Mesoamerica, Polynesian *tapa* bark cloth differs significantly from the Celebes-Indonesia and the Mesoamerican complexes (Tolstoy 1993:661, 1991, 2008:49). Therefore, Tolstoy infers that the paper-making was carried through the Pacific before Polynesian colonizations were completed in the early second millennium CE. Mesoamerica did not have the critical step for making true paper: beating the soaked bast fiber into a pulp and drying the stretched pulp on a frame or board. Mexicans did make fine paper by hard beating of the soaked fibers, but technically, the pulp state is defined as necessary to term the product true paper.

Tolstoy's research was meticulously scientific. He began with close examination of bark beaters in the American Museum's collections from South America and Mesoamerica, the Pacific, and Asia and Island Southeast Asia. Celebes and Java used a heavy stone block, grooved on one side, and not—or very slightly—grooved on the opposite side, hafted in a cane loop, so that it swings like a racquet. The two faces are used in sequence in beating bark. Virtually identical racquet beaters were used in Mesoamerica, with one excavated archaeologically at El Riego rock shelter in central Mexico, and dated about 700 CE (Tolstoy 1991).

Turning to ethnographic and historical descriptions of the craft of making bark cloth and paper, he listed sequences of steps for each region, again finding the greatest number of similarities between Indonesia and Mesoamerica. Among these are the way the inner bark (the bast) is harvested, alkanization of the soaked, boiled bast with wood ashes, decorating finished paper with black gum (rubber in Mesoamerica), and using paper for writing, priests' vestments, banners for processions, and tax or tribute paid in paper (Tolstoy 1963:659). Later, Tolstoy similarly analyzed and compared bark cloth making in Fiji and Polynesia, the results supporting his rejection of a Polynesian conveyance of bark cloth to America (Tolstoy 2008). Laying out his analyses in tables, distribution maps, and cladistic diagrams (branching tree diagrams of relationships), Tolstoy defends his inference that the process of producing bark cloth and paper from inner bark of mulberry trees was carried from Indonesia to Mesoamerica in the first millennium

BCE. He notes that this dating puts the voyaging earlier than the invention of true papermaking in the Han period in China, thus the absence of that end-of-the-chain sequence of manufacturing steps, pulping the soaked beaten fibers, and drying as sheets on frames.

We have a nested set of Asian technologies here: felting; felting technique used on bast fibers to make bark cloth; fibers processed toward producing thin flat sheets (paper); paper used for writing, priests' vestments, and processional banners; and the art of paper cutting to create effigies of deities and spirit beings employed in rituals. All these were known in Eastern Asia and through Indonesia two thousand years ago. Bast fiber cloth and paper making and paper cut-out effigies were practiced in Mesoamerica before 1492, with archaeological evidence of beaters going back a millennium. Writing in ideographs developed in China in the second millennium BCE. Writing in hieroglyphs in Mexico appears at the very beginning of the first millennium CE, following the carving of symbols of places—probably tribute-paying towns—at Monte Albán in Oaxaca.

The earliest full hieroglyphic text so far found is in the Isthmus of Tehuantepec region, from Tuxtla, with what looks like the date 143 or 156 CE (if its similarity to Maya written dates is correct) (Evans 2004:240). The Isthmus of Tehuantepec in southern Mexico, linking Chiapas and Oaxaca on the Pacific side with Veracruz on the Atlantic side, is the center of the area where earliest preserved writing, bark beaters, and wheeled figurines have been found. Acapulco, the port for Spain's Manila galleons and the China trade beginning in 1565, is a little farther north along Mexico's Pacific coast; the huge galleons needed its superb harbor, from which goods were transshipped on to the Isthmus and across it to Veracruz. To a geographer, the clustering of apparent Asian/Island Asian technologies in the region of the Isthmus of Tehuantepec fits hypothesizing voyages from Indonesia and the Philippines along the Manila galleons' eastward route. Thus, the criterion of collocation of items—wheeled animal figurines, paper—in time and place on each side of the Pacific increases the probability that they were carried from Asia, where they have long histories, to Mesoamerica, where they were later and limited in area.

## Resist-Dyed Fabrics

The procedure known as ikat weaving is mind-boggling. Sections of threads are wrapped with string or covered with beeswax, then dipped into a dye solution, so that only the unwrapped sections of the thread get dyed. The process can be repeated with a series of different color dye baths for different sections of the thread. Dyed threads are warped on the loom and may be wound on bobbins or shuttles placed beside the weaver's loom. As she weaves, she picks up one or another of the bobbins to use its thread for weft in her cloth. Designs appear as different-colored threads lie one beside another. To perform ikat, the weaver remembers an intricate sequence of threads, often a dozen or more, generally choosing them without a pattern or key to look at.[6] In Asia, very experienced older women do the thread dyeing and warp the looms. Ikat cloths are not flamboyant, as brocades and embroideries can be, but subtle in the very slight blurring of the outlines of the designs. Connoisseurs value ikat cloths according to the fineness of the weave and complexity of the designs; Indonesians appreciate the dedication inherent in the "extremely complex and time-consuming" work in ikat (Hauser-Schäublin, Nabholz-Kartaschoff, and Ramseyer 1991:195).

Related to ikat is the procedure known as batik. For batik, sections of a finished cloth are wrapped or waxed, and the cloth dipped in the dye bath to leave a design formed by the undyed, or differently dyed, sections. Making batik cloth can be complicated, but compared to ikat, with its precise loom warping and its array of bobbins to create designs from hours of throwing the shuttle through the warp, batik seems less difficult. Its common name is tie-dyeing, popular for colorful sunburst designs on T-shirts.

The word *ikat* is from Java, meaning "to tie" or "to bind." Radiocarbon dating of ikat textiles in Indonesia shows that some date to the fifteenth century CE (Barnes 2010:36, 38, 250).[7] An extraordinarily fine example, dated 1403–1501, has these motifs woven as figures, some tiny, in an intricately interlocking pattern: ancestors; four-petaled diamond lotus; cosmic tree; human figure stylized as new growth sprout; stepped-diamond yantra; birds with long or foliate tails; stag; "endless knot"; scorpion with new-growth tail; and decapitated humans with three growth sprouts or trees from their necks. Gold threads and silk warp, as well as the quality of the weaving, indicate the cloth was owned by wealthy nobility (Solyom 2010:49). Whether this masterpiece was woven in Sumatra where it was collected, or in Java, can't be determined; fine ikat was produced in much of Asia as well as Indonesia during the medieval heyday of the Silk Road, both land and sea. Its motifs are common in mainland Asia as well as Island Asia where, additionally, ships are woven designs symbolizing lineage houses and communities, and carrying rituals (Gavin 2010:237, van Dijk 2010:74). Medieval India produced and exported such prized textiles (Crill 1998:16–20), while in Indonesia, noble women themselves wove luxury cloth, one sign of the leisure their wealth bestowed (Kahlenberg 2010:14).

Ikat is historically woven in Guatemala, where it is called *jaspe*, in Ecuador, and in Peru. Pictures of Mexican rulers' garments, in Postclassic art and early Colonial manuscripts, show a mantle and hip cloth that appear to perhaps be ikat, but careful analysis of accompanying descriptions in Colonial depictions indicates that the mantles were netted, with turquoise beads fastened to the knots in the netting, and similar beads were sewn onto the hip cloths (Aguilera 1997). Apparently, the ikat technique of resist-dyed threads (as different from resist-dyed woven cloth), to be woven so that a pattern appears from the juxtaposition of sections of threads, was not known before the Spanish invasions of Mexico.[8] Once the Manila galleons began their annual voyages across the Pacific, 1565–1815, men and women from China, the Philippines, and Indonesia entered Mexico, many as slaves, some as deserters from the crews. Slaves with skills such as weaving were in demand; there was also an attempt to develop a silk industry, initiated by the conqueror Hernan Cortés, that failed to flourish against the competition from established sources in Asia (Davis 1991:312).

Whether ikat was indigenous in Peru seems ambiguous. Gauzy cloth fragments identified as ikat were recovered from Max Uhle's 1898 excavation of cemeteries associated with the coastal Peruvian shrine of Pachacamac (Van Stan 1957). Resist-dyed cloth (batik) also was recovered. Pachacamac cemeteries were used for a millennium, even after Spanish conquest, and later interments disturbed previous ones. Possibly, the ikat fragments postdate Spanish colonization. Four other reported ikat specimens from Peru are even less well provenanced: a surface find from the Virú Valley, and three with only general locations (Van Stan 1957:157). Junius Bird, an anomaly among male field archaeologists in that he became expert in studying textiles, discussed the Virú specimen, noting that other fragments were seen in the desert valley, and that the analyzed piece used a locally traditional weaving method clumsy for ikats, displays ineptitude in figuring the complex counts of warps and their resist sections, and was painted after weaving, somewhat obscuring the ikat design. He concluded, "ikat was not traditional in this area" and footnoted that an ikat had been found associated with a glass trade bead in a grave, therefore post-Columbian (Bird 1947:77, 74). Ann Peters, an archaeologist currently studying coastal Peruvian sites and their textiles, cautioned me:

. . . in natural cotton plain weaves I often see differential fiber deterioration in patterns that look a bit like pattern-dyed yarns, since it results in shades of brown that vary in a repeated pattern along each yarn. Differential fiber deterioration also can produce a stripey or plaid-like effect.

I suspect this is due either to a powdered earth used in spinning cotton, or to storage of balls of yarn before weaving, with one side exposed to the sun. Looking at the fiber under a hand lens or microscope, the effect is associated with areas of fiber deterioration, without evidence of a dye present. Such an effect might have confused someone in the past. (Peters, pers. comm. October 2, 2014)

Resist-dyed cloth seems pre-Columbian in Peru, while ikat more likely is post-conquest.

Ikat is woven on backstrap looms and on fixed looms. Backstrap (tension) looms cannot produce cloth wider than the width of the weaver's body, a limitation compensated for by sewing lengths of cloth together to make a wider cloth. Backstrap looms are commonly associated with village women who can pick up the loom with its unfinished cloth and put it away while doing other domestic chores. They are not "primitive" so much as handy; an alternative is the portable frame loom pegged out or held stretched by the feet when in use, that can be lifted, rolled up, and stored until time for it is again available. Pegged looms are used in Indian villages in the Andes. Industrial-quantity production of cloth is facilitated by larger fixed looms creating fabrics wider and longer than can be managed on a backstrap or portable frame loom. Backstrap looms are found throughout Asia and Latin America, definitely pre-Columbian on both continents, and in western Oceania (Broudy 1979:78). They didn't come with Paleoindians over Bering Strait, since they have not been seen in northern North America, where twining predominated for making fabrics, attested as early as 9,400 years ago by the fine large shrouds and carrying bags preserved in dry Spirit Cave in Nevada (Kehoe 2001). To conclude this section, it seems that ikat is a post-Columbian import from Asia to Mesoamerica and probably to Peru, whereas the histories of backstrap looms and indeed most handlooms are imperfectly known (Broudy 1979, numerous pages).

## Blowguns and Panpipes

Two instruments made of cane or reeds are found in Southeast and Island Southeast Asia, and in South America: blowguns and panpipes. Blowguns may appear to be simple and obvious, like their late derivative, the boys' pea-shooter, but they are serious and effective weapons in forests. Like gun barrels, blowguns must be straight and smooth. Deadly outcome is usually attained by tipping the dart in a poison such as curare; hard pellets are also used, effective for smaller game. Blowguns seem to be indigenous to Malaysian peoples in Southeast and Island Southeast Asia, and they are also common in northwestern South America, described by Spanish invaders in 1541, in Mexico in 1520, and seen in both Maya art in Mesoamerica (Coggins 2002:64 nt. 59) and Moche art in northern Peru, in the first half of the first millennium CE.

Stephen Jett, the geographer who has most recently studied the distribution of blowguns, interprets his data as suggesting contacts between Malaysia-Indonesia and northwestern South America two or possibly three thousand years ago (Jett 1970, 1991). Rising sea levels at that time would have inundated low-lying coastal areas in the Malayan peninsula and Indonesia, forcing people to seek other localities to settle (Jett 1991:98). Tropical forests in northern South America would have attracted Malaysians and Indonesians, accustomed to such environments. Jett's compendium of historic and ethnographic records of blowguns, and their varieties, is impressive, as is his explanation that these weapons are not simple pea-shooters. Actual blowguns not preserving in archaeological sites, so far as may be recognizable, makes dating the proposed diffusion from Island Southeast Asia to northern South America a matter of plausible antiquity rather than laboratory science. Given Jett's presentation of the technicalities of the weapon, the case for parallel independent inventions is not compelling, while the problem of dating for perishables leaves the time of contacts indeterminable.

Panpipes that look similar and are similarly tuned are found in Polynesia and South America. Hopewell sites in the American Midwest, dating two thousand years ago, have panpipes preserved through copper sheathing of the pipes, although I have not found information on their tuning. Debate has raged over comparing the tuning of African and Indonesian panpipes, where the settlement of Madagascar by Austronesian speakers, specifically likely from Borneo, gives good reason to accept transmission between the regions. Crux of the debate is that tuning systems follow harmonics valued by the musicians; adjustments are made to eliminate what the musicians consider disharmonies (Blench 1982:84). (Listen to a guitarist or violinist tune the instrument before playing.) Contrasted to weapon blowguns limited to, and adapted to tropical forest hunting, using certain similar plants for the blowgun tube and for dart poison, panpipe similarities are not a strong case for ancient transoceanic contacts.

## Metalworking in Northwestern North America

Both the Inuit, in the Arctic, and Northwest Coast First Nations were forging and hammering artifacts of iron and copper before historic European contacts. Although they didn't smelt metal from ores, analyses of many metal objects older than European documented contacts show that Inuit and Northwest Coast craftsworkers did use a variety of metallurgical techniques, suggesting familiarity gained through trade with northeast Asia. Inuit in eastern Canada traded for iron with Norse since eleventh century CE Norse settlements in Greenland, but they also forged iron directly from meteorites (McCartney 1988).

Iron and bronze artifacts likely were traded across Bering Strait around 600 CE, on the evidence of two bronze objects excavated in a Birnirk period house on Cape Espenberg, on the coast in northwest Alaska (Jarus 2015), and iron artifacts in Ipiutak village near Point Hope, Alaska, dated 300–600 CE (Larsen and Rainey 1948, Rainey 1992:82). In the same Cape Espenberg house, excavators found obsidian sourced to the Anadyr River in Siberia (Jarus 2015), direct evidence of Siberian connection. Dramatically, an iron bit was the working point in a tool in a leather pouch carried by Kwaday Dan Sinchi, "Long-ago Man," an Indian man who froze crossing the mountains between the coast and interior British Columbia about 1450 CE (Acheson 2003:227, 229).

Considering that iron and copper were worked not only in Alaska but also in British Columbia, maritime Siberians could have traveled across the North Pacific to trade for American products, in addition to the recognized two-way trade across narrow Bering Strait (Acheson 2003:216–217). Copper was mined in the Copper River valley in southern Alaska and mid-continent in the Great Lakes, and worked also from nodules in river drift. Both American and Eurasian copper were used in the American Northwest, as shown by trace elements indicating ore sources. A similar technique sourced some obsidian excavated in Alaska to a Siberian source. Direct trade between China or Japan and the Northwest Coast and Alaska is not evidenced, in spite of many finds of Chinese coins from periods before Magellan's voyage. Grant Keddie of the Royal British Columbia Museum checked out a number of finds of Chinese coins in Northwest Coast villages, discovering that Chinese prized ancient coins as tokens of longevity—the older the coin, the longer its longevity, of course. Old coins were hoarded and given as gifts, and when coins went out of date, traders bought bagsful and traded them to Siberians and American Indians as ornaments. Keddie concluded that Chinese coins in western America are most probably from historic Chinese immigrants, plus some representing trade along the North Pacific Rim (Keddie 1990).

## Ceramics

In 1961, Ecuadorian avocational archaeologist Emilio Estrada and Smithsonian archaeologist Betty Meggers published a claim that their excavation at the mound site Valdivia in Ecuador had revealed the earliest pottery known in the Americas, sherds at the bottom of the mound of occupation layers. The style of the sherds, and some other artifacts in the lower levels of the mound, resembled pottery of the Jomon period in Japan. They inferred that the art of ceramics was introduced into the Americas by Japanese sailors arriving at the Guayas coast of the Gulf of Guayaquil. Four years later, a full report on the Valdivia excavations was published by the Smithsonian, with the authors repeating their interpretation that the site exhibited the introduction of pottery to America by Japanese Jomon voyagers (Meggers, Evans, and Estrada 1965:vii).

Sharp criticisms of the claim stressed that, first, pottery had been excavated in northern Colombia radiocarbon-dated to 3100 BCE, somewhat earlier than the lowest level at Valdivia (several authors including Lathrap 1967:97, 1973:1761–1762); second, Meggers and her collaborator husband Clifford Evans had "cherry-picked" Jomon pottery decoration that resembled Valdivia out of a much larger range of Jomon pottery shapes and decorations (Pearson 1968); third, and most damning, by excavating in 30-cm. (one foot) arbitrary levels measured from a base line, Meggers and Evans had mixed the actual stratigraphic occupation layers (Bischof and Viteri Gamboa 1972, Lathrap 1967:97). The mound is hill-shaped, so that the later layers slope from the central top down to ground level at the edges, meaning that an arbitrary horizontal level at the bottom of the mound will have the oldest materials in the middle and much later material at the edges. The bottom level collection mixed sherds from a series of occupations on the mound.

How could well-trained archaeologists such as Meggers and Evans not see this problem with their method? At the time they were trained, in the late 1930s, some leading professors of archaeology taught that it was more scientific to create an arbitrary stratigraphy by measuring from a base level, that trying to follow visible natural stratigraphy is often difficult and confusing. It is, indeed; nevertheless, as the flawed Valdivia work showed, painstakingly observing actual stratigraphic layers in a site is the only method that reveals sequences through time.

Estrada, who had originated the Jomon hypothesis, died in 1961, soon after the project finished. Evans died in 1981. Meggers, who lived until 2012, continued to argue for Asian—Shang Chinese as well as Jomon Japanese—voyages significantly influencing Latin American history. From the standpoint of Critical Thinking, her later papers, like the Jomon hypothesis, are deductively researched from an initial hypothesis, rather than inductively formulating an interpretation from observed empirical data. In her 1975 paper suggesting Shang Chinese invaders created the Olmec civilization in Mesoamerica, she averred a "break . . . with the earlier village farming culture" in Mesoamerica, coupled with "speed with which the new elements spread over most of Mesoamerica. This rapid dispersal implies . . . some form of coercion was exercised," presumably by the Chinese invaders (Meggers 1975:6). Mesoamerican archaeologists were quick to refute both the alleged break and speed. Since the 1970s, a multiplicity of archaeological projects in Mesoamerica have demonstrated continuity between earlier cultures and those of the Olmec period, second millennium BCE, with far more variation of societies participating in trade within and beyond sites labeled Olmec. "Olmec" itself is more and more differentiated as new data come from many excavations. "Shang" also has become more differentiated through increased archaeological explorations in China. There may have been some contacts, perhaps around the North Pacific Rim rather than across the central Pacific (Birket-Smith 1967, 1971), but present knowledge of "Olmec" is too much in development to assert foreign sources.

# Chapter 8

# Art, Architecture, and Mythology

Some of the most striking similarities between pre-Columbian Asia and Mesoamerica are in art, architecture, and mythology. These topics are closely related, especially in Asia, where "Hindu-Buddhist" art and its subjects diffused throughout the continent's literate urban societies. "Hindu" and "Buddhist" are hyphenated because Hindu mythological figures were often incorporated into Buddhist art. Local styles and preferred venerations gave great variety to expressions of Buddhist worship; this tolerance for local traditions and for innovations may have facilitated appearances of Hindu-Buddhist art conventions in Mesoamerica.

Siddhartha Gautama was a prince born in Nepal probably between 485 and 450 BCE (Leidy 2008:1–2). He forsook the worldly luxuries of the court to meditate outdoors, finally achieving a breakthrough enlightenment on life and salvation. His sophisticated philosophy attracted intellectuals, while his compassion brought multitudes to the temples and monasteries they founded across Asia. Perhaps because the Buddha ("the Enlightened") was a prince who renounced competing for a crown, kings were comfortable with supporting his teachings. In kingdoms great and small, statues and bas-reliefs silently instructed worshipers to respect the Buddha's gentle leadership, and to recognize evils portrayed as demons. Originating from Hindu India, the religious iconography was broadened with figures from Hinduism such as Vishnu, Shiva, and female devas (minor goddesses or divine attendants). Lotuses, shells, thunderbolts, and other traditional symbols clued viewers' identifications of scenes and figures, and were entwined in ornamental borders. Overall, Hindu-Buddhist art and architecture was ornate, baroque, and naturalistic.

Diffusion of Hindu-Buddhist art and architecture, with its mythology, is perhaps our grandest example of diffusion, incontrovertibly historic, covering most of a continent and its island chain into the western Pacific. Well documented in some instances, for example, several Chinese monks who traveled to India to learn from priests there, in other times and areas there is considerable uncertainty, although diffusion and its ultimate source in India are not in doubt. "Lost Kingdoms: Hindu-Buddhist Sculpture of Early Southeast Asia, 5th to 8th Century" [CE] is the title of an exhibit in New York's Metropolitan Museum of Art; the exhibit's first object was a merchant's clay seal from eastern India picturing a typical Indian Ocean sailing vessel of the time (www.metmuseum.org/.../lost-kingdoms). Although this period and region manifest intriguing similarities to the contemporary time period, the Classic, in Mesoamerica, uncertainties in Asian histories becloud comparisons. Again, the Early Postclassic period in Mesoamerica, the second period of intriguing similarities, is met in Southeast and Island Southeast Asia with "much [that] can be inferred but next to nothing affirmed" (Keay 2006:89–90).

Architectural historian Jacques Dumarçay extracts from the buildings themselves, what must have been known models for temples, lamenting the lack of information on master builders or preserved plans (Dumarçay 2003:9, n. 3). His understanding of how apprenticeship and experiential learning create a master builder fits recent investigations into neurology, how observation and practice physically affect the brain. Humans and other primates have "mirror" impulses, provoking copying what one sees (Onians 2007).[1] With so little detailed documentation of Asian sea trade and so profuse proof of vigorous dissemination of Hindu-Buddhist art and religious ideas, blanket denial of the possibility of extension across the Pacific would be unscholarly.

## Gordon Ekholm's Work

Gordon F. Ekholm (1909–1987), born in Minnesota, was Curator of Mesoamerican Archaeology at the American Museum of Natural History in New York from 1937 until he retired in 1974. In his later years, he was considered a foremost authority for authenticating Mesoamerican artifacts, or disproving claims of antiquity. His knowledge built on both the extensive documented collections of the American Museum, and his numerous excavations in eastern, central, and western Mexico.

Sober, hard working, a careful scientist, he developed pioneer cultural sequences in Sinaloa and Sonora, in the West, and especially for the Huasteca in the East. Territory of Maya and of less-known nations including Teenek, Otomí, Totonacs, and the Olmeca-Xicallanca, (who conquered Cholula in Puebla c. 900 CE, ruling until driven out by allied Toltecs and Chichimecs about 1200 CE), Huasteca's humid jungles, bordered by the steep Sierra Oriental mountains, make archaeology generally difficult. Marguerite Ekholm, Gordon's wife since 1937, assisted her husband in the field in Mexico and in researching museum collections and records. Gordon Ekholm served as president of the Society for American Archaeology in 1953–1954, an office reflecting his peers' high regard for his scientific work and collegial cooperation.

World War II brought to New York a refugee specialist in the art and archaeology of Southeast Asia, Robert Heine-Geldern. Welcomed to the American Museum, Dr. Heine-Geldern was intrigued by similarities in its American collections to artifacts he knew from his Asian work. He and Ekholm began to collaborate on refining this line of research, each impressed with the other's scholarly approach. For the 1949 meeting of the International Congress of Americanists, scheduled for New York, Ekholm and Heine-Geldern prepared a temporary exhibit[2] in the American Museum displaying the series of transpacific parallels they had identified (Heine-Geldern and Ekholm 1951; Heine-Geldern 1950). The Museum's curators of South American archaeology and ethnology, Junius Bird and Harry Tschopik, and independent scholar of Asian ethnographic arts, Carl Schuster, assisted with the exhibit. It stimulated interest, bringing Ekholm invitations to lecture and prepare papers on the issue.

After a flurry of these opportunities, traditional denial of transoceanic contacts resumed its default position. In the eyes of mainstream archaeologists, Ekholm and Heine-Geldern had failed to unequivocally, incontrovertibly prove contact before 1492. That his very recent efforts to move toward recognition of probable contacts did not diminish his reputation for good science is shown by his election as Society for American Archaeology president shortly after the Americanist Congress exhibit and his publications related to it. Heine-Geldern was honored by dedication to his memory the publication of a three-volume set of papers from a Columbia University conference, *Early Chinese Art and Its Possible Influence in the Pacific Basin* (Barnard and Fraser, eds., 1972).

Ekholm explained:

As far as possible I try to maintain an analytical attitude. I do not strongly hold to a 'belief' that transpacific contacts occurred, only that the problem is an exciting and important one and should be thoroughly examined from all points of view (Ekholm 1953:72). One must always beware of basing broad historical interpretations on varyingly incomplete archaeological pictures (Ekholm 1953:88).

When he first discovered wheeled figurines in his excavations, he considered "contact with the cultures of the Old World . . . quite un-likely" (Ekholm 1946:225). "Pure invention," he surmised, "not put to practical use in the culture. Such a situation appears to be extremely un-common in the so-called primitive cultures of the world, for I can find no case comparable to it" (Ekholm 1946:225). It was when guest schol-ar Heine-Geldern expressed surprise at similarities between Mayan and Southeast Asian art that Ekholm realized the wheeled animals were not the only artifacts in his primary area of expertise, the Huasteca, that look like Asian parallels. He postulated a complex, or set, of similar-ities, that in the aggregate makes "pure [independent] invention" less probable than transpacific contacts (Ekholm 1953). This is what Need-ham and Lu termed the criterion of collocation, when traits or artifacts appear together in groups in the localities postulated to have been in contact (Needham and Lu 1985:10–13). Paul Tolstoy used the criterion of collocation in arguing that his complex of many discrete steps in making inner-bark cloth and paper weighed heavily in favor of trans-pacific carriage from Island Southeast Asia to Mesoamerica (chapter 7).

Collocation led Ekholm to recognize that the western Maya area at the Isthmus of Tehuantepec, the Mexican states of Chiapas, Tabasco, and Campeche, show more Asian similarities than other regions, the similari-ties extending northward from the Isthmus into the Huasteca, and south to Central America. Palenque, a Late Classic Maya (600–800 CE) city in Chiapas, seems to have more of the complex than do other Mesoamer-ican sites. Especially intriguing is the pagodalike three-story tower rising above the royal palace; nothing like it is known elsewhere in the Americas (Pohl 1999:88). Palenque is one of the most studied Maya cities, its hiero-glyphic texts, read in the 1960s, a breakthrough in decipherment that gave us a list of its kings. There is no question that these lords and their culture were Maya, nor about the exquisite artistic taste of Palenque's greatest rul-er, Pakal, and his son Chan Bahlum. Patrons of gifted artists, architects, and learned priests, the kings may have welcomed foreign talent.

**Figure 8.1.** Palace of Lord Pacal at Palenque, with pagodalike tower. Photo by Alice Kehoe

Ekholm's list of Late Classic Maya art similarities suggestive of trans-pacific influence is as follows (Ekholm 1953):

- Trefoil arches "over doorways and as a framing for niches in the upper walls. . . . Not as a corbelled arch, but as a framing for decorative panels, that same form is also used extensively during the Angkor period in Cambodia" (Ekholm 1953:74).

- "*Sacred tree or cross.* The motif of a stylized cross or tree occurs in America only at the site of Palenque and without known antecedents at earlier Maya sites. That from the Temple of the Foliated Cross has a kind of monster mask at its center and a bird in it upper branches" (Ekholm 1953:74–76).

- "*Lotus panels* . . . at Chichen Itza and at Palenque . . . rhizome of the lotus plant forms a sinuous pattern along the length of the design area, curving back and forth across the width of the panel and leaving spaces which are filled with leaves, buds and flowers . . . not a natural feature of either the Asiatic lotus or the American water lily.. . . Fish are seen eating lotus flowers at the ends of one of the Chichen panels. The placement of the fish is identical to that of the makaras or fishlike monsters in the lotus panels of Amarāvati [in India]. At both Chichen Itza and Palenque the lotus rhizome is seen to emerge from the mouth of a monster head or mask—an

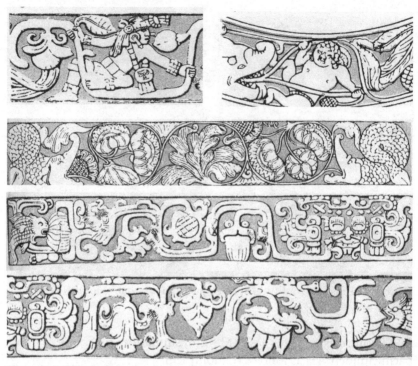

Figure 8.2. Ekholm's comparisons of decorative panels. Upper left and lower two panels from Maya Yucatán; upper right and second-from-top panel from Amarāvati, India. Courtesy American Museum of Natural History, New York, Natural History 59(8):345

extremely common feature of the Hindu-Buddhist lotus designs. Examples occur in both areas where the rhizome proceeds from a jawless mask placed in the center of the panel [as at] Santa Lucia Cozumalhuapa" (Ekholm 1953:78).

- "*Seated lions or tigers* . . . from the ball court of Tula . . . [and] flanking the staircase of the monolithic temple at Malinalco of Aztec date. . . . They are placed as if they were guardians of the temple . . . quite similar to their common method of use in southeast Asia" (Ekholm 1953:84).

- "Serpent columns and balustrades" at Chichén Itzá and Tula and "on some of the smaller and earlier 'Hindu' temples of Java . . . [and] in one of the reliefs of the Borobudur" (Ekholm 1953:84).

- "phallic representations" [i.e., lingams, common in Hindu-Buddhist sites] only at [Puuc-style sites of] Uxmal, Labna, Chacmultun (Ekholm 1953:81–82).

**Figure 8.3.** Top: Lion-dog guardian statues flanking entrance to temple at Wat Phnom, Phnom Penh, Cambodia. Bottom: Note naga balustrades along stairs to temple, their long serpent bodies forming the balustrades ending in multiple feathered monster heads. Photos by Alice Kehoe

Figure 8.4. Sri Ranganathaswamy Temple in Srirangapattana, India. National Informatics Centre, Guntur District, Government of India, Andhara Pradesh

We could add the Amareswara temple to Siva in Amarāvati, with a massive base like a monumental gate, topped by four stories each with a central doorway, and a fifth storey like a columned building; the effect is strikingly like Maya temples such as the Pyramid of the Magician at Uxmal.

Ekholm's list, significantly, comprises a distinct set recognized in the spread of Buddhism throughout Asia. Elements such as the makara monster are conventional in the set although not part of Buddhism per se; they show the Hindu cultural base from which Buddhism developed. At the same time, the art would have appealed to Mesoamericans who since Olmec times (1500–700 BCE) had symbolized the power of the watery world by a crocodile, and who were familiar with lotuses in their own tropical waters.[3] Similarly, Asian "lion-dog" temple guardian figures fit with Mesoamerican jaguar symbols of earthly power, plus dogs' guardian role in ordinary life.

## Paul Shao's Studies

A generation after Ekholm, a Chinese-American professor of fine arts used his bilingual fluency and skills in stylistic analyses to carry out a unique field project, recording both Chinese and pre-Columbian Mesoamerican art in original settings. Paul Shao (Shao Pang-hua, as Joseph Needham preferred to cite him), born 1940 in China, came to the United States with his family as political refugees, an experience that inclined him to hypothesize earlier voyages of elite officials deposed by new regimes in China (personal communication, November 1977). He notes that Chinese histories seldom recorded overseas ventures, which unlike those of early modern Europe, were private enterprises rather than state-supported. China, a large kingdom investing heavily in productive technologies within its domain, let international shipping often be carried out by peripheral small kingdoms of Southeast Asia and India, where absence of bureaucratic structure left few historical records (Shao 1976:11; see also Lieberman 2003, 2009, Shi 2014:107).

Shao's professional training in design and art history enabled him to discern and draw significant details in baroque art of each side of the postulated Pacific connections. His sections on dragons, on agnathic (no lower jaw) monster faces, and on elephants particularly benefit from the clarity he can picture. The final section in the 1976 book, on gestures, is perhaps the strongest. Shao and, independently, Mexican anthropologist Samuel Martí (1971) cite Hindu dance gestures called mudrā, featured also in Buddhist art.[4] Each gesture or posture is named and performed carefully, identifying emotion or an action such as blessing.

In Mexican art, rulers and lords central to a scene sit on bench thrones with one leg tucked under, the other leg dangling down, *padmasana*, the lotus posture; this in a society where people normally sit cross-legged (Coggins 2002:54, note 34). A variant in Buddhist art has the Buddha or bodhisattva sitting cross-legged with the left foot above the bent right leg, a rather uncomfortable position that is seen also in Maya art.

Hindu dance manuals list and picture dozens of named hand gestures and postures; Martí shows a page from the precontact Codex Nuttall in which a seated woman faces a seated masked figure or deity, the woman's two hands giving the mudrā gestures *varamudrā* (conferring boons) and *patakamudrā* (savior). The figure opposite her holds one arm across the chest, the other hand with index finger pointing and other fingers folded under, a common gesture in the Mesoamerican codices signifying instructing (Martí 1971:55, 1992:74–75).

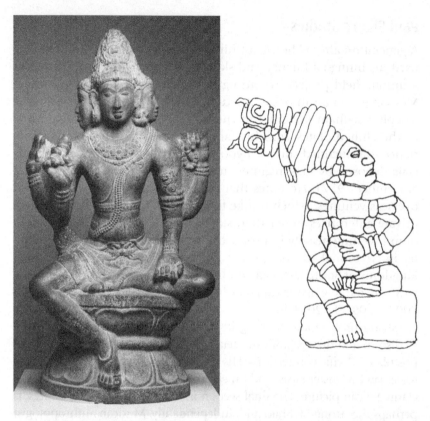

**Figure 8.5.** Figures seated on thrones, with one leg dangling, represent deities in both Hindu-Buddhist and Maya art. See also Shao 1976:94–95. Left: Hindu god Shiva, Chola period, India (c. 860–1279 CE). Right: King of Maya kingdom of Copán, Honduras, portrayed as deified forefather of King Yax-Pac, whose accession to the throne is the subject of the carved panel, c. 775 CE (G-M-T correlation, or 983 CE in Kelley's correlation). Shiva: Metropolitan Museum of Art, New York, photograph by Schecter Lee; King: Drawn by Kehoe, after plate 36a in Schele and Miller 1986:131

Mudrā and ceremonial postures form a set of visual symbols repeated over and over in Mesoamerican art media, similar to the repetition of the same mudrā and postures throughout Hindu-Buddhist art and dance in Asia. Many of the mudrā hand formations are highly stylized, uncomfortable to hold. Rulers or holy persons sitting with one leg dangling over a bench, the other tucked under, have a comfortable posture but one at odds with the Western convention of rulers and deities sitting stiffly on chair thrones, both feet firmly together on the floor.

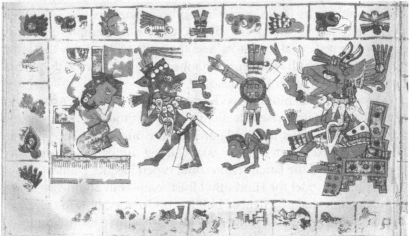

**Figure 8.6.** Top: The Buddha using mudrā represents asking Prithvi, devi of the earth, to witness his enlightenment (bhūmisparśa mudrā). Bottom: Page 64 of pre-conquest Maya *Codex Borgia* shows dancers performing before the god of dance, both the dancers and the deity using mudrā-like hand gestures, as in Indian dance. The deity's hand positions signify giving help or favors (Martí 1971:49). Buddha: Gallo-Roman Museum, Lyon, France; Codex Borgia: from 1898 facsimile, Fondo de Cultural Economica, Mexico

## Architecture

Hindu-Buddhist architecture features temples on platforms, usually with ornamental, monumental gates to the holy precinct. Temples are ornately designed and ornamented, customarily with a vertical series representing a series of heavens. Feathered serpents, called *nagas*, are carved at ends of balustrades along entrance walks. *Nagas* look like cobras and may have multiple cobra heads; Mesoamerican feathered serpents look like rattlesnakes, a difference likely to reflect lack of cobras in America and respect for the rattlesnake as America's most deadly serpent.

Comparing Asian and Mesoamerican architecture requires looking at the whole precinct of temples, courts and courtyards, approaches, boundary walls, and the placement of symbolic figures such as the feathered serpents forming balustrades. These precincts represent cosmological models; in Asia, holy Mount Meru in the center of the world, its terraces being a series of heavens, its base having concentric rings of mountains and oceans until the outermost is the infinite Cosmic Ocean. Beings such as nagas and nature spirits abide on the terraces. Generalizing, "Maya temples can . . . be identified: a temple has a high platform topped by small chambers; access is limited and is usually by a single staircase, although a few examples have other arrangements. . . . Although clearly associated with specific deities, these Maya temples primarily commemorated royal ancestors and the gods with whom the kings were united in death" (Miller and Taube 1993:161; to view these temples and palaces, see Proskouriakoff 1963).

Maya temple architecture is closest to Hindu-Buddhist Asian style. Specialists in Mayan research discuss the multitude of regional, and even local, variations in temple architecture, just as do specialists in Hindu-Buddhist architecture in Asia. Cutting through the trees to see the forest, one of the latter, architectural expert Jacques Dumarçay, discerns a basic model for Hindu-Buddhist temples in Southeast Asia, a mental picture that experienced builders understood how to construct. Dumarçay premises that kings and other wealthy patrons employed master builders to lay out and supervise commissioned work; almost never is the name of the master builder inscribed, only that of the patron (Dumarçay 2003:9, footnote 3).

Over the course of centuries, thousands of miles of space, and hundreds of ethnic traditions, innovations were added—sometimes to accommodate different building materials (Dumarçay 2003:25, 31), sometimes to honor a different deity. Traditional conventions in

**Figure 8.7.** Top: Bakong in Angkor area, Cambodia, built 881 CE. Bottom left: Temple of the Magician, Uxmal, Yucatán. same century (G-M-T correlation, or eleventh century CE, Kelley correlation). Bottom right: Temple of the Inscriptions, Palenque, Mexico, built over the tomb of Lord Pacal who died 683 CE (G-M-T correlation, or 891 Kelley correlation). Photos by Alice Kehoe

**Figure 8.8.** Naga, Siem Reap, Cambodia. Note the feathers behind the monster faces, and that the faces are toothed demons, not cobras as one would expect from the cobra body. Elsewhere in Southeast Asia, nagas sometimes have feathered dragon heads. Photo by Alice Kehoe

structure and ornamentation were often retained, giving scholars clues to the evolution of regional forms. Mayan researchers have a range of time comparable to that of Hindu-Buddhist architecture in Asia, if a somewhat smaller geographical range—the Asian tradition diffused over 7,000 kilometers (4,000 miles), the Mayan region covers about 1,000 kilometers (700 miles) north to south, and 700 kilometers (500 miles) west to east.[5] Dumarçay's concept of master builders, thousands of them through time and space, actualizing a basic cosmological model provides a perspective for the great number of variations around a recognizable basic form. Most importantly for our purpose in this text, a very few (maybe only one!) master builders on a ship from Asia to Mesoamerica could transmit the Hindu-Buddhist basic model.

**Figure 8.9.** Corbelled roof buildings in temple precincts. Top: Preah Khan in Angkor area, Cambodia, built 1191 CE. Bottom: Puuc-style temple with corbelled roof, Chichén Itzá, Yucatán, built probably in tenth century CE (G-M-T correlation, or twelfth century CE, Kelley correlation). Photos by Alice Kehoe

In Campeche state in west-central Yucatán, Mexico, a relatively small site, Nocuchich (Adams and Jones 1981:311, Andrews 1997), has, amid a few nondescript ruins, two towers that uncannily resemble medieval Asian ones. Most striking is the tower with a huge human face carved in the middle, as if a personage is overlooking the site, very much like the face towers at Bàyon in Angkor, Cambodia,[6] themselves unique in Asia (Sharrock 2007:25, comparing Bàyon face towers with Nepalese towers with painted eyes). On the same site, 38 meters (125 feet) away, is a very slender tower like a pagoda symbolizing sacred Mt. Meru. Another pagodalike tower stands at Pacal's palace at Palenque, this one more like the Chinese pagodas that people could climb up inside. So far as is known, these towers resembling pagodas are unique in the Americas (Andrews 1996:19 mentions a similar tower in Chanchén, in the same region as Nocuchich).

Nocuchich's pair of Asian style towers in an otherwise unimpressive site suggests, much more than other American sites do, the possibility of a party of Asians attempting to build a temple complex in the foreign land. One possibility could be Buddhist monks fleeing (1197–1207 CE) massacres and the destruction of their monasteries in the Ganges Valley, India, as Muslim armies conquered northern India (Sharrock 2007:29). Thousands of Buddhists flooded the kingdoms to the north and east that continued in their faith; those who arrived in the coastal kingdoms of Southeast Asia, Malaysia, and Indonesia would have been able to purchase an ocean-going ship to seek refuge in a remote eastern land, beyond the tumultuous Philippines and Indonesia.

Asia to America works for the model Mayan temple of a small sanctum on a cosmic-mountain platform, topped with false storeys. That master plan is basic in Asia. Another model is indigenous to the Americas: a small temple on a four-sided platform with stairs in the center of one platform side. These temples do not have the upper storeys resembling the terraces of the cosmic mountain. Instead, the massive platform *is* the mountain, at Teotihuacán and Cholula, contoured to replicate holy mountains seen from the city plain. Here, the deity resides on top of the mountain. At Chichén Itzá in Yucatan, this central Mexican style was used for the elegantly simple Castillo that contrasts with the ornate native Maya style of other temples in the city.

Surprisingly, a temple strongly resembling the Castillo was built in central Java in the fifteenth century, in the kingdom of Majapahit (Jumsai 1988:121, Plate 2, Shaffer 1996:64). It is called Candi Sukuh. Princes and nobles of that kingdom vied with one another to gain merit by ordering the construction of a temple, each to be distinctive enough for its

**Figure 8.10.** Towers with huge human faces at midpoint are unique to Bàyon and Nocuchich. Nocuchich also has a pagodalike tower near the human-face tower. Top left: Bàyon in Angkor area, Cambodia, Top right, and below left: Nocuchich, Yucatán. Photos by Teobert Maler, 1889; Bàyon: photo by Alice Kehoe

**Figure 8.11.** Top: Candi Sukuh temple in central Java, Indonesia, built 1437 CE. Bottom: Castillo temple, Chichén Itzá, Yucatán, built probably in tenth century CE (G-M-T correlation, or twelfth century CE, Kelley correlation). Candi Sukuh, Jogja Petualang photo by friends member KKN UGM 2013; Castillo: Photo by Alice Kehoe

patron to be noticed. Majapahit, founded 1293 CE, became the dominant power in Indonesia until the end of the fifteenth century. Its ports handled the highly lucrative medieval spice trade from its eastern subordinates, the Moluccas Islands (present day Maluku), out to mainland eastern Asia and India. Considering the Moluccas are the easternmost islands of Indonesia, and Majapahit's ships were state-of-the-art in maritime Asia, it seems plausible that one of the Majapahit princes employed a Mexican builder to construct a temple that would outdo all rivals for distinction. Whether the prince himself had visited Mexico is not the question; if we follow Dumarçay's argument, we need only one man traveling with a Majapahit ship returning from an exploratory trip across the Pacific.

If Candi Sukuh is the work of a Mexican Postclassic builder adventuring aboard an impressive Javanese ship, it seems unique in Asia, as the Nocuchich slender pagoda and face tower are in America. In contrast, the Hindu-Buddhist temple model seems to have been creatively used in a number of Maya temples, and significantly, the architectural model is part of the set of art motifs argued by Ekholm and Heine-Geldern and the mudrā presented by Martí and Shao. We need not invoke dramatic scenarios: one or a few merchant ships exploring for luxury cargo could have carried artisans ready to create beautiful temples and treasures for Maya nobles ready to pay with gold and jade. Temples on steep, high platforms, and palaces on lower, broad platforms, go back to second millennium BCE on both sides of the Pacific, a bauplan (basic structure) that might simply reflect notions of deities "on high" and kings' "extensive" domains (Lakoff and Johnson 1980 explain such fundamental metaphors). One other caution should be kept in mind: that in addition to Classic and Postclassic Maya and Central Mexican temples, the Americas during the last two millennia before European invasions had several other distinct regional art and building traditions. Huge mounds, presumably part of religious sites, go back in both North and South America to the third millennium BCE. If they had buildings upon them, they would have been of wood, long since decayed away.

## Mythology and Astrology

Hindu-Buddhist art and architecture alike illustrate a rich trove of scriptural stories, deities and spirits, cosmologies, icons, and theological concepts (Bonnefoy 1993). Although Buddhism postulates one prophet, Prince Gautama who achieved perfect enlightenment, centuries of meditation and discussion by monks and teachers led to a number of schools variously portraying the Enlightened One, his disciples, and spiritual beings in the layers of heaven. Hindu deities, plus local spirits in the vast regions to which Buddhism spread, were incorporated into many of the schools calling themselves Buddhist. Buddha himself, or his avatars, seems not to have been portrayed in the Americas, while elements of Hinduism do have parallels in Mesoamerica. The strongest parallels comprise a set used in astrology.

Both Hindus and Mesoamericans postulated a series of world ages, *yuga* in Hindi, ending in catastrophes. Hinduism has four, of which we are in the fourth, Kali-yuga. Mesoamerica had five ages, the present being in the fifth, and all likewise ending in catastrophic destruction (Miller and Taube 1993:70; Evans 2004:34–35; Kelley and Milone 2011:494). Similarity here would carry little weight, except that the world ages are part of calendar systems that do include detailed parallels, with the calendar systems themselves the necessary foundation for astrological horoscopes on which Asians and Mesoamericans placed great value. What could be more fantastical than believing that the conjunction of stars and planets at the exact moment of a person's birth would forecast his or her life fortunes? Surely, seeing how different outcomes are for persons born at the same moment would end that fantasy? No; believers can say that errors were made in determining the crucial moment of birth, or the precise conjunctions in the heavens, or people are forewarned and alter their fates by avoiding predicted dangers.[7] Persistence of astrology from our earliest records in Babylon and Assyria four thousand years ago, to today's newspaper and online horoscopes, is a remarkable testament to humans' anxiety over their lives (Kelley and Milone 2011:500–502).

David H. Kelley (1924–2011) was an archaeologist and linguist best known for his collaboration with the Russian scholar Yuri Knorozov and the American, Floyd Lounsbury, in "breaking the code" of Maya hieroglyphs, demonstrating they can be read phonetically in Mayan. Mayanists know Kelley for his identifications of portrayals of the Mayan Lords of the Night (deities) in the tomb of Lord Pacal of Palenque; for the genealogies he worked out for historical figures in the surviving Mesoamerican native books; and for interpreting Mayan astronomies.

Mesoamerican nations developed sophisticated mathematics for their astronomical calculations, supported by rulers wanting astrological predictions. Broadly interested in the history of astronomical knowledge, Kelley compared astrological systems and calendars in early Western Asia, their diffusion to Greece, India, and China, and the Mesoamerican systems. The several systems in Eurasia, clearly historically connected, varied in many details, such as which animals are in the zodiac, or their order; so did the several systems in Mesoamerica. Kelley compared the Eurasian and Mesoamerican calendar astrologies and saw that Mesoamerican systems differed from Eurasian systems *to about the same degree* as any two or three systems on either continent differed. Paul Kirchoff, who resided in Mexico and studied these systems, strongly agreed (Kirchoff 1964). Presumably, a Eurasian calendar astrology became known in Mesoamerica, likely about two thousand years ago.

Mesoamerican calendars are complex systems of interdigitating units, with a base of twenty (Miller and Taube 1993:48–54; Kelley and Milone 2011:355–359). In their calculations, Maya used a zero, likely the first in the world to do so (Maya glyphs of zero, a stylized snail shell circle, go back a little earlier than evidence of zero in India). Kelley surmised that about 200 CE, a learned Maya astronomer met an astronomer from, or in, India, and brilliantly coordinated his own calendrical system with that in India, creating the elaborate Mesoamerican calendar of a 260-day period, possibly derived from agricultural calendars, with the sidereal year of 365 days.

A meticulous scholar, Kelley never felt his huge compilation of calendar astronomies was completely finished.[8] Meanwhile, he worked on related questions, one being correlations between Mesoamerican calendrical dates and the European calendar, another being the dating of historical events and personages recorded in the surviving pre-Columbian books and inscriptions and in early Colonial documents.

Correlation challenged scholars for centuries, usually by trying to find European dates for astronomical phenomena recorded by Mayans. By mid-twentieth century, archaeologists and historians generally accepted the correlation equation known as the Goodman-Martinez-Thompson, Thompson being a preeminent Mayan archaeologist. Kelley found too many discrepancies between dates in this correlation and astronomical data, as well as with events recorded in the indigenous books and with genealogies of rulers he worked out from these books. His best correlation is 208 years later than the G-M-T.

Two younger scholars, Bryan Wells and Adreas Fuls, worked out a correlation very close to Kelley's (Kelley and Milone 2011:360), as has Mayan archaeologist Arlen Chase (1986). Most Mesoamericanists prefer to stay with the G-M-T rather than revise conventional dating. The correlation problem directly affects discussion of possible pre-Columbian transoceanic contacts, particularly in the last few centuries before 1500. For example, when the Chinese king of Wuyue sent out thousands of miniature stupas to every land, 965 CE, was it the time of the collapse of lowland Maya kingdoms, as the G-M-T would have it, or was it the flourishing Early Postclassic, as Kelley, Wells, and Fuls have it?

Part of the Mesoamerican calendar systems is division of the year into 20-day months. Each day of the month is named, that is, a total of twenty names per month (Kelley and Milone 2011:356). No two local Mesoamerican lists of twenty day-names coincides completely with any other, i.e., each nation had its own calendar traditions. Comparing these lists, Kelley drew out a list likely to represent an early source from which the later day-name series varied.

Asia has series of names similar to those of the Mesoamerican days, the Asian names given to the set of lunar mansions (stations of the moon as it moves along the ecliptic each month). Since there are twenty-eight lunar mansions, each seen as a constellation, there could not be an exact copy if the concept of a regularly repeating sequence was used for names of the twenty days of a month (that is, Eurasian "month" relates to the moon's phases, while the Mesoamerican day names do not). Commonalities among the Mesoamerican lists suggested to Kelley that the Mayan astronomer took a list of lunar mansions used in India two thousand years ago—where the mansions have mostly animal names corresponding to constellations—and rearranged some of the names to structure relationships such that as the prototype twenty-day series proceeds through the year, day 4 Earthquake is winter solstice, day 4 Fire is spring equinox, 4 Rain is summer solstice, and 4 Wind is fall equinox. These names are the names of the four eras separated by cataclysms, and the four elements Earth, Water, Fire, and Wind (air), common to India (and Greece, sharing Indian astrology) and Mesoamerica.

Lunar mansion day-names in India referred to principal deities. Taken from India to China, the deities were dropped, indicating the direction of borrowing for this astrology. In Mesoamerica, the names that do not occur are those of domestic animals (horse, sheep, cow, pig, and elephant) unknown in America. Another telling link is that in India, one of the days is named for the intoxicant Soma, while in the Mesoamerican prototype, the Day 8 is Rabbit, symbol of drunkenness (Wicke 1984, Kelley 1990). Asians see a rabbit in the moon—in China, standing on its hind legs pounding with a pestle into a mortar, making the elixir of immortality; in Mesoamerica, the rabbit in the moon is pounding to make pulque.[9]

**Table 8.1.** Aztec Names of Days Compared With Chinese and Greek Lunar Month Mansion Animals (D. H. Kelley, 1960)

Aztec days are listed in the order of occurrence in the 20-day month. For Chinese and Greek names of days, numbers indicate their position in the 28-day month.

| Aztec Days | Chinese Days | Greek Days |
|---|---|---|
| 1. Crocodile or Swordfish | 1. Dragon | 9. Snake or Dragon |
| 2. Wind | | |
| 3. House | Purification Temple Constellation | |
| 4. Lizard | 4. Serpent | 9. Snake or Dragon |
| 5. Snake | 4. Serpent | 9. Snake or Dragon |
| 6. Death | Piled-up Corpses Constellation | |
| 7. Deer | 5. Little Deer; 7. Big Deer | 20. Deer |
| 8. Rabbit | 27. Hare | |
| 9. Water | Gemini Constellation, "Accumulated Water" | |
| 10. Dog | 9. Wild Dog; 15. Dog | 7. Dog |
| 11. Monkey | 10. Little Monkey; 11. Big Monkey | 15. Baboon |
| 12. Twisted (broom plant) | Lunar Mansion *liu* "Willow" | |
| 13. Reed | | |
| 14. Ocelot | 24. Leopard; 25. Tiger | 16. Cat; 17. Lion; 18. Leopard |
| 15. Eagle | 12. Crow; 13. Cock; 19. Swallow | 5. Hawk |
| 16. Vulture | 12. Crow; 13. Cock; 19. Swallow | 2. Vulture |
| 17. Earthquake | | |
| 18. Flint | | |
| 19. Rain or Turtle | Tortoise Constellation | |
| 20. Flower | | |

Note that lists will not be identical because Mesoamericans had a 20-day month, whereas Eurasians had a 28-day month. For examples of variations in Eurasian calendar astrology, see Kelley and Milone 2011:494–498.

## Discussion

Kelley's comparisons of Eurasian and Mesoamerican calendar astrologies follow linguistic methods to infer an earlier prototype. He and his colleague Floyd Lounsbury used these methods when deciphering Maya hieroglyphs, to work back from contemporary Maya languages, of which there are about thirty, to what was probably spoken by elite Maya in the first millennium CE, that is, the sounds denoted by the phonetic glyphs. Change through time, incrementally dropping, substituting, adding phonemes, words, grammatical practice, ideas, and expected behavior, happens everywhere in human societies; trends or patterns can be detected through careful documentation.

What demonstrably works in linguistics and historical studies was how Kelley charted earlier and later aspects of calendar day-names, astronomical references, and astrology practices across Eurasia and Mesoamerica, and compared the two continents. Imperfect matches are to be expected because variations through time and between cultures are normal. Some of Kelley's work was to see substitutions such as Mesoamerican Rabbit, denoting drunkenness, for intoxicating Soma in the Hindu day-name list, and Lightning for Rain. He then discerned that the Maya genius who formalized their interdigitating set of calendars repositioned some day-names so as to make oppositional pairs across the seasons or years in a calendar cycle.

Can this story be true? We can never know; we ask whether it is plausible, and whether it is probable. Plausible it is, given the extensive maritime voyaging around Asia in seaworthy ships two thousand years ago, and the rewards merchants could gain. Probable is another argument: How likely are repeated independent inventions of a mystical system based on the fantasy premise that human fortunes are linked to astronomical conjunctions at the exact moment of birth? Kelley attacked that question by comparing all Eurasian astrologies and showing borrowings linking them all to the earliest known, from Mesopotamia. Mesoamerican calendar astrologies, too, show linkages. Therefore, the logical parsimonious inference to best explanation is that Eurasian and Mesoamerican calendar astrologies were linked, in the manner of those in each continent linking to a prototype.

Rabbit in the moon is part of the overall calendar astrologies links, much more easily understood, and seen, than more esoteric signs of deities and constellations (Kelley and Milone 2011:494). Chinese popular culture still enjoys seeing the rabbit in the moon pounding elixir of immortality. Mesoamericans painted rabbits in the moon, rabbits giving a cup of drink to a ruler, and sculpted rabbits making out with the beauteous young moon goddess. Is it plausible that on two sides of a sea, people would independently see a white rabbit in the moon, see it pounding an intoxicating drink in a large mortar?

## Summary

Alleging meaningful similarities in art and intellectual creations between Asia and Mesoamerica carries us into an uncomfortable realm of postulating basic ideas realized in varieties of actual structures. On the one hand, we have innumerable examples around us of transoceanic contacts producing examples, among them the styles of houses in North America: Tudor, Georgian, gothic, Flemish Renaissance, English cottage, and so on. As Dumarçay said in his study of Hindu-Buddhist building similarities in Asia, the master builder knew the basic plan but was not compelled to exactly copy the prototype, perhaps did not know the details or have workmen capable of reproducing them. Perhaps, like American builders, he wanted his distinctive stamp on the building.

Only Nocuchich in Campeche looks like an effort to reproduce an Asian prototype, Báyon, and it is somewhat of an anomaly for Yucatán, rather crude compared to the region's great, artistically refined cities, Chichén Itzá and Uxmal. Some other Mayan sites appear to represent artist-architects' borrowings of Hindu-Buddhist architecture, so powerfully diffused throughout Asia, to enhance established Mayan style.

Ekholm and Heine-Geldern, and Kelley, suggested gifted individuals becoming familiar with Asian styles, not migrations of Asians to Mesoamerica. These individuals could have been passengers on an Asian merchant vessel seeking new sources of valuables, or less plausible but possible, Mesoamericans going west on the return of such a vessel, then finding means of returning home following some years in Asia.

Critical Thinking always seeks new data, ready to revise or perhaps reject interpretations that at one time appeared to fit available data. A good example is Robert Heine-Geldern's hypothesis that metallurgy in South America derived from that in Southeast Asia, specifically, the region of Viet Nam (Heine-Geldern 1972, a paper published after his death in 1969). When he wrote that paper, in 1967, archaeology supported the idea that metallurgy developed in central China by 2000 BCE and spread to Southeast Asia during the first millennium BCE. Metallurgy appeared in Peru, it seemed, about 1000 BCE. Heine-Geldern's hypothesis, drawing upon similarities in small bells, mace heads, pins, elaborate bracelets, and a few other artifact types, was reasonable.

Half a century of archaeology in both Asia and South America renders Heine-Geldern's hypothesis no longer tenable. Hundreds of excavations and surveys document widespread use of copper, and then development of bronze work, across Asia, beginning by late third millennium BCE near sources of ores, extending to contacts across the steppes with eastern European metallurgists (Linduff and Mei 2008). In South America, discovery of a necklace of tubular gold beads in a burial in the Andes near sources of gold ore, dated late third millennium BCE, indicates independent invention of metallurgy in Peru (Aldenderfer et al. 2008). Bronze (that is, copper alloys) was favored in eastern Asia, gold in Peru. While it remains possible that contacts in later centuries between the two metal-using continents added techniques to each other's repertoire, this question has not been pursued as issues of times and places of earliest metallurgies dominate research.

# Chapter 9

# The Atlantic World

Why is so much attention given to possible pre-Columbian contacts across the Pacific, and so little to Atlantic possibilities?

The best answer would be this: because Polynesian colonizations even to Remote Oceania proved these peoples' impressive seafaring capabilities, whereas there are no comparable records for Atlantic voyaging. That good scientific reason isn't all the story. The myth of Columbus focuses on the Atlantic, the theater of that Admiral's exploits and suffering, portrayed as bordered on the east by progressive civilizations and on the west by savages in wildernesses. Had there been prior contacts, the supposition goes, America would not have been such a wilderness—see how quickly it was cleared after Europeans landed! Related to that notion is that contact with Europeans infected American natives with devastating epidemics of Eurasian diseases; if no evidence of such devastation is recognized, it means no contacts. "Knowing" this, evidence suggesting pre-Columbian epidemics is attributed to indigenous pathogens. Power of chartering myth is especially apparent when it hits so close to home.

Transoceanic contacts across the Atlantic before 1492 could happen across the North Atlantic where island-hopping shortens open-sea distances, across the middle Atlantic where Columbus sailed with prevailing winds westward and returned on the Gulf Stream current, or between West Africa and Brazil, where the distance across is shortest. This chapter will give a section to each. Not discussed is the evidence for European commercial fishing on the Grand Banks off Newfoundland beginning perhaps 1481. Competition between fishermen, and in

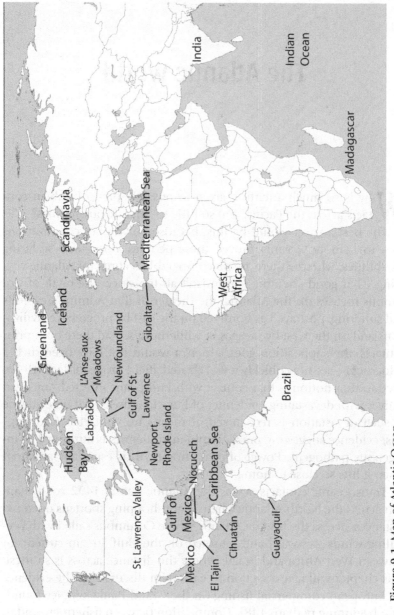

**Figure 9.1.** Map of Atlantic Ocean

some cases, sponsoring merchants, seems to have kept these enterprises scantily documented until Englishman John Day wrote that the city of Bristol had already equipped ships to sail to the land Columbus claimed to have discovered (Quinn 1974:17–18). In any case, by 1500, there were dozens of European fishing boats on the Grand Banks, going ashore in southeastern Canada to dry their catches and replenish supplies.

## North Atlantic—Norse

The most secure proof of transoceanic voyages to America before 1492 is in the Northeast: the Canadian Maritimes and New England. Here we have a well-excavated Norse settlement radiocarbon dated to 1000 CE, conforming in many details of buildings and artifacts to Scandinavian settlements of that date. Not only is the site, L'Anse aux Meadows, clearly Norse, it fits narratives of Norse colonization in the North Atlantic at that time.

Two sagas preserved in Iceland, *Eirîks saga rauða* (Saga of Eric the Red) and the *Grænlendinga saga* (Greenlanders Saga), tell how Bjarni Herjólfsson sailed in 986 from Scandinavia to his parents, whom he believed were living in Iceland. There he was told they had moved to Greenland, newly colonized by Erik the Red (bloody Erik, he had killed several men and been banished). Bjarni set out for Greenland but lost the way in a storm. When it cleared, he saw land that he realized couldn't be Greenland, that he was too far south and west from his course. Already late in the summer sailing season, Bjarni did not land but corrected course and made Greenland, where he told settlers of land farther west.

Erik's son Leif determined to go explore it, hoping to find land less harsh than Greenland. His party saw grassy meadows suited to cattle and grapes that could be made into wine, so called it Vinland. Several other groups led by Erik's family attempted to settle in Vinland. One received a friendly visit from local Indians wanting to trade; they received red cloth and milk, but no Norse weapons. More often, natives attacked the intruders. Quarrels among the settlers also led to violence. So far as the two sagas tell, colonization of Vinland was given up within the lifetimes of Erik's children.

Icelandic sagas are family histories, handed down orally for a couple of centuries before they were written. On the one hand, trained bards memorized these histories for formal telling; they were expected to be accurate. On the other hand, the bards were supposed to recall and keep straight names and deeds of hundreds of men and women living in two or three centuries, moving about, marrying, and remarrying.

**Figure 9.2.** L'Anse aux Meadows, Newfoundland, Canada, Norse occupation at 1000 CE. Photo by Alice Kehoe

Enough in the two sagas is similar to give us some confidence that actual historical happenings are described, melodramatic though some of them are.[1] If over the five centuries of Norse settlements in southern Greenland, there were other efforts to colonize Vinland, no one wrote sagas telling us.

Archaeology validates and expands the Norse sagas. For seven seasons, Norwegian archaeologist Anne Stine Ingstad, assisted by her anthropologist husband Helge Ingstad and experienced crews, excavated L'Anse aux Meadows, a site on the northern tip of Newfoundland that had been recognized in 1956 by Danish archaeologist Jorgen Meldgaard as fitting the sagas' descriptions. Turf-covered Norse-style houses, a boat shed, smelted bog iron, and artifacts such as a Norse type of spindle whorl and a woman's brooch unequivocally identified the occupation, radiocarbon dated to the same time that the sagas gave for Leif's and his family's ventures, as a Norse settlement, not Indian. That it was one of those described in the sagas is reasonable.

Other archaeological projects in northeastern Canada, particularly by Patricia Sutherland, a curator at the Canadian Museum of History, have found what appear to be medieval Norse hunting camps on the Canadian mainland and Baffin Island. Compared to the houses and associated structures at L'Anse aux Meadows, these camps are paltry, yielding few artifacts and rough hunters' shelters. Still, they don't resemble the camps of native Inuit. We know from Scandinavian history that Greenland Norse traded American furs and walrus products for European manufactures brought annually by a ship from Norway. For their own economic security, the Greenland Norse should have supplemented trading for furs with Inuit by themselves hunting for these export products. A few native carvings of bearded men wearing Norse hooded coats have been found in the eastern Canadian Arctic (Pringle 2012, Schledermann 1980, Sutherland 2000, 2015).

Besides the definite Norse community at L'Anse aux Meadows in Newfoundland and the archaeological evidence for Norse hunting camps on Baffin Island and the Canadian Eastern Arctic, a stone tower in Newport, Rhode Island, looks very much like buildings in western Europe in the eleventh century CE. For example, in the Bayeaux Tapestry portraying William the Conqueror's invasion of England, 1066 CE, one section shows the defending English lords dining in a round two-storey tower. "Norman" means "Norse-man;" William and his companions were descended from Norse invaders of northern France.

Attempts to firmly date the Newport Tower have not been successful, as of this writing; being stone, not organic, its masonry cannot be radiocarbon-dated, and efforts to date the mortar have been inconclusive. Late in the nineteenth century, the town of Newport had the tower stabilized, a procedure that interfered with later assessments of the origin of the tower. Mainstream American opinion asserts that the tower was constructed in the later seventeenth century to be a windmill by the first governor of colonial Rhode Island. Perhaps the governor utilized the tower to be the base of the mill the colony needed, if it was built by Norse before 1492.

Given lack of conclusive documentation that the governor built the entire tower, and the solid evidence of Norse in the Gulf of St. Lawrence, the *possibility* that the Newport Tower was built by medieval Norse should not be dismissed. It is *plausible* that it is medieval Norse. *Probability* that it was Norse is equivocal: for a colonial governor's windmill it is odd, for an eleventh-century building it would be in style, so the basic question is whether Governor Arnold indulged in novelty, copying a medieval style tower to mount his windmill on, or whether he mounted his windmill on a tower built by Norse attempting settlement, conveniently located in what became Rhode Island Colony's Newport.

Figure 9.3. Top: Newport Tower, Rhode Island, resembling medieval Norse towers. Bottom: Scene from the Bayeux Tapestry showing English King Harold dining in similar tower house before the battle with William of Normandy, 1066 CE. Newport Tower: Photo by Matthew Trump, 2004; Bayeux Tapestry: Reading Museum, UK

Before we move on from Norse Vinland, a related question exists about the disappearance of Norse from Greenland, about 1450. Their two settlements in southern Greenland had survived for nearly five centuries; why were they abandoned only decades before Columbus sailed? Most probably, worsening climate imperiled their small communities. Erik the Red had colonized during the early part of a climate era called the Medieval Warm Period, about 950 CE to about 1250, when the northern hemisphere temperatures were comparable to mid-twentieth century.[2] After about 1250, the climate became colder—the Little Ice Age—until around 1850, when it again became generally warmer. Onset of the colder period brought heavier storms along northern coasts, making coastal settlements dangerous and destroying their pastures and farms. Cold also shortened the growing season for crops and for pasturing livestock outdoors. First one Norse Greenland settlement was abandoned, then the second one, neither with any indication of rapid catastrophe. Some people may have immigrated to Iceland or Scandinavia, some may have joined Inuit communities, living their hunting life. If any contemplated seeking Vinland to settle, no clue remains. They may have thought about the attacks by natives upon the eleventh-century efforts to found colonies, told in the sagas.

Inland from Vinland, there apparently was one effort by medieval Norse to reconnoiter sources for the luxury furs that brought wealth when sold to southern Europe and western Asian markets. In the mid-fourteenth century, the Black Death plague hit Scandinavia, causing the kingdoms of the region to lose one-third to one-half of their people. Soon after the plague abated, in 1360, merchants of the Hanseatic League in Baltic cities organized an army of three thousand German mercenary troops to invade the Norwegian port of Bergen, Scandinavia's best all-weather port and its terminus for the trade in Russian furs that brought wealth to Scandinavian entrepreneurs. The Hanse forbade Norse to use Bergen and cut them off from the fur trade.

A stone found in 1898 in northwestern Minnesota, U.S.A., has an incised inscription in Norse runes stating that a party of Norse on an acquiring expedition west of Vinland had camped at that place in 1362, and ten of the men had been killed by natives. The stone slab was erected on top of a knoll as a memorial to those men. Given what was happening in Scandinavia at that time, it makes sense that a party of traders experienced in the grueling long-distance fur trade through northern Russian forests might have sailed to Greenland and on, as advised by the Norse there, to America to find a new source of luxury furs. They could have sailed through Hudson Strait into Hudson's Bay, the route used after 1670 by the Hudson's Bay Company of England, and used small boats to go inland, again the standard route of the later traders. If any of the party succeeded in returning home, they would have arrived when, in 1363, the three Scandinavian kingdoms had mounted a joint campaign to recover Bergen from the Germans. Surely these men would have joined the Norse army fighting to regain the Russian fur trade, rather than return to source American furs.

Although the *history* of Scandinavia, 1345–1363, describes a unique crisis that offers a motive for Norse traders to seek American furs, no one of the many investigators and evaluators of the Kensington Runestone, as the inscribed stone is called, had noticed that crisis. I was asked by a Danish-American engineer with advanced degrees in mathematics and materials science to advise him on archaeological aspects of the find, as part of a project to scan the stone with modern microscope technology. As an anthropologist and ethnohistorian, I looked into fourteenth century Scandinavian history: the crisis of the Norse fur trade jumped out as the smoking gun, a motive.

When the scanning project confirmed weathering around the edges of the incised runes, the geologist in the project went on to pull out from Minnesota Historical Society archives a 1910 commissioned but disregarded report by Minnesota's eminent geologist Newton Winchell, providing both his expert opinion and affidavits from his interviews with the local farmers and Kensington village citizens about the 1898 find. All affirmed the honesty of Olof Ohman, the farmer who found the stone, and his neighbors. Winchell consulted with Wisconsin's state geologist and with the best-known glacial geologist of his time, both men agreeing with him that weathering indicated the runes could not have been inscribed within the then half-century of Euro-American settlement in Minnesota. Another line of argument, over language professors' allegations, around 1900, that there are errors in the text inconsistent with medieval Norse, was rejected when the recent project submitted the text to a contemporary Danish expert on Norse. He recognized the "errors" to be a dialect known to be spoken in coastal Sweden in the fourteenth century. Altogether, the geologists' studies of the stone, in 1910 and 2000, the affidavits from Winchell's interviews, the resolution of alleged errors in the inscription language, and the unique historical circumstances in Scandinavia in 1362, correlate physical, linguistic, and historical data all weighing the *probability* of authenticity and finding it *plausible* (Kehoe 2005).

Figure 9.4. Olof Ohman, center, who found the Norse runestone beside him on his farm in northwestern Minnesota (1927 photo). Photo courtesy of Ohman family

## North Atlantic—Speculative Claims

Television addicts may have seen films on the so-called History Channel 2, or a series on that channel called *America Unearthed*, claiming medieval Knights Templar crossed to America when their order was banned by a French king. With them, say some of the writers of mostly self-published books used in the television films, the Templars carried the legendary Holy Grail, either a golden chalice or the young descendant of the marriage of Jesus of Nazareth and Mary Magdalene. Neither the chalice nor trace of Jesus' descendant[3] have been found, nor any evidence of medieval Knights Templar in America. Instead, carvings in the chapel of Rosslyn Castle near Edinburgh, Scotland, are claimed by some of these writers to represent American plants and secret symbols of Templars and Freemasons, related to a voyage to America by the grandfather of Rosslyn's builder, Henry Sinclair Earl of Orkney, at the end of the fourteenth century (i.e., a century before Columbus).

Henry Sinclair held the title to Orkney from a king of Norway who ruled the islands at the time. Hence, he would have been familiar with Norse voyages to Greenland—ships sailing there stopped at Orkney to stock up on water and supplies, and it was a regular landfall on return voyages—and he would have known there was land west of that island. No contemporary record has been found of any transatlantic voyage by Henry Sinclair. Instead, the sagas and historical documents relating to Orkney in his time are full of bloody contests between Norwegian and Scottish barons, including Sinclair himself fighting cousins disputing his holding. Sailing to America would have unwisely left his earldom easy prey to those cousins.

Prince Madoc of Wales is another proclaimed voyager to America. His story is that he was one of the many sons of King Owain of Gwynedd, in Wales. Upon Owain's death in 1170, a struggle ensued over which son would be heir to the kingdom. A medieval romance sang that Madoc, fed up with his half-brothers' fights, took a colony to a peaceful and abundant land over the sea. This story was revived in the reign of Elizabeth I of England (1533–1603) by some of her courtiers as a counterclaim to Spain's claim to America. Elizabeth was canny enough to refuse to make use of the vague story. It didn't die, inspiring Welsh among United States traders and explorers to try speaking the language to Indians they encountered, never with any but rumored success.

Stories of blond natives were analyzed by anthropologist Marshall Newman, who concluded that between the wintering residence of European and Euro-American traders in Indian towns, leaving offspring behind, and a genetic trait among Northern Plains Indian people producing light-colored (gray) hair and eyes, "blond Indians" can be accounted for without invoking any legendary Welshmen, particularly a Madoc whose name does not appear in the historical documents of the sons of Owain Gwynedd (Kehoe 2005:55, Newman 1950, Williams 1980).

## North Atlantic—Prehistoric Contacts?

Similarities between northwestern European prehistoric coastal artifacts, and artifacts in more or less contemporary prehistoric northeastern North America have stimulated a few archaeologists to hypothesize transoceanic contacts. Best known is the proposition by Dennis Stanford of the Smithsonian Institution and colleague Bruce Bradley that paleoindian Clovis flint-knapping derives from Upper Paleolithic Solutrean culture in southwestern Europe. Less discussed is my own hypothesis that the earliest pottery in northeastern America, called

Vinette 1, derives from Late Neolithic/Bronze Age ceramics of north-western coastal Europe. My hypothesis is *not* that Bronze Age Europeans came to eastern North America, built mounds, left inscriptions, and mined American copper to ship to Europe, longstanding ideas perennially put forth by citizens impressed by the sophistication of American mound-building societies. We can quickly dismiss the notion that three thousand or more years ago, Europeans shipped copper overseas from Lake Superior; many Bronze Age metal artifacts have been assessed for sources of copper, and all assays indicate European ores.[4] The other propositions bear discussion.

Stanford and Bradley's hypothesis is that Solutrean hunters pursuing seals followed the margins of Arctic ice across the North Atlantic, eventuating in America where, several millennia later, their descendants' flint-knapping skill had developed the Clovis type of spear point. The two archaeologists, both expert knappers themselves, allege that Solutreans and Clovis mastered a difficult technique to manufacture biface blades (knapped on both sides of the blade, in contrast to blades produced by a different technique that didn't require further finishing on the face). Telling clue to the technique, they said, is a hingelike edge, technically called overshot flaking. Their hypothesis challenges the standard explanation that North America was first populated by hunters moving eastward from Siberia across what is now Bering Strait, during the Late Pleistocene when lower sea levels due to so much water locked up in huge glaciers left the Strait a dry tundra land bridge. Stanford and Bradley emphasize that more Clovis blades have been recovered from eastern North America than from northwestern, where they are few and later than in the East (critics point out that the oldest Clovis sites are in the Southwest). To say their hypothesis was not well received is an understatement (Straus 2000, Straus, Meltzer and Goebel 2005). Strong criticisms have been:

1.  Solutrean in western Europe dates 23,500–20,000 BCE (radiocarbon dates calibrated to our calendar), and Clovis in America dates 13,500–12,900 BCE (calibrated). Five thousand years separate Solutrean from Clovis. The few well-excavated sites in America somewhat earlier than Clovis do not contain Solutrean-looking artifacts.
2.  Overshot flaking is not unique to Solutrean and Clovis, nor is it frequent on Clovis blades.
3.  Solutrean sites have a wide range of stone blades, large and small, and many other stone artifacts, of which few occur in Clovis sites in America. If Solutreans colonized eastern America, we would expect to find more of the kinds of artifacts common in European Solutrean.

4. Solutrean sites have few or no bones from sea mammals (seals or whales) or deep-sea fishes, even in sites only a few kilometers from the seashore of their era. Seals and whales did, and do, inhabit the Bay of Biscay in a region of Spain rich in Solutrean sites.

Other studies emphasize the difficulties and dangers of hunting seals on sea ice, hardly an enticement to people with a relative abundance of game, river fish, and plants in southwestern Europe (Phillips 2014). As with most interpretations of American data with some resemblance to Eurasian or African cultures, a *possibility* of transoceanic migration or contacts exists. In the Solutrean→Clovis case, the five-thousand-year gap between European Solutrean and American Clovis is the critical factor that makes Stanford and Bradley's hypothesis *implausible* and improbable.

Pottery, on the other hand, has a wholly different history, appearing in northeastern Asia as early as 14,800 BCE, only a few millennia later than Europe's Solutrean (Gibbs and Jordan 2013:7, 9). Greatly upsetting long-accepted theory that pottery was invented by farmers, northern Asian ceramics were made by hunter-fisher communities in a region that even today is at the northern edge of agriculture, or beyond. Pottery spread very slowly westward across northern Eurasia, reaching the Baltic and Scandinavia around 4500 BCE (Gibbs and Jordan 2013:17, Philippsen and Meadows 2014:1.1). Cooking residue on the early sherds from both Japan and Scandinavia, and also from the earliest northeastern American sherds, demonstrate that marine fish and mammals were cooked in these pots (Craig et al. 2013:33–53, Philippsen and Meadows 2014:1.1, Taché and Craig 2015).

On the eastern side of the North Atlantic, a maritime adaptation to the skerries-and-fjords landscape appears to have spread rapidly after 9500 BCE, once boats adequate for sea fishing had been developed (Bjerck 2008:37). Agriculture moved into Scandinavia around 4000 BCE, with a population related to Central European farmers and, with their ceramics, distinct from the native hunter-fishers who used pots derived from the northern Eurasian boreal forest wares (Malmström et al. 2015, Hallgren 2008). These, called Pitted-Ware Culture people, of third millennium BCE Sweden, depended on seals and fish, supplemented with wild boars whose tusks and teeth were made into ornaments (Fornander et al. 2008:292–295; Papmehl-Dufay 2009;439; Eriksson and Lidén 2013 [unpaged online]).

Cod, abundant around the North Sea and Scandinavia during the warm period 7000-3000 BCE, and in archaeological sites, continued to be important food as the cooling climate influenced the species' habits

(Enghoff, MacKenzie, and Nielsen 2007:174–175). Ertebølle, in coastal Denmark, 5400–3950 BCE, like later hunter-fishers of Sweden and Norway, hunted seals; early Ertebølle sites contain also bones of hunted sea-dwelling killer whales, dolphins, swordfish, and sharks. Red deer were the principal land game, with wild boar, elk, and aurochs taken as well (Enghoff n.d.). Ertebølle traded with farmers for stone axes, likely selling furs including pine marten skins, a northern fur much in demand historically (Layton 2001:296), polecat (a weasel), and squirrel. This marine-oriented hunter-fisher culture disappeared in Denmark as farming took over, while continuing farther north in Sweden and Norway as agriculturalists became established inland (Stillborg and Holm 2009:361, Van de Noort 2011:96).

On the western side of the North Atlantic, there also were hunter-fishers whose boats took them out for deep-water fishing, bringing in swordfish and cod. Beginning 1100 BCE, coastal settlements in southeastern Canada and adjacent New England had pottery called Vinette I, remarkably like the Eurasian boreal pottery.

On a map with dates, this type of pottery—conoidal jars with pointed bottoms—looks like it spread westward slowly and steadily, continuing across the North Atlantic to appear, with no antecedent ceramics, in northeastern America. Earlier pottery exists in Mesoamerica and southeasternmost United States (Savannah River area, Georgia), but these are quite different in styles and techniques from Vinette I (Taché 2005:169). Vinette 1 pots are typically coarse grit tempered, coil constructed and paddled, thick, interiors smoothed with horizontal wiping, exteriors smoothed, some over cord impressions, or especially for upper portions, cord impressions left visible (Taché 2005:177, 200). Decoration, if any, may be simple punctates in a band (Jackson 1986:393–394,Taché 2005:189–190).

From Vinette I, what is called Early Woodland pottery spread westward into the Midwest during the first millennium BCE. If that is the terminus of the dissemination of the earliest northeast Asian pottery, it leaves a gap of the western half of North America without pottery, except for Alaska where it appeared about the same time as Vinette 1, apparently diffused across the Bering Sea from Siberia (Anderson, Boulanger, and Glascock 2010:3).

If not for the ocean between Scandinavia and Canada, Vinette 1 and its Early Woodland offshoots could be simply explained as the extension of the wavelike movement of ceramic technology from an origin in Late Pleistocene northeast Asia. Supporting the postulate that these boreal zone ceramics compose a single technological tradition are the

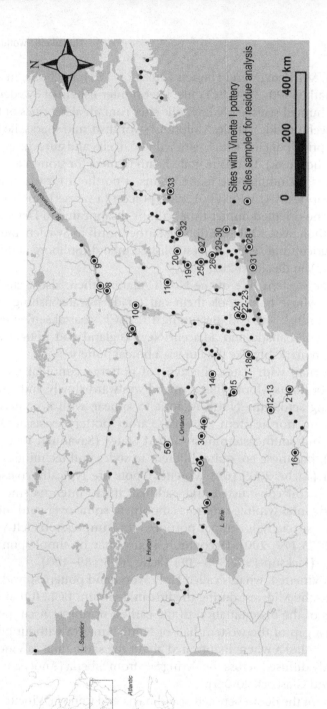

**Figure 9.5.** Map of Vinette 1 pottery sites, clustered in Maritime Canada and adjacent northeastern United States. Courtesy of Karine Taché, original in Taché and Craig 2015

sherd residues indicating the same primary use for these pots: cooking fish. The probability of Vinette 1 deriving from the Eurasian boreal ceramic tradition depends upon evaluation of Neolithic coastal Scandinavians' maritime capabilities, and considering their possible motive, or impetus, to sail so far. That they had seaworthy boats, very likely curraghs, is indubitable (Gjessing 1973:88, 90; Bjerck 2008; Garrow and Sturt 2011:65; see Severin 1978 for demonstration of such boats, and Johnstone 1980:121–139 for full discussion).

Motive, or impetus, may be tied to the expansion and consolidation of farming in Scandinavia. Around 1400 BCE, agricultural societies there had developed to the point that aristocracies ruled, contesting power. Noblemen journeyed to the cities of the eastern Mediterranean, bringing home gold and bronze and perhaps religious rituals (Kristiansen and Larsson 2005). Pressure mounted on commoners to produce more food and goods to support the ostentatious life of the nobility. Earlier trade between coastal hunter-fishers and their inland farmer neighbors was likely devalued as citizens' diets became nearly completely composed of farmed grains and livestock (Eriksson and Lidén 2013). Two hypotheses seem reasonable: either expansion of Bronze Age agriculture and decline of the value of marine products threatened the Late Neolithic economy of hunter-fishers, motivating some families to sail away seeking a country where they could continue their free, traditional way of life, or conversely, Bronze Age markets for seal products and fish stimulated fishermen to go farther to richer fisheries and adjacent shores where furs might be obtained—an early version of the historic fisheries-and-furs commerce around 1500 CE (Jordan 2003:33, see also Morrison and Junker 2002, for long-term symbiotic relationships between hunter-gatherers and market-economy societies). Either way, the Scandinavians needed their accustomed pots to boil their fish.

Gutorm Gjessing (1906–1979), a Norwegian anthropologist, in 1944 proposed a circumpolar cultural adaptation including pottery and ground slate knives, two traits that were used by maritime peoples in the boreal and north-temperate zones as well. Gjessing's work has been discussed and commented upon ever since, mostly to add new data from the multitude of regions in the circumpolar zone. Northeastern American early pottery has not received much interest, in contrast to ground slate knives which are argued to have developed independently in these regions from bone and antler knives (Fitzhugh 1975, 2010:120, but see Kehoe 1971:286[5]). Slate knives are especially effective for cutting fish. Techniques for cutting and polishing bone and antler wouldn't transfer easily to slate. Ground slate knives appear on

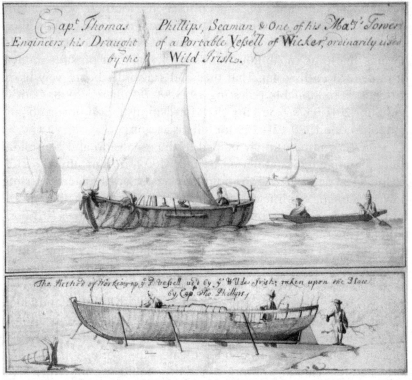

Figure. 9.6. Irish seagoing curragh, drawn by Captain Thomas Phillips, 17th century. Original in Pepysian Library, Cambridge, UK

both sides of the North Atlantic at about the same time as Vinette 1 in America. Fishermen using the conoidal Eurasian pots for cooking fish would have liked the knives for processing those fish.

Independent inventions in similar ecological conditions? Or transmissions of useful inventions through ecological zones? Gjessing, in a 1948 publication that built upon a year he spent as a visiting scholar in America, considered Early Woodland pottery and slate knives in northeastern America to derive from circumboreal ceramics (Gjessing 1948:299). Diffusion, that is to say, transmission of inventions through contacts between societies, was taken for granted by mid-twentieth century Scandinavian anthropologists (Klausen 1960), and generally by European archaeologists. Americans in the twentieth century, in a society lauding inventions, instead assumed independent invention as default interpretation. After mid-century—that is, after World War II—American anthropology experienced a resurge of cultural evolutionism, seeing it now not so much as humanity's mystical Progress toward civilization, as adaptations to varied environments (multilinear evolution). Its most popular and strongest version was ecological determinism (Kehoe 1998:107–111, 128–131; Trigger 2006:407–410). Proponents saw their work as natural science, following the concept of natural selection in evolutionary biology. Inventions, or artifact innovations, would therefore be cultural mutations, spontaneously arising, then persisting if advantageous in the community's environment, otherwise disappearing.

Suggestions of borrowing, particularly long-distance, were disparaged as "history," less valid than "science." Under this paradigm, artifact innovations are manifestations of a natural process like genetic changes in populations. Given similar environments, pre-modern peoples would be expected to react by inventing tools and practices suited to surviving and prospering in their locales. Apparently, slate knives and conoidal grit-tempered pots sooner or later would be figured out by maritime fishermen.

Opposed to this natural-science paradigm is culture-historical research, also called historical particularism. Practiced by Franz Boas (1858–1942), one of the founders of anthropology as a discipline, historical particularism focuses on directly observed communities (ethnography), documenting contacts between societies to explain similarities between them. Adapting to environments is a given for survival, ground for *stimulus diffusion*—taking an idea from contact, then expressing it in a local style—as well as impetus for direct borrowing. With myriad documented borrowings with contacts, historical particularism is powerfully empirical. Notably, Boas refused to propound reductionist general theories, insisting that we need far more observational data from a wider range of living, historical, and earlier societies to draw generalizations. Absent such quantities of good data, we seek to chart undeniable historical societal contacts and to indicate probable earlier contacts, alert to stimulus diffusion as well as clear borrowings. With the wealth of ethnographic and historical instances of borrowings from contacts, contrasted with the paucity of actual observations of spontaneous independent inventions, a scientist should premise borrowing rather than independent invention to explain similar artifacts in two or more areas at approximately the same time period.

Basically, this is the premise Stanford and Bradley use to argue for Solutrean origin of Clovis blades. Their thesis fails because Solutrean and Clovis are five thousand years apart, and Clovis-type blades are not found in Solutrean sites; it is not the method and premise of historical particularism, but quality of data that renders their argument implausible.

Vinette 1 pots overlap in time with Scandinavian coastal hunter-fishers' pots and are very similar in technology, function, and style. They appear first along the northeast American Atlantic coast and waterways debouching into it, then diffuse westward as Early Woodland ceramics, a relatively complex technology unknown before that in northern America. Weighing these points against the rare documentation of independent invention, deriving Vinette 1 from the ancient Eurasian boreal ceramic tradition via fishermen in seagoing curraghs is a plausible explanation.

Bruce Trigger wrote, in his magisterial *History of Archaeological Thought*, "The enduring value of a culture-historical approach is not its emphasis on ethnicity or on diffusionist and migrationist explanations of culture change but its ability to trace real lineages of the development of material culture in the archaeological record" (Trigger 2006:313).

## Middle Atlantic

Columbus's voyages are one indication of the feasibility of ships crossing the mid-Atlantic, westward from southern Europe or North Africa, or eastward from the Caribbean and U.S. Southeast, catching the Gulf Stream current. Most recent adventurers trying for records in small boat crossings (see Table 1) take the mid-Atlantic with its warmer waters.

One candidate for a pre-Columbian crossing is the head of a little figurine that looks, and tested as, second century CE Roman manufacture. It was discovered in 1933 during excavations at Calixtlahuaca in the Valley of Toluca, west of Mexico City in central Mexico, in a burial under a floor in a Postclassic building. Although the excavator, José García Payón, was a reputable Mexican archaeologist, he did not record the exact location of the figurine head in the detail demanded since mid-twentieth century (Smith 2003), nor publish the find until years later. Many Aztec and other Late Postclassic small figurines were found in the site, for the most part, with burials like that containing the Roman figurine head (Smith 2003:16). Implication of a Roman visit to Mexico provoked accusations of excavator's negligence, even a story that a student had planted the figurine head to embarrass the excavator. Sixty years later, efforts were made to directly date the figurine by using thermoluminescence and by consulting a Classical scholar expert on Roman terracotta figurines. From photos, the expert confirmed that the head looked like Roman manufactures of the second century CE. Thermoluminescence yielded a broad range of possible dates, from first millennium BCE to early second millennium CE, allowing for the stylistic dating to second century CE; note that it dated the object, not its find location.

Given that the small head is probably Roman, it could have come from a Roman ship that reached Mexico, become an heirloom, and eventually was offered with other treasures in a Late Postclassic Calixtlahuaca grave; it could have been dropped by a Spanish invader or colonist who had carried it from home, and it being so small, worked down through soil or rodents into the grave area; it could have been planted as a joke; it could have been carried to India by Roman merchants, then across the Pacific to become an heirloom in Mexico. Summary: We can't use the figurine head as evidence of Roman-period transatlantic contacts. Neither can we definitively rule that out; its probability is low due to uncertainty about details of the find, and the gap between its date of manufacture and dating of the burial it was reported from.

Another Roman possibility is the use of cement and concrete, and dome roofs, at El Tajín in Veracruz, near the Gulf of Mexico. Famous for the unique Pyramid of the Niches, with 365 niches in its seven-storey platform, Tajín flourished from about 600–1230 CE— the later Classic and the Epiclassic (or Early Postclassic) periods of Mesoamerica. Its relatively small valley did not permit the expansive layout usual in major Mesoamerican cities. Instead, it has major temple-topped pyramids, ball courts, and plazas on the valley floor, rather close together, and an acropolis above with buildings believed to be palaces and rulers' temples.

Very unusual in the Americas, cement and concrete were among Tajín's building materials. Analyses show that they were pozzolanic cement, the same kind of mixture used in Classical Rome (Olmos 2009:109, 111–112; Ward 2008:118). Furthermore, this material was used to construct low domed roofs over rooms, structures not found elsewhere in Mesoamerica (Olmos 2009:111). Only the cement and its use for domed roofs resembles anything Roman. Interestingly, García Payón left Calixtlahuaca in 1938 to go to work at El Tajín, where he continued working until the end of his career. Could he have picked up the little Roman head at Tajín and mistakenly put it with his Calixtlahuaca collections?

Comalcalco in Tabasco is identified as the westernmost Mayan site, flourishing in the Late Classic until the late tenth century CE (Andrews 1989). Located on a river flowing, at the time, to the southern Gulf of Mexico, Comalcalco traded widely, manufacturing and exporting mold-made clay figurines and probably cacao, since it is in a prime cacao-growing region. Its architecture and art resemble those of Palenque, an important Maya city to the southeast, inland (Andrews 1989:141, 150).

**Figure 9.7.** Pyramid of the Niches, El Tajín, Mexico. Building A, with a low dome roof (destroyed during restoration) using pozzolanic cement, overlooks this central pyramid temple on the site. Photo by Alice Kehoe

In all respects but one, Comalcalco looks Mayan; after initial building in lime aggregate, its major structures were constructed of fired bricks set in mortar (Littman 1958, Andrews 1989:31–36). No other Mesoamerican city used fired brick. Many bricks have symbols on the back side that may be makers' marks; others have hieroglyphs, figures in low relief, or graffiti-like sketches (Andrews 1989:133–137). Because fired brick construction is an anomaly in pre-Columbian Mesoamerica, Roman contact has been postulated; Roman brickmakers (and those in other societies, too) marked their personal symbols on their bricks, and some of the Comalcalco ones look like some Roman marks. Fired bricks were also used in Asia, for example, in Cambodia in the tenth century (Uchida, Tsuda, and Shimoda 2014). As it stands, Comalcalco's use of fired bricks might be explained by the locality's lack of limestone suitable for building (Andrews 1989:141). Or, one could conjecture that this trading center was visited in the ninth century CE by a European who suggested and demonstrated substitution of fired brick for unobtainable stone. Given the dates for Comalcalco brick structures, such a European was centuries too late to be a Roman.[6]

Phoenicians have been suggested as possible voyagers to America. They were a strong alliance of city-states in the eastern Mediterranean from about 1500 to around 300 BCE, although their city-states likely continued to operate later (Herbert 2003). Specializing in trade, their cargo vessels supplied cities around the Mediterranean, with a daughter city-state, Carthage (814–146 BCE), in North Africa. Because Phoenicians carried British tin to bronze-making foundries in the eastern Mediterranean, it has been assumed that their ships sailed through the Straits of Gibraltar at the western end of the Mediterranean, directly to Britain's tin mines, but a recent search of museum collections failed to locate any Phoenician artifacts found in the tin mines region (Wear 2012). Therefore, so far as documents and archaeology attest, the Greek explorer Pytheas was the first Mediterranean seafarer to sail through the Straits and explore Atlantic Europe, about 325 BCE. British tin may have been exported by Celtic traders into the Mediterranean, to the Phoenician port of Tarshish (its Biblical name), probably Tartessos near Cádiz in southern Spain (Aubet 2001:291–293, 321).

Phoenicia and Carthage, Rome's arch-enemy in the second century BCE, built economic strength on their merchants' businesses, in contrast to Rome's military power focus or Athens' fame for philosophy, art, and literature. Like in Asia, merchants were private entrepreneurs whose records were seldom archived. Their cargoes came from many producers around the Mediterranean, rather than mainly from their own manufacturers, making for few items unambiguously Phoenician. Then, when Alexander the Great overran Phoenician cities, 325 BCE, and later, Rome destroyed Carthage, 146 BCE, the conquerors not only massacred people, they deliberately wiped out texts and monuments, leaving little definitively Phoenician or Carthaginian in the archaeological record. Hence, we today have too few data for confidently assessing the probability of Phoenician voyages to America. Possible, yes; plausible, maybe; Phoenician voyages having been private ventures means less documentation than if most were state enterprises, so lack of clear evidence leaves the question open.

It seems a bit odd that from 1492 on, the middle Atlantic becomes a busy seaway, even the most usual route for extreme small-boat crossings (see Table 1), yet there is so little reasonable evidence for Phoenician and Roman-period crossings. Perhaps there were enough challenges and opportunities in extending Mediterranean economics into "tribal" Europe, then in the first millennium CE, enough turmoil from invading Huns, Goths, and others riding overland from the East, that no states, and few, if any, merchants, looked to explore the western ocean.

## South Atlantic

Between West Africa and northeast Brazil, the Atlantic is narrowest: 2,575 km (1,600 miles). Flowing westward from Africa, the South Equatorial Current would seem to facilitate voyaging from Senegal or Guinea in Africa to Brazil. Neither region displaying eye-catching architecture or globe-shaking empires, their populations were labeled "primitive." Add to that denigration the real difficulties of archaeological and paleobotanical research in humid tropics forests, their early histories were little known until after mid-twentieth-century.

Donald Lathrap was a pioneer in investigating the Upper Amazon region on the Brazil-Peru border, using ethnographic observations and discussions with local people to flesh out his archaeological data. Arguing that Upper Amazon First Nations such as the Shipibo devised sophisticated adaptations to what temperate-climate people perceive as a difficult environment, Lathrap saw deep time depth to their agriculture, interpreting it as fully developed by 3000 BCE (Lathrap 1977:744). Lathrap enjoyed provoking staid colleagues demanding solid data for his challenging interpretations. The early agriculture he proposed was based on manioc; cultivated manioc has no seeds or wood that might preserve in a site, it doesn't require fully cleared fields, it is cultivated with wooden digging sticks, and it is harvested out of the ground whenever wanted rather than kept in storehouses; *it leaves practically no traces in the archaeological record.* Key to its presence were tiny stone chips that would have been fixed into wooden graters as teeth. Clay griddles for baking manioc meal flatbread could be another clue, although the griddles could have been used for other baking. Picture the archaeologist in a jungle clearing excavation, looking for scattered tiny chips in the layers of occupation . . .

Lathrap died in 1990, as paleobotanists were beginning to recognize ancient manioc by phytoliths, microscopic silica casts formed inside plant tissue (Piperno 2006, Sandweiss 2007). Starch granules left on sherds can also be clues, although the ubiquity of starch granules in laboratory buildings easily contaminates samples. Manioc and yams are now documented back to 5800 BCE in Panama, northern South America, and Brazil (Iriarte 2007:177–179, Sandweiss 2007:3021), and bottle gourd even earlier, 8000 BCE, the gourd a domesticate originating in Africa (Kistler et al., 2014).

These data, and those on the early appearance of other domesticates in the Americas, Asia, and Africa, displace Lathrap's bold speculation that agriculture first originated in tropical Africa before the

Holocene modern climatic era, and was carried from Africa to Eurasia and to America (Lathrap 1977:722).[7] Phytoliths indicate that bananas in Cameroon, 1500 BCE, transported over several millennia from the plant's homeland in New Guinea-western Melanesia (see Chapter 6), were added to indigenous African cultigens apparently only centuries after agriculture became established in West Africa (Blench 2007:414, 2009:376). Lathrap's hypothesis that tropical forest Africans cultivated yams for millennia, the practice being invisible to archaeologists because in the humid forest no trace could remain of the plant, its cultivation tools (digging stick), or its processing, was an audacious dare to his peers. How far can logical argument be extended? How should we deal with gaps in archaeological records likely due to decay, not to mention behavior that doesn't produce material objects? It seems improbable that Terminal Pleistocene West Africans went by dugout to Brazil,[8] bringing yams and bottle gourds and, in time, cultivating the manioc they noticed in their new homeland. If yam phytoliths were to be recovered in West African excavations dating that early, in sites suggesting cultivated gardens, then the balance of probability would shift. Provoking though he was, in-your-face to his colleagues in his 1977 essay, Donald Lathrap did reflect as a scientist on his observations in his Upper Amazon projects, raising issues over the paucity of data in the archaeological record when compared to living communities' lives he carefully noted.

Claims for pre-Columbian contacts across the South Atlantic are numerous but not well supported. One is a letter sent to a Brazilian scholar in 1872 by a resident of Paraíba in northeast Brazil, the area closest to the most narrow portion of the South Atlantic. In the letter is a long inscription said to be copied from a stone the writer's slaves found on his plantation. At the time, and since, the inscription was identified as Phoenician, recording a voyage to that "unknown coast" by Canaanites seeking trade. As with the Kensington rune stone discovered in 1898 in Minnesota, the Paraíba inscription was denounced as a hoax. Unlike the Kensington stone, safely curated and on public view in Minnesota, the Paraíba stone has never been seen, other than by the 1872 letter writer and his slaves (if true). A 2012 posting on the Wikipedia website "The Paraíba (Parahyba) Stone" suggests the "stone" may have been a rock art site with several thousand years of indigenous art, now partly covered with sediment from a dam (http://anais.sepex .ufsc.br/anais_3/trabalhos/581.html, accessed 2/13/2015). The consulting archaeologist assessing the rock art site makes no mention of the alleged Phoenician inscription.

## Conclusion

Claims for pre-Columbian transoceanic contacts more often are made for Pacific crossings, rather than Atlantic. Perhaps that's an aspect of "Orientalism," Westerners' proclivity to see "the East" as full of hidden mysteries; perhaps it's only a spin-off from the myth of Columbus, the idea that the Americas are the nearer shores of Asia. This chapter began with the North Atlantic where incontrovertible proof of Norse discovery at 1000 CE raises the probability that sites in the Canadian Northeast Arctic may represent Norse hunting furbearers and walrus. Tim Severin's demonstration that a large cargo-carrying curragh can cross the North Atlantic makes more plausible the hypothesis, drawn from strong similarities between Eurasian boreal pottery and the earliest pottery in northeast America, that the craft of pottery was introduced to American maritime communities by voyagers from Scandinavia, forebears of the Norse.

When we look at the Middle Atlantic, there is a longstanding discussion among historians about islands shown in medieval world maps. Are they America, not yet known to be a continent? Or are they the Canaries and Azores, islands in the mid-Atlantic? The Canary archipelago is only 100 km (62 miles ) off Morocco, the northeast tip of North Africa; the Azores are much farther: 1,360 km (850 miles ) west of Portugal. Romans and Phoenicians knew of the Canaries, and the Azores were (re)discovered by Portuguese in the fourteenth century CE, although chambers (*hypogeum* artificial cave type) and coins indicate North African Iron Age (Carthaginian) inhabitants (Ribeiro, Joaqunito, and Pereira 2012). Maps showed a large island named Brasil west of Ireland, possibly an effect of Arctic mirage (*hillingar* effect), that can show land or sea as much as 500 km (311 miles) distant from the observer (Sawatzky and Lehn 1976:1301) appearing much closer. The phenomenon could have encouraged exploration toward the ephemerally rising land. Whether accounts of it confused medieval mapmakers, we don't know. We do know that for several centuries before 1492, Europeans, including Muslim Moors in Spain, speculated there was land beyond the Canaries—in a few instances, it was reported, sailing toward it without returning (Hamdani 2006).

Did Phoenicians or Romans cross the Atlantic? For Phoenicians, a maritime nation built on seaborne trade, it is plausible but without documentation, Roman conquest of Carthage having deliberately obliterated its history and related Phoenician history. Romans were land-oriented, building great roads instead of great ships. Documents that have come down to us describe explorations into the European North, rather than into the western sea. One brief, ostensibly historical, composition by Plato (early fourth century BCE), likely meant to be read as a parable, describes Atlantis, a city on a plain ringed by mountains, out beyond Gibraltar, destroyed by flood. Medieval scholars debated where exactly Atlantis had been, adding to curiosity over what might lie west of Europe; strangely, fascination with finding that legendary long-gone city still incites adventurers and investors in their quests (Adams 2015).

Mesoamerica bordering the middle Atlantic contains more intriguing similarities to Asia than to western Europe. These cluster along the Gulf of Mexico north and south of the narrow Isthmus of Tehuantepec bridge between the Pacific and Atlantic. The most intriguing similarities to Europe are respectively just north and just south of the cluster, near the Gulf: El Tajín with Roman-type cement and domed roofs, and Comalcalco with fired brick structures. Both are later than the Roman Empire and the Phoenicians, Rome's hated rivals. Other than the building technology, neither displays European features.

Why should there appear to be more resemblances to Asian, not European, pre-Columbian cultures, even in eastern Mesoamerica? The answer may lie in ships and trade. Asian merchant ships were larger and more seaworthy than European ships of the times, and private ventures into long-distance oceanic trading long and well established. As was also true of European private trading ventures, these were largely outside state affairs, less documented and less archived than official state activities. If the archaeological record is sparse and impoverished, so are archives of ancient documents compared to the myriad activities going on in their times.

## Chapter 10

# Critically Examining
# pre-Columbian Seas

A wise professor taught, "Never say 'never' or 'always.' We never can know the entirety of the past, nor of possible exceptions to 'always.'" Her caution applies to the question of whether the seas were "peculiarly empty," in David Quinn's words, before the Admiral of the Ocean Sea sailed in 1492.

We know that men and women together crossed ocean straits by boat (or raft) back in the Pleistocene, 50,000 years ago, to reach and settle Australia and Indonesian islands. We know that Austronesian traders and colonists sailed from Indonesia westward to Africa in the first millennium BCE, and a millennium earlier into Near Oceania, already inhabited by Melanesians. We know that Polynesians sailed to and colonized every habitable island in Remote Oceania, reaching an eastern limit in Chile in the fourteenth century CE. We know that Norse had two permanent settlements in Greenland from the tenth century CE, crossing Davis Strait to northeastern Canada for timber, furs, and at least one attempt at settlement. These facts established by sound, scientific archaeological research demonstrate that many human societies have not hesitated to venture upon open seas.

We know, too, that fluctuations in sea level over the past 50,000 years have destroyed or drowned ancient coastal zones. Both sides of the Americas have underwater coastal shelves that once were dry, resource-rich habitable land. We cannot confirm ancient long-distance voyaging along these coasts or to them; neither can we deny the possibilities. Astoundingly long open-sea voyages did take place millennia ago to colonize islands, proven beyond doubt by the populations on these islands (Matisoo-Smith 2014). Experienced seamen live in a reality different from landlubbers: Paul Johnstone, a BBC producer who researched watercraft, wrote of curraghs:

> Soon . . . one comes more and more to appreciate the reassurance of its sea-keeping quality, the extraordinary liveliness and vigour with which it rises to and surmounts the seas. It is only when one has had some experience of these craft in the open sea that its long history of usage becomes readily understandable. (Johnstone 1980:139)

A conference on histories of seafaring led to a summary of factors to be discussed in research on the subject: time, in terms of climate and other conditions (such as demography of homelands) affecting voyages; the crew; the lands involved; the sea itself; and vessels with their cargoes (Barrett and Anderson 2010:305). "Both seafaring and its absence require explanations that make sense in terms of human motivation," the conference organizers emphasized (Barrett and Anderson 2010:307). Historical accounts tend toward Great Man explanations: a leader forced into exile (for example, Eirik the Red), or choosing to embark upon an expedition to gain riches or establish a colony. Archaeology seldom divulging information about individual leaders, archaeologists have looked at data available on impersonal factors such as climate change or depletion of resources to interpret cultural happenings. Extremes, in ecological determinism and behavioral ecology drawn from nonhuman populations, are such poor fits to particular cases that they push to the front historical contingencies, including the power of charismatic leaders. That leaves us, again, acknowledging the wisdom of never saying "never" or "always."

## The Three Ps: Possibility, Plausibility, Probability

Blanket denial of the possibility of pre-Columbian transoceanic contacts flies in the face of numerous record-making modern crossings, deliberate or drift (Table 1). A posture of denial is exemplified in a paper in the prestigious journal *Proceedings of the National Academy of Sciences*. The topic is early dating, 8000 BCE, of domesticated bottle gourds in Asia and in Mexico. The authors suppose bottle gourds with seeds could have drifted across the Pacific, like objects thrown into the waves by Japanese tsunami that land in northern California or British Columbia, or:

Paleoindian groups could have carried bottle gourds and still-viable seeds through the northern noncultivation zone along the south coast of Beringia, either on foot or in near-shore water craft, rapidly enough to have introduced domesticated L. siceraria [bottle gourd] to the New World along with the dog.. . . . In contrast, any scenarios involving straight line, long-distance trans-Pacific transport of domesticated bottle gourds from Asia to the Americas by open-ocean seafaring vessels can be considered as having a close-to-zero probability, given the absence of evidence for watercraft capable of making such a voyage in the Late Pleistocene time frame required for bottle gourd to have reached the interior southern highlands of Mexico by 10,000 B.P. . . . we favor a Paleoindian near-coast (land and/or water) introduction as representing the most plausible alternative. (Erickson et al. 2005:18319)

How long are bottle gourd seeds viable? According to *Seed Storage of Horticultural Crops*, a standard work, "Viability decreases to 50 percent after 12 months, and none of the seeds germinated after 24 months of storage under ambient conditions," although they retain viability at low temperatures, 5°F and −20° C, for as long as ten years *when stored in polyethylene pouches or laminated aluminum foil pouches* (Doijode 2001:302–303).[1]

Let us analyze this scenario that passed muster with reviewers at the National Academy of Sciences: *"Paleoindian groups" from tropical or subtropical Asia carried bottle gourd seeds thousands of miles north along Asia, around the North Pacific Rim with near-Arctic conditions, down along thousands of miles of northwestern American coast to Mexico, and inland to highland Oaxaca.* This immense journey through extremes of climate would be completed without harming gourd seeds that deteriorate in less than a year under everyday ("ambient") conditions and are vulnerable to cold unless packaged in modern industrial materials.

Then there is the question of "Paleoindians" living where bottle gourds grew in Asia. Around 8000 BCE, that would have been in Hoabinhian territory, characterized by pebble tools and Austro-Melanesian people (Bellwood 1997:85, 162). Compared to postulating that Austro-Melanesians paddled along so many thousands of miles of coasts from subtropics through temperate and near-Arctic conditions, and down through those zones on the eastern side of the Pacific, changing physically into northern Eurasian type Paleoindians so quickly that bottle gourd seeds remained viable in their boats—a transpacific voyage in inter-island boats, picking up the Japan Current off Taiwan, is more *plausible*.

Given the improbability of gourd seeds remaining viable for the years it would take to paddle circumpacific from Southeast Asia to Mexico, and the lack of any genetic data for Austro-Melanesian heritage in Paleoindians, not to mention Paleoindian stone tools being very different from Hoabinhian pebble tools, Erickson et al.'s "close-to-zero probability" must be rejected. A few years later, even some of the authors of this paper realized the *zero* probability of their scenario, engaged in more extensive laboratory research on bottle gourd genetics, and published a new paper affirming African, not Asian, ancestry for early American bottle gourds, suggesting gourds drifting across the Atlantic from Africa as the source of the American plants (Kistler et al. 2014).

Valid argument in historical sciences calls for "the strength of building and testing models based on multiple lines of independent evidence," stated Patrick Kirch, a leader in Polynesian archaeology (Kirch 2010:142). Our arguments are most often inductive, leading to conclusions that seem *plausible* or *probable*, not to certainty (Hurley 2012:33–34), and admit to degrees of probability (Hurley 2012:50). Statements that something is impossible or "near-impossible" need to be argued from evidence, just as much as positive statements on possibility. To distinguish probability from plausibility, evidence must be scrutinized in detail. It isn't enough to say that mound-builders must have been connected; the particulars of mounds should be closely compared. Such historical particularism is counter to a goal avowed by many anthropologists that we seek universals in human behavior, a goal assumed on the model of the physical sciences.

Looking for universals in human societies has been linked with unilinear cultural evolution, setting up stages of accomplishments on the road to civilization. From these efforts comes a sometimes unstated premise that "more advanced" societies likely stimulated "less advanced" ones into moving up to a higher stage, even if an ocean lay between them. Especially with regard to the appearance of pyramidal constructions, large plazas, statues, elegant ceramics, expert lapidary work on stone beads and figurines, and agriculture in tropical Mexico, postulates abound of stimulation or even migration from Asia or Egypt.

One of the better-reasoned books is Stephen Compton's *Exodus Lost* (2010), arguing that the Olmec of southern Mexico absorbed significant aspects of their culture from a colony of Hyksos refugees from Egypt, c. 1550 BCE. Hyksos came from small kingdoms along the eastern Mediterranean, active maritime traders and ship builders who expanded south into Egypt, ruling as pharaohs from 1674 to 1549 BCE.

They were defeated by Egyptian rivals at the Hyksos capital of Avaris, a large seaport in the Nile Delta. Compton suggests that, having many good ships, defeated Hyksos sailed across the Atlantic to settle in the fertile lowlands at the Isthmus of Tehuantepec in Mexico. In support of his thesis, he adduces similarities between Hyksos Egypt and contemporary Olmec sites in Mexico, where for want of texts such as are abundant for Egypt, the meanings of images can only be guessed.

Underlying the argument is the premise of disjunction on the American side: "Not only did all of these features exist among the Hyksos before they suddenly appeared at San Lorenzo" (Compton 2010:218). To the contrary, as archaeologist Hector Neff notes, "As of approximately 1600 BC, Early Formative populations with similar pottery occupied the lowland area stretching from the Gulf Coast to western El Salvador. Large residences, ball courts, and other [elite prestige] archaeological manifestations appeared in parts of this region between 1700 and 1500 BC" (Neff 2011:114).

San Lorenzo, the largest Olmec town of this period, is very favorably situated on a plateau overlooking a riverine network leading to the Gulf—facilitating trade and also transport of the huge stone blocks wanted for the massive portrait heads and thrones—and forming highly fertile levees. Four crops of maize can be raised each year on these soils in the warm, humid climate. Initially, exploitation of riverine fish, plants, and animals supported burgeoning populations divided locally into aristocrats and commoners, evidenced by architecture, while trade and shared religious icons integrated populations from the Basin of Mexico to Honduras, centered on the Isthmus of Tehuantepec Gulf lowlands (Joyce and Grove 1999, Neff 2011:117). As improved (or better adapted) varieties of maize were bred, people moved from riverine flats to upland fields (Arnold 2009), and competition for prime lands increased, leading to San Lorenzo's climax, about 1000 BCE, of larger structures and spectacular sculptures. There seems little, if any, evidence of sudden intrusion into this Mesoamerican heartland.

Olmec have been postulated as recipients of Chinese refugees, and their Ecuadorian neighbors to have hosted Japanese bearing Jomon culture. Betty Meggers, the archaeologist with the Smithsonian Institution, and Paul Shao, the Chinese-American artist who went into the field to draw and photograph Chinese and Mesoamerican similarities, saw a number of particular similarities between Olmec and Shang, considered to be the first empire in China, 1600–1046 BCE. Chinese annals give a long history of dynasties preceding and following Shang, including their rulers and wars.

Shao saw a pattern of deposed aristocratic families fleeing threatening new power, as his own family did in coming to America (Paul Shao, personal communication, November, 1977). His book (1983) argues that China developed a religion celebrating dragons associated with rain, ancestors, royal authority, and a cosmology built on dual and quadruple complementary ideas. This "dragon cult," he avers, was carried to America from Shang China, powerfully spreading to become foundational to Mesoamerican and to western South American cultures (Shao 1983:49).

Meggers (1975) saw close parallels between high valuation of jade in both societies; Shang jade batons held by royal and feudal lords, and clublike objects in Olmec figures' hands; feline deities and agnathic (lacking lower jaw) monster masks; serpents and birds in iconography; and mountains as holy places, replicated as pyramidal mounds in Olmec. In her view, Olmec, the class-stratified kingdom(s) with imposing ritual centers, fine pottery and art, and trading extensively throughout Mesoamerica, appeared suddenly from dispersed kin-based villages making a simpler pottery. Why Shang persons should have emigrated to America, rather than, say, Korea, she doesn't speculate. Meggers later criticized a report on sourcing Olmec-style pottery excavated from various Mexican sites because the authors had not discussed the Shang resemblances she had published; her commentary was politely countered with reference to the long development of Olmec culture at San Lorenzo, and the point that the resemblances cited from the later Olmec center at La Venta date about three centuries after the demise of Shang (Blomster 2005).

Prior to her paper on Shang and Olmec, Meggers had teamed with her husband, Clifford Evans, and an Ecuadorian avocational archaeologist, Emilio Estrada, to excavate Valdivia, a site near the Pacific coast in Ecuador (see Chapter 7). Estrada had recognized a number of artifacts in his excavations in coastal Manabí province to resemble Asian items: clay model houses resembling Asian houses, neck rests (instead of pillows for the head), a style of seated figurine, rectangular pottery net weights, "golf-tee" earlobe insertions, and panpipes. Radiocarbon dated the complex to late in the third, early in the second millennium BCE. (These dates were run early in the use of radiocarbon, before refinements in the process produced narrower dating ranges, and before radiocarbon dates were usually calibrated to Western calendar years.)

After the Valdivia period came the Bahía, dated to late first millennium BCE. In their 1961 paper, Estrada and Meggers postulated the Asianlike objects to be part of the Bahía culture, claiming that this marked the shift from smaller communities not yet fully agricultural to larger, agricultural polities with increased trade—receptive, they assumed, to foreign ideas. Then Meggers and Evans published, in 1965, a thick monograph in which they focused on the Valdivia phase, interpreting it as a regional culture that had picked up pottery-making from Jomon Japanese fishermen drifted on the Japan Current from Kyushu (Meggers, Evans, and Estrada 1965:167–168). The crux of the interpretation was the apparently sudden appearance of well-made pottery in the Valdivia sequence, and the ceramics' resemblance to some in Jomon, the long prehistoric period in Japan. Donald Lathrap finetuned the occurrences of "Jomonlike" sherds in the 1965 monograph, noting that some came from levels above that stated to be the earliest appearance of pottery (i.e., the level of the supposed Jomon intrusion) (Lathrap 1973:1762). The postulate of Jomon fishermen introducing the ceramic art to America could not be accepted.

Whether from the East or the West, postulates of voyages jump-starting Mesoamerican or South American civilizations in the third or second millennium BCE have not proffered either close enough correlations in dating or substantiated claims of "sudden" change. What half a century ago seemed to be sudden shifts from subsistence-based villages to class-stratified polities trading fine artisan-made luxuries, were the result of gaps in archaeological work. Two generations of fieldwork from an increased number of archaeologists spreading farther into the tropical lowlands and highland valleys have chronicled developments of agricultural societies in many regions, linked by trade and by adaptations of crops and cultivation techniques from originating locales.

A dragon cult? Olmec and South Americans knew only too well several kinds of large venomous snakes; likewise, Asia has large dangerous snakes. Fear of them is instinctive after millions of years of natural selection for primates to react with fear of big snakes. Mesoamerican cosmic serpents look like rattlesnakes, an animal that in addition to its fatal bite, bears rattles that warn of its approach, as distant thunder sounds the approach of storms. Asian serpents and dragons look more like cobras—that continent's most visible deadly serpent. Pythons are pictured on both continents' tropical iconography. Two thousand years after Olmec, details of Mesoamerican cosmic serpents do resemble details of Asian dragons. At that time, later in the first millennium CE, a cluster of Asian inventions is known in Mesoamerica, of which wheel-and-axle mounted animal figurines are the most telling.

Possibility, plausibility, probability. Contrary to the myth-of-Columbus idea that only Europeans had seaworthy boats, since the dawn of history, human habitants of thousands of islands prove the *possibility* of transoceanic travel, as do hundreds of verified long-distance drift voyages and the long table of Guinness records of ocean crossings in small boats. *Plausibility* is the next hurdle: the postulates discussed in this chapter are plausible, unlike the rich trove of implausible claims of aliens from other galaxies or planets, drowned Atlantis or Mu, exiled Templars' Holy Grails, or Bronze Age Europeans importing copper from America. Plausibility is lessened when transfer is alleged for concepts based on common human experiences such as fearsome serpents, raptor birds, trees that (seem to) reach heaven, or sky+land+under-earth making a cosmology. *Probability* applies when possibility and plausibility have been satisfied by empirical evidence that comparable operations did occur, however difficult or strange they strike us—men and women *did* cross open sea to Australia thousands of generations ago, to Remote Oceania and the Azores, centuries before 1492. Probability is not a yes-or-no question; it weighs *degree* of support for an interpretation. Mathematician E. T. Jaynes explained:

> By "inference" we mean simply: deductive reasoning whenever enough information is at hand to permit it; inductive or plausible reasoning when—as is almost invariably the case in real problems—the necessary information is not available. But if a problem can be solved by deductive reasoning, probability theory is not needed for it; thus our topic is the optimal processing of incomplete information. (Jaynes 2003:xix)

And he warned, "When a data set is mutilated (or, to use the common euphemism, "filtered") by processing according to false assumptions, important information in it may be destroyed irreversibly" (Jaynes 2003:xxvii).

## A Higher Degree of Probability For Transpacific Contact

Reasoning from probabilities of Atlantic pre-Columbian contacts, the preceding chapter presented the incontrovertible probability of a Norse settlement at L'Anse aux Meadows at the beginning of the eleventh century; the equivocal probability of domed roof, Roman-type cement and fired bricks at El Tajín and Comalcalco, having been introduced by Europeans in first millennium CE; and the lesser probability, though plausible, that the little Roman figurine head came to Mexico in late Roman Empire times.

Transpacific contacts before Magellan similarly can be ordered by degree of probability. This chapter adduced Mesoamerican data on Olmec-period shifts to agricultural societies—data not available to

Meggers, Evans, and Estrada in the early 1960s—that contradict the earlier picture of a sudden introduction of foreign ways. A time gap between Shang China and Middle Olmec reduces the probability of the latter having received Shang visitors, nor are the resemblances between cosmological serpents in China and Olmec close enough to demand direct import from China to Mexico.

A very different situation exists for Early Postclassic Mesoamerican contacts with Asia.

Here we have a set of contemporary Asian features clustered along the Gulf Coast north and south of the Isthmus of Tehuantepec.

Wheel-and-axle have been found *exclusively* in the Americas within this cluster, from the Huasteca to Cihuatán in El Salvador, at the southern edge of Mesoamerica. Wheel-and-axle, invented in the steppe region of Eurasia about 4000 BCE (Anthony 2007:64–65), by this medieval period in European terms, had diffused throughout Eurasia and Africa—a stark contrast to its late and very restricted appearance in the Americas. Even starker is that the American version is in only one form, a toylike animal, contrasted with the ubiquity and range of the device in Eurasia from chariots and wagons to millstones.

At Cihuatán, what is interpreted as a temple precinct is marked by stone statues of snarling felines *with collars of bells*, very much like the "lion-dog" guardian statues of Asian temples that also wear collars of little bells (Ekholm 1953:84, Fig. 21) (personal communication, Karen Olsen Bruhns, January 2014[2]). The pre-Columbian provenance of these finds in excavations by respected archaeologists cannot be questioned.

Still within the restricted American southern Gulf Coast provenance are sculptured reliefs, Late Classic-Early Postclassic, singled out by Gordon Ekholm as showing strong contemporary Asian parallels: the ruler or deity sitting with one leg under, the other dangling, on a throne; thrones that are snarling tigers (jaguars, *tigres* in Mexican Spanish) wearing collars; cosmic trees with monster mask face in the middle; copper bells with wirework decoration *unlike South American metal bells*; and several other parallels, somewhat less exact (Ekholm 1953: 76–77, 75, 87–88). The strange Nocuchich tower with a face and companion pagoda tower may fit in here.

Narrow collocation in space and time in Mesoamerica, with extremely broad distribution and great time depth in Eurasia, strengthen the probability that this set identifies transpacific voyaging from Southeast Asia in the tenth or eleventh centuries, perhaps continuing to the thirteenth. Paper and ritual paper cutouts may have come to Mexico at this time, leaving no preserved examples from archaeology. Probability of contact at this time is heightened by the period being a time of competition in the Indian Ocean-Island Southeast Asian region for Moluccas spices, driving voyaging into the eastern end of the Indonesian chain.

The case for calendar astrology is not so straightforward. Its validity leans more to the *im*plausibility of two complex systems built upon fantasy becoming so similar. David Kelley painstakingly researched and compared all the major calendar astrology systems of Eurasia, listing the variations between them and between several of them and several Mesoamerican variants, finding that within-continent variants differed from each other about as much as any Mesoamerican one differed from an Asian one. Since scholars agree that the Eurasian systems were linked—diffused—it logically follows that the Mesoamerican systems like them fall into the same linkage. Note that the comparisons are not limited to historical records or archaeology; many versions are actively practiced and can be directly observed (e.g., Tedlock 1982).

An inkling of the thousands of Maya books on astronomy, calendar dates, and astrology is glimpsed in the Dresden Codex, the only one of these books to be saved from conquering Spaniards' iconoclastic book burnings. Maya calendar notations can be read on stone stelae and bas-reliefs from early in the first millennium CE. Kelley inferred from his extensive researches[3] that probably in the second century CE, a learned, brilliant Mayan amalgamated components from four Asian systems (from India, Southeast Asia, China) into the Mayan calendar system, selecting from the Asian sequences of twenty-eight named lunar mansions to make a twenty-day sequence fitting his existing calendar system (Kelley and Millone 2011:498).

That the sign for zero and the concept of place-notation figuring including zero place is attested in Maya slightly earlier (so far as is documented) than in India in the first millennium CE, implies that voyagers from India arrived in southern Mexico-Guatemala, communicated with peers in Maya science, and returned to India. This would have been at the beginning, or a century or so before, the creation of the Gupta Empire (320 CE), considered a Golden Age of art and learning in India, and certainly of expansion. For the Maya, it was the early portion of their Classic period of ambitious kings, great cities, and art. Plausibility lies in the congruence of fine arts, learning, science, and grand political ambitions on both sides of the Pacific; India and Southeast Asia had strong maritime traditions and large seagoing vessels. What degree of probability can be given to Kelley's hypothesis?

Ekholm's work on Hindu-Buddhist art motifs and styles resembling Mesoamerican art can complement Kelley's work on calendrics. In

Asia as in Mesoamerica, astronomers and mathematicians were associated with rulers' courts, standing in the audience when envoys and foreign merchants paid their respects. Hindu-Buddhist art and beliefs overspread Asia, in a remarkable example of true diffusion, with initial major impetus in the Gupta period of Indian history. Architects, artists, craftspeople, theologians, and ritual specialists traveled to, settled in, and voyaged back and forth to the farthest reaches of Island Southeast Asia. A reasonable probability exists that a few ships, forerunners of Spain's Manila Galleons, used the Japan Current and equatorial tradewinds (Montenegro et al. 2014:245) to reach beyond their competitors. Evangelical Buddhists could well have been on board, as they were on ships within the Indian Ocean-China maritime world. Some of Ekholm's art parallels are earlier than the Early Postclassic cluster with wheeled figurines, and could have traveled with the Gupta-era waves of diffusion. Here, probability is heightened by the indisputable spread of art-architecture-icons throughout Asia's civilizations. Its force little abated for centuries, its carriers frequently on ships, the probability that it reached Mesoamerica in the Gupta era should not be rejected, although is not as strong as the probability of American landings by medieval spice trade ships.

## Chapter 11

# Dubitanda

Critical Thinking deals with dubitanda. Yes, that is Latin for *what is doubted*. Philosopher Stephen Pepper used the Latin term to jolt us into realizing everyday knowledge—"common sense"—is accepted without reflection, and not the result of critical examination. Intelligent, responsible people refine inferences from data, testing against more and more varied data, thinking out logical inconsistencies, seeking corroborative data. Pepper drew out how refining knowledge leads to, "On the one side, irresponsible but secure common sense; on the other, responsible but insecure critical cognition" (Pepper 1942:47).

Anthropologists study how practices and beliefs are ingrained in people as they grow up within their societies. Darrell Kipp, a sophisticated and well-educated Blackfoot Indian, remarked that he would no longer talk about "cultures." His people, he said, don't "have a culture"— they live in a "reality" that differs from that experienced by Euro-Americans (Kipp 2010). Blackfoot reality has massive mountains that live very long, very slow lives, their movements almost imperceptible to humans. Many kinds of peoples live in this reality, each with its language, traditional ways, gifts, and foibles—bison, hawks, squirrels, mice, elk— every species is a "people" in the way Blackfoot and Europeans are peoples. Living in this world, one senses an Almighty Power vitalizing the universe; it cannot be seen although it may manifest to humans as apparent beings. The life-supporting sun is one of its manifestations. Such a reality is at odds with a Western reality of hierarchy, a structured world of superior and subordinate beings inventing technologies to conquer and dominate.

Alice Beck Kehoe, *Travelling Prehistoric Seas*, pp. 173-182. © 2016 Alice Beck Kehoe. All rights reserved.

Belief that no one could cross the oceans before Europeans developed the caravels that Columbus used, together with his navigation instruments, is common sense knowledge in the United States. It is part of the ideology justifying and legitimating Anglo invasions and wars of conquest against American First Nations, charged with being inherently inferior to White Europeans. Schools teach, even at the college level, that America had no history before 1607 when Anglo settlement took hold (Kehoe 1990, 1998, Schmidt and Mrozowski 2013). This book takes that common knowledge as *dubitanda*.

## The Bugabear: Diffusion

In a study that won the Scholarly Book Award given by the Society for American Archaeology in 2007, Scandinavian archaeologists Kristian Kristiansen and Thomas Larsson wrote:

> A mature archaeology should be able to encompass all phenomena of historical change, including travel and population movements. This calls for a widening of the theoretical repertoire of archaeology to include diffusion and interaction. (Kristiansen and Larsson 2005:30)

They conclude, "the theoretical and interpretative repertoire of archaeology should be derived from the general field of culture-historical studies" (ibid., 372).

How did archaeology lose its grounding in culture-historical studies? From its nineteenth-century foundation modeled on geology, archaeology strove to use scientific practices as counterweight to romantic associations (Kehoe 1998, 2013). Archaeology collected, and increasingly produced, material data that are proxies for past societies. It was valued for constructing local and regional histories where no other data are known, except, sometimes, orally transmitted chronicles.

Archaeologists embedded in academia have been expected to go beyond sequences of data to illuminate projected universal "laws" of human existence. Straight culture-historical interpretations and, for historical and contemporary peoples, historical particularism have been disdained as lacking theoretical worth (in spite of Franz Boas explicitly stating that we do not have sufficient data, from all times and places of human existence, to scientifically sample and to justify generalizing universal regularities (Boas in Stocking, ed., 1974:61–71)). Disjunction came to a head in the 1970s with the crusade led by Lewis Binford to make archaeology conform to a physics model of science. "Diffusion," although a respectable necessary term in chemistry and medicine, was laughed out of the arena; it was associated with crackpot non-archaeologists seeing Egyptian sun gods everywhere.

Interestingly, that cartoonish image came out of a hardnosed competition for major institutional and research funds in 1920s London, between G. Elliot Smith and Bronislaw Malinowski (Crook 2012:54, Smith 2011:109). Both men were excellent scientists: Smith, one of the most skilled and knowledgeable anatomists of his generation; Malinowski, sophisticated in using evolution principles to distinguish human biological necessities (food, water, sex, shelter) from cultural habits. A debate was set up between the two, published in 1927 with comments by two American anthropologists (Smith et al. 1927). Each man endeavored to disarm his opponent by seeming to cede some of the other's position. Elliot Smith said, rebutting multiple independent inventions:

> It is utterly unjustifiable to assume, as modern ethnological theories implicitly do, that human behaviour was totally different before writing was invented. There is not a scrap of evidence to suggest that our unliterary predecessors had a remarkable aptitude for invention far transcending that of modern man. (Smith 1927:13–14)

To which Malinowski challenged, "What precisely an 'invention' is . . .", and then listed a string of discoverers, beginning with Galileo, whose contributions were necessary to the invention of the "wireless" (radio):

> Diffusion and invention are always mixed. . . . The process is always one of adaptation in which the receiving culture has to re-evolve the idea, custom, or institution which it adopts.. . . Diffusion . . . is always a readaptation, a truly creative process, in which external influence is remoulded by inventive genius. (Malinowski 1927: 28, 30, 46)

Commentator Alexander Goldenweiser concluded:

> No one doubts the *reality* of diffusion nor its importance in the building up of culture complexes . . . the real issues: Is there such a thing as independent invention? (Goldenweiser 1927:102, his emphasis)

As the two recent biographers of Elliot Smith make clear, what was at stake was not a preference for tracing elements of cultures versus an ethnographer's commitment to holistic analyses of actual societies. Granted over a million dollars by the Rockefeller Foundation to build an Institute of Anatomy in London, Elliot Smith subsumed anthropology with the medical sciences into a Human Biology program stressing evolution (Crook 2012:53–54). Malinowski was at the London School of Economics, where his attention to praxis through fieldwork fit well with LSE's strength in political science, attracting students. Anthropology came to be seen as a social science, useful in that heyday of administering colonies, while Elliot Smith's biologically oriented program was estranged.

Contextualizing the rejection of "diffusion" with Malinowski's battle to establish his version of anthropology against Elliot Smith's biologically oriented program, "diffusion" can be seen to be at odds with the Anglo colonial administrations that engaged many British anthropologists. Both Britain, in Australia and Africa, and the United States colonized regions lacking large cities, monumental stone architecture, elaborate royal courts, written legal codes, and historical ties to the Roman Empire. France and Spain, in contrast, had to deal with such civilizations in their colonies. Anglo nations could maintain that their "wards" were savage or childlike, incapable of engaging in global trade. Malinowskian structural-functionalism looking at non-Western communities as small, closed societies fulfilled this colonial picture and provided colonial governments with information for policies working against resistance built through alliances in the colonies. Ending overt colonial rule after World War II allowed postcolonial movements to develop, often drawing upon suppressed histories (Johansen 2003). Contacts between precolonial societies could no longer be denied a priori.

Franz Boas's influence in America kept biological anthropology within the discipline—Boas himself carried out notable research in the subfield, along with his ethnographic and linguistic work—while his historical particularism (and no doubt his fieldwork with living communities) steered him and his students away from the old-fashioned singling out of objects and traits to compare, regardless of where and when found. Boas's contempt for grand theories divorced from committed long term ethnographic fieldwork damned Elliot Smith. It is a classic case of a baby thrown out with the bathwater. "Diffusion" became a term of ridicule, with Malinowski's as well as with Boas's students.

For Americans, extending "diffusion" studies to the Americas hits the myth of Columbus. Having Egyptians, or Asians influenced by them, bring pyramid building and sun deities to America meant Egyptians should claim the right of first discovery under the Doctrine of Discovery that legitimated Anglo governments. Thinking they knew, in Pepper's "common sense" mode, that the Americas had never been

visited by Eurasian ships before 1492, prompted Americans to imme-
diately reject all "diffusionist" suggestions of pre-Columbian contacts.
Coupled with British rejection of outmoded trait distribution studies,
"diffusion" was no longer tenable in reputable anthropology programs.

## Diffusion Studies in Other Disciplines

"Diffusion" continued to be in the basic vocabulary of chemistry and
a label for studies in sociology, geography, and history of technology.
Its chemistry usage furnishes a metaphor, that an introduced artifact
or idea comes to permeate a society, as introduced particles intermin-
gle with other molecules in a gas. In the other fields, subfields were
developed: for sociology, Everett Rogers's 1962 text that went through
several revised editions; for geography, Torsten Hägerstrand's dissertation published in 1967; and for history of technology, the founding
of the journal *Technology and Culture* by the Society for the History of
Technology (*SHOT*).

Hägerstrand's work tracing the spread of innovations quantitatively
by mapping locales or spread through time is an early version of GIS,
geographical information systems. Rogers began as a rural sociologist
tracing the adoption of hybrid corn in his native Iowa, discovering
that, as he stated in his textbook, "subjective evaluations of an innovation, derived from individuals' personal experiences and perceptions
and conveyed by interpersonal networks, drives the diffusion process"
(Rogers 1995 ed.:208; for an overview see Palloni 1998). History of
technology initially was the mirror image of sociologists' studies of diffusion, in that writers focused on inventions and adaptations of technology, but social historians expanded its scope (Bijker 2009). Animal
behavior research also uses "diffusion" for studies of social learning in
nonhuman groups (Whiten and Mesoudi 2008).

"Diffusion" continues to be a standard term for spread of people
into a new area, for example, Han Chinese moving southward into
better farming areas, "diffusing" their genes into the indigenous population (Wen et al. 2004), and "male diffusion" into Neolithic Europe
(Lacan et al. 2011). One research paper on genomics cautions that "po-
tential migration movements described from the spreading of some
material culture could in fact be revealed to be just the consequence of
cultural diffusion" (Olalde and Lalueza-Fox 2015:6).

Diffusion of Hindu-Buddhist beliefs and practices, including art
and architecture, throughout Asia even to Farthest India in the Pacific,
has been on a scale so large—the elephant in the room—it has not, so

far as I can find, been discussed as exemplar in diffusion studies. To begin with, Hinduism and Buddhism are supposed to be separate and indeed opposing religions. Their mixing in art prompts art historians to use the hyphenated label. Anthropologist David Gellner presents an ethnographer's view of the categories:

> South Asian religious boundaries were conceived in ways very different from the dominant modern model of one-and-only-one religious identity per individual . . . people recognize that there are an enormous number of holy people and sites, all of whom and all of which deserve respectful worship . . . common in Asia as a whole, it is very hard to divide people up and allocate them unambiguously to discrete religious categories. (Gellner 2005:756)

He notes that, "What Hinduism and Buddhism have in common is, in many cases, underpinned by a shared basis in Tantrism" (Gellner 2005:760). Within such a worldview, diffusion could be easy; instead of others' icons and practices being forbidden, they were welcomed to enrich local ambience.

Maritime trade, at least as much as the overland Silk Road, facilitated diffusion of Tantric practices along with Hindu and Buddhist ideas. Speaking of the southern Chinese port of Quanzhou between 1000 and 1400 CE, economic historians Pomeranz and Topik noted:

> In its heyday, the port's foreign merchants included Muslims, Hindus, Theravada and Mahayana Buddhists, Catholic and Nestorian Christians, Jews, and Parsees; one can still find in the city images of Shiva and Vishnu, the ruins of a twelfth-century Muslim cemetery endowed by a merchant from the Persian Gulf, a tenth- or eleventh-century Hindu stone phallus (delicately redesignated a "Stone Bamboo Shoot" in Chinese texts), and a bilingual Tamil/ Chinese religious inscription [that] espouses Hindu teachings. (Pomeranz and Topik 2013:24)

Recent archaeology, supplanting traditional texts, brought "all regional specialists [to] agree that acculturation in this region, whether one wants to call it 'Indianization,' 'localization,' or 'convergence,' was clearly linked to expanding trade networks and more especially to the maritime routes" (Bellina and Glover 2004:68; Higham 2001).

Merchants as primary agents allied themselves with crafts guilds, relatively free agents acting as investment and credit organizations cross-cutting urban states such as the Mauryan empire in India and Southeast Asia's small polities' river ports (Bellina and Glover 2004:70).

As early as the Augustan Age, first century CE, cloves from the eastern Moluccas Islands were carried to Rome. For more than a millennium, Indian (Tamil, Bangladesh, Kalinga), Southeast Asian (Funan, in the Mekong Delta), and Indonesian kingdoms and trade organizations competed to transport Moluccan spices into the international markets, as well as expensive carnelian and agate beads, fine ceramics, jade, dammar resin, camphor, bronze cauldrons, drums, mirrors, silk, and cotton (before the cotton gin and mechanized spinning, cotton was a luxury cloth produced in India) (Bellina and Glover 2004, Theunissen, Grave and Bailey 2000, Hung et al. 2007, Burger et al. 2009).

Early in the first millennium CE, trade between India and China portaged across the Malaysian peninsula, with Indonesian products transshipped there. In the fourth century CE, invasions of north China drove thousands of Han Chinese families south, stimulating markets and trade in southern China (Wolters 1967:76; Wen et al. 2004). Shippers discovered a sea route through the Straits of Malacca between the Malay peninsula and Island Southeast Asia, specifically Sumatra; the Straits are long and take ships southward rather than straight east-west, but avoiding the overland transshipment was (and is) advantageous (Singapore is at the southern end of the Straits, which remain a highly important shipping lane). By the seventh century CE, the Srivijaya kingdom in southeastern Sumatra became the principal entrepôt for Indonesian products shipping direct to both India and China, plus a major port for replenishing supplies and exchanging cargoes. Not incidentally, Indonesian seamen manned most of the ships, some of which were built in Indonesia (Wolters 1967:158).

Srivijaya's rulers prospered by charging fees, as their subjects prospered by charging merchants for warehousing, supplies, ship repairs, agents' services, and so on. To protect its prosperity, Srivijaya waged wars against competitors along the Straits. Over time, more and more shippers ventured direct to Indonesian producers of spices, resins, and other goods, bypassing Srivijaya, and the kingdom could not prevent ports from developing along the Straits. By 1350, Srivijaya on the western end of the Indonesian archipelago no longer dominated long-distance in what had become a three-cornered maritime world: India, China, and Indonesia (Wolters 1967:252). From the fifth to the fourteenth centuries, Asian ships increased in numbers, in exploring for new sources, and in creating new routes. The Western Pacific was anything but empty.

With these steadily expanding mercantile enterprises came passengers. Buddhist priests traveled to teach, Chinese and other Asians traveled the other direction to India to learn about Buddhism. Artisans traveled, independently or at the behest of foreign patrons. Aristocrats and envoys traveled with entourages to the great courts of Indonesia as well as mainland kingdoms. Experiencing the richly detailed baroque architecture and art of Indian centers of sanctity and power, visitors associated their styles and icons with rulership and ritual potency. Stephen Bokenkamp notes, of Chinese theologians translating Buddhist texts in the fifth century CE:

> New worlds, striking new divinities, new postmortem possibilities, new spiritual threats and ritual solutions, new moral imperatives, new modes of religious organization—all were contained, for the first time in [Chinese scholars'] experience, in a *written* language that could be translated into Chinese. (Bokenkamp 2014:184) (his italics)

"Indianization" was more than its material expressions seen today: it carried so rich, so cosmopolitan a world that its elements became signs of superior knowledge and character. Its richness allowed wide choice to its admirers; it was not a cult, but a universe.

The Gupta kingdom covering the northern half of the Indian subcontinent, 328–467 CE, was the epitome of "Hindu-Buddhist" culture. One historian says, "The Gupta period saw the spread of Indian ideas to the far reaches of the known world" (O'Reilly 2007:179). Even a metallurgical sourcing study concludes that the coasts of Southeast Asia, "particularly Iron Age (c. 500 BC–c. 500 AD) sites (e.g. Khao Sam Kaeo, Prohear), appear to be involved in maritime exchange networks spanning thousands of kilometres, with diverse material strongly suggesting cultural and economic interactions, if not actual migrations, between China, India, and other intermediary littoral populations" (Pryce et al. 2014, online unpaged, accessed 2/28/2015). The impetus loosed by Gupta kings' ambitions, building on the previous millennium's development of ports, entrepôts, extraction and manufacturing centers, and ship capabilities, may have extended the world known to a few as far as Mesoamerica. There, as throughout Asia and Indonesia, ruling families and their advisors may have selected a few striking elements reflecting both Hindu and Buddhist practices, such as mudrā. Perhaps, as David Kelley inferred, this was when the complex Mesoamerican calendar, incorporating astrology, was perfected.

A second period of contacts with Asia is likely to have been the Early Postclassic of Mesoamerica, which, whether using the conventional Goodman-Martinez-Thompson calendar correlation or Kelley's, two centuries later, falls within Asia's medieval period, eleventh to fourteenth centuries. This was the era of Angkor in Cambodia, where the unique face towers of the Bayón resemble the equally unique face tower in Nocuchich in Yucatán. Both continents saw an unprecedented expansion of merchant trade, on the Asian side relying heavily on shipping. Indonesia and the Philippines were very much involved, along with the South China Sea and Japan, raising the probability of a Japan Current route north of Central Polynesia to America. Wheeled figurines, paper and rituals using it, and "lion-dog" temple guardian figures may have come to Mesoamerica in this period; Candi Sukuh, the Mexican-like temple in central Java, suggests a nobleman of Java's Majaprahit kingdom made a round trip to Mexico.

Are these cases of "diffusion"? Not really; the objects noted did not *permeate* the societies of Mesoamerica. They appear to have been restricted to state constructions, religious rituals, court display. Polynesian transport of sweet potatoes to Central Polynesia a thousand years ago was diffusion, for the plant became a basic cultivar in the island societies; it permeated their subsistence. Culture contacts, borrowings and stimuli, are not necessarily diffusion. In the cases of transoceanic voyaging before Columbus, there was little true diffusion—tropical bark beaters for bark cloth, long before the process led to paper, may be an example. Blowguns may be another. More of the cases seem to have been ruling-class adoptions of beautiful labor-intensive objects, just as in European Bronze Age transmissions (Kristiansen and Larsson 2005) and much of the Hindu-Buddhist "Indianization" of Asia, although the two religious movements did really diffuse throughout the populations of this vast area. A distinction between diffusion versus limited elements of a foreign culture reaching a limited set of people is a step toward valid histories.

Overall, a remarkably balanced and well-informed discussion of the issues of diffusion or independent invention, specifically in the transpacific cases, was written by art historian Douglas Fraser (1965; Barnard and Fraser 1972). As he noted, "within the Americas innumerable traits are assumed to have diffused from one area to another . . . the logical consistency of a theory that stops at the water's edge is difficult to defend" (Fraser 1965:476–477). Cases for independent invention are seldom argued, "psychic unity" is taken for granted, and it's "common sense" that before 1492, no one could cross oceans to America. None of these positions are scientific.

## Epilogue

"Objects arouse curiosity, resist implausible manipulation, and collect layers of information about them. Objectivity can only refer to a relationship between persons and these fascinating things; it cannot reside outside of persons. . . . We have redefined historical objectivity as an interactive relationship between an inquiring subject and an external object. Validation in this definition comes from persuasion more than proof, but without proof there is no historical writing of any worth" (Appleby, Hunt, and Jacob 1994:260–262).

In my research on the Kensington Runestone in Minnesota, I and my predecessors Robert Hall, the Cornell linguist, and Newton Winchell, the geologist, sought proof in examining data within the methods of historical linguistics, forestry, geology, settler history, and medieval European history. We thought we had amassed enough proof to validate the authenticity of the rune inscription of 1362. Our several publications failed to persuade our colleagues. A Smithsonian curator told me he wouldn't read my book because he knew, already, the stone was a hoax—it couldn't possibly have been left by medieval Norse. This he knew in spite of his years of fieldwork along Davis Strait where Greenland Norse came over during five centuries before 1492. He told me that the data he studied are "prehistoric" and that historical facts about medieval Norse are of no relevance to America. Thus one sees how dubitanda persist, dictated by "common sense."

This book does not waste your time on ill-informed popular assertions that archaeologists conspire to hide data that would revolutionize history. Transoceanic voyages before Columbus are possible. Some of those proposed are plausible. I have focused on those best supported by empirical data, evaluating their probabilities. Reasonable persons do not dismiss these cases because since kindergarten, they've known that Columbus was the first to sail the ocean blue.

# Notes

## Preface

1. Bob Dylan's line is apropos here.

## Chapter 2

1. Linguist Johanna Nichols suggests the myth of unknown, uninhabited wilderness discovered by progenitors of a present nation may be common among Indo-European speakers (Nichols 1997:262, note 5).

2. In the early eleventh century, the Arabic scientist al-Biruni had correctly calculated the circumference of the earth, using geometry and his own measurements of longitude at a number of sites. Realizing there is a huge area on the globe not recorded in the geographies of his day, al-Biruni suggested there is likely a large land mass in the ocean between Asia and Europe. This postulation of inhabited lands should earn al-Biruni the title of discoverer of America, one historian urges, even though the Central Asian scholar never sailed to find it (Starr 2013:375–377).

3. First Nations refers to the indigenous nations invaded by Europeans following Columbus's voyage. Canada officially uses this term for its indigenous peoples. The United States still officially uses "tribe," a term associated since the Roman empire with smaller nations invaded by empires. Most First Nations citizens say they are American Indians, or Indian people, rather than Native Americans, a term contested by some European-descended U. S.-born citizens.

4. Early in the "modern" period in Europe, so labeled by many self-confident writers in the sixteenth century there, three inventions were singled out as the key innovations launching "modern" progress: firearms, printing, and the nautical compass (Boruchoff 2012). Ironically, all three were Chinese inventions used there for centuries before diffused to Europe (Needham 2004:20, 53, 204).

5. Originally a phrase taught as a placebo by French pharmacist Émile Coué (1857–1926).

## Chapter 3

1. Archaeologist A. Sampson reported habitation on the Aegean island of Agios Eustratios in the Middle Paleolithic, around 80,000 to 35,000 BCE (Laskaris et al. 2011:2475). What look like Early Paleolithic stone tools have been found on other islands in the Mediterranean, suggesting the people were using boats on the open sea as early as 130,000 years ago (Runnels 2014, Simmons 2014).
2. This paragraph uses extended discussion and classifications in McGrail 1997, and Doran's classification in Doran 1973.
3. Mark Twain's Huckleberry Finn describes a rich variety of boat people on the Mississippi as Huck and Jim raft down from Missouri.

## Chapter 4

1. Archaeological finds on Agios Eustratios, an Aegean island, and other Mediterranean islands suggest Middle Paleolithic voyaging in that sea, around 80,000 to 35,000 BCE (Laskaris et al. 2011:2475; Runnels 2014). The Agios Eustratios excavation was not yet published when this book was written in May 2015, so it could not be evaluated.

## Chapter 5

1. Sampling of human genetics, particularly of male Y chromosomes, in today's Melanesian and Polynesian populations is affected by a colonial practice between the 1870s and early 1900s called blackbirding, in which native men were forcibly taken from Pacific islands to work on plantations in Australia. As many as nearly half the males in some islands were removed, never to return. Thus Y chromosomes of thousands of islanders did not reproduce into today's populations (Matisoo-Smith 2014:8).
2. The name of the last Inca emperor, Atahualpa, killed by Pizarro in 1533, means "chicken" in Quechua, the language of Tawantisuyo (the Inca empire). Presumably, it brought to mind fighting cocks.

## Chapter 6

1. Kuhn used "paradigm" to mean a model of proper scientific research.
2. Müller, Roberts, and Brown 2015 caution that bacilli related to the tuberculosis vector may have been incorrectly identified as evidence of tuberculosis in laboratory tests of ancient DNA, due to these bacilli in soil in which skeletons lie, or later contamination.
3. I asked Arthur C. Aufderheide, M.D., co-editor of the 1998 Cambridge Encyclopedia of Human Paleopathology, whether he considered it a reasonable hypothesis that Norse introduced tuberculosis to northeastern American Indians during the Vinland explorations. Dr. Aufderheide replied, May

24, 2005, "Do I think it's a valid hypothesis? Yes, certainly the hypothesis is valid. . . . In the 1960s, I had the good fortune to live through several winters with the Canadian Arctic Inuit. There I learned quickly the tuberculosis-transmitting power of the igloo environment on the family members living in it." He added that to confirm my hypothesis, a researcher would need "A Norse (or, probably more realistically, a European DNA marker in the M. tuberculosis complex genome that is unique to European strains from that period , and test the New World strains both before and after A.D. 1000." This would require, he said, " a special program for which this would be the focus."

4. When I lived in an Aymara village in Bolivia during an ethnographic project, the matrons of the community invited me to join them after work chewing coca and chatting. They chewed the dried leaves with sugar. The experience was very much like tea-time in Britain.

5. Sauer's and Johannessen's work was totally ignored in a massive tome, 678 8"x11" double-column pages titled Histories of Maize: Multidisciplinary Approaches to the Prehistory, Linguistics, Biogeography, Domestication, and Evolution of Maize (2006, Academic Press [now published by Left Coast Press]). The volume takes for granted that maize was known only in the Americas before 1492; the topic of pre-Columbian transoceanic distributions is not raised.

6. Francesca Bray (1984:518) concluded after careful assessment that peanuts were most likely introduced into Fukien in China by Portuguese in the early sixteenth century. She similarly concluded that maize was brought to China at that time, its earliest Chinese documentation, in her opinion, in 1511 (Bray 1984:456, 458). The Yangling tomb peanuts had not been discovered when Bray wrote.

7. Johannesen included grain amaranths in his list of medieval likely imports, but Jonathan Sauer, the leading authority of amaranths and son of Carl Sauer, concluded after years of study that Asians cultivated Asian species of amaranths, primarily to use the leaves as stew vegetables. By the eighteenth century, American grain amaranths had been taken to Asia and became widespread (J. Sauer 1993:9–14).

## Chapter 7

1. Pellagra results from niacin (vitamin B3) deficiency. Poor people in South Carolina were eating mostly maize not processed with lime or ashes, as American Indians did, a process that adds niacin to maize flour. Hospitals and asylums for the insane were filling up with people dying of pellagra. The 1940s government campaign to add niacin to bread and other foods used by the poor halted this health crisis. Dr. Lu told me that she felt her role in ending this scourge of the poor was her greatest achievement.

2. He didn't mention, but China and Mesoamerica also shared series of courts separated by walls with gates, creating a set of barriers between commoners and the priests and rulers in the inner courts. The "Avenue of the Dead" in Teotihuacán, Mexico, leading past the Pyramid of the Sun, offset on the east side, to the Pyramid of the Moon is a good example.

3. Uto-Aztecan is a major language family in the Americas, from Paiute, Ute, and Shoshone in the western U.S., down through northwest Mexico into central Mexico, where it includes Nahuatl, the language of the Aztecs.

4. As an aspect of postcolonialism, some archaeologists have been arguing that the label "prehistory" is unjustified for the histories of non-Western peoples (Schmidt and Mrozowski, eds., 2014).

5. I queried S. Frederick Starr, a scholar familiar with medieval Central Asia and its relationships. He replied, "I had always assumed that the game was Turkish, and that the name refers to the 'pieces' that are moved around" (personal communication, July 1, 2014). According to Google Translate, Turkish "parça" means "piece," as a component or part. "Pachisi" is translated as "a four-person board game . . . the favorite game of the rulers of India" (accessed 7/1/2014). It would seem unlikely that "pachisi" is of Turkish origin, or named from the Turkish word for "piece."

6. In some areas of India, ikat cloth is produced in workshops staffed by men. They may use patterns drawn on paper.

7. Specifically, two between 1419 and 1520, one between 1403 and 1501 (Barnes 2010:36, 38), and one between 1390 and 1480, possibly even 1320 to 1350 (Barnes 2010:250).

8. I queried several Mayanists about pre-Columbian textiles, and the linguist Nicholas Hopkins about the Tzotzil word ikatz. I am grateful to Karon Winzenz, Susan Milbrath, Matthew Looper, Patricia McAnany, and John Justeson for answering my query on evidence of ikat before Cortés, and Nick Hopkins for his exposition of ikatz, which with its cognates in Mayan refers to "load" (carga in Spanish), not to a textile (pers. com. Nicholas Hopkins, September 30, 2014).

## Chapter 8

1. "Monkey see, monkey do" has been scientifically watched and the brains of the observed monkeys scanned, revealing excitation of particular neural areas. That "mirroring" is not necessarily conscious movement can be seen in the way we tend to mirror body posture of those we are conversing with. Notice how you may move your hands, arms, or head when the person beside you does so.

2. Apparently no catalog or work plans for this exhibit were preserved (personal communication Kristen Mable, April 2014).

3. The Osage, a nation in the Midwest that may have descended from the prehistoric city Cahokia, had mothers of newborn Osage go to a marshy lake to procure the root of the lotus, symbolizing food to sustain life (La Flesche 1928:55).

4. Also became a hashtag on Twitter: #Mudrā (accessed 8/4/2014).

5. Maya area is about 1,269,094 square kilometers (490,000 square miles); Asian Hindu-Buddhist area is about 41,000,000 square kilometers (about 16,000,000 square miles).

6. I am grateful to Diana Zaragoza for informing me about the Nocuchich tower.

7. There have been several efforts to demonstrate astrological principles by correlating biographies with moments of birth and sky phenomena. To make a scientific test, one would need to collect hundreds of thousands of detailed biographies from random samples of populations. Weak correlations may reflect weather conditions experienced in infancy and early childhood, in that infants born at the beginning of a cold season have less experience of outdoor exercise and pleasure than those born at the beginning of the pleasant season. So suggested my children's pediatrician, predicting the child born in early April would be more inclined to outdoor activities than his brother born in late October. This is true, with the third brother born in July outdoors less than the April one and more than the October one. One trial of a hypothesis does not, however, make for a scientific conclusion.

8. As a personal friend since 1965 until his death in 2011, I saw the growing manuscript pile of this magnum opus, and in his last years, begged Kelley to see it published. He refused because he had not been able to find data to resolve one correlation gap.

9. The rabbit in the moon is the light parts of the full moon, the opposite of the European man in the moon which is the dark parts. With a little effort, one can easily see the white rabbit and its mortar.

## Chapter 9

1. Literature professor Annette Kolodny teaches a History of American Literature course that she begins with the two sagas, arguing that they are about America, have literary value, and have been used by many later American writers. See her well-written *In Search of First Contact: The Vikings of Vinland, the Peoples of the Dawnland, and the Anglo-American Anxiety of Discovery.* (2012).

2. Medieval Warm Period temperatures were not quite as high as the rapid warming that began in the 1980s. Causes of that warm period, or of the colder period that followed until about 1850, or of the warming from 1850 to the 1980s, are not yet well understood.

3.  A contributor to an evangelical Protestant magazine noted, some years ago, that Jesus the Christ would have had God's own Y chromosome, since he had no earthly father. So if Jesus had a son, and that male lineage continued, God's own Y chromosome would have continued on earth for generations. Thus the sons in the lineage could have been called, mystically, the Holy Grail.

4.  Popular misinformation indicates that huge amounts of copper were taken from the Lake Superior mines, and occurrences of copper artifacts in prehistoric America cannot account for such quantities. Archaeological investigations of the Lake Superior mining pits indicate the quantity of ore removed was not millions of tons. Native copper artifacts are numerous in eastern North America, dating from five thousand years ago to historic times.

5.  An earlier version of this is Kehoe 1962, originally a seminar paper for a course taught by Stuart Piggott when he was a Visiting Professor at Harvard, 1961. Professor Piggott set the topic, suggested by similarities he saw between Vinette 1 and Late Neolithic ceramics from coastal northwestern Europe; by the capabilities of Irish curraghs he had ridden in; and by an Inuit kayak found near Aberdeen, Scotland. Years later, another Piggott student, Ian Whitaker, discovered that Dutch whalers picked up adventuresome Inuit men off Greenland and gave them transport to the Netherlands territorial line twelve miles offshore, then set them down in their kayaks to paddle themselves to land, because Dutch port authorities forbade them to land. Some landed in Scotland (Forbes 184–186).

6.  During the Roman Empire period, relatively large cargo ships carried grain and olive oil across the Mediterranean from colonies to the capital in Italy. The "Pax Romana" made a strong navy unnecessary; on the few occasions when a fleet was wanted, the cargo ships were added to the regular fleet. In the later third century CE, disintegration of the Empire let pirates prey on cargo ships; in the next century, Constantine and his successors built coastal fortresses rather than keep patrols on the seas to prevent piracy and barbarian raids. By the sixth century CE, the Ostrogoth king Theodoric, who ruled Italy, began building up Mediterranean maritime trade in two-masted ships, but Celtic kingdoms held power in the Atlantic from the Northern Isles off Scotland south to Spain. Whether they explored beyond Iceland isn't known (Lewis and Runyan 1985:1–15).

7.  Mention should be made of Amazonian ethnoarchaeology carried out after Lathrap's death. Argentine archaeologist Gustavo Politis worked with a botanist to record the economy and beliefs of Nukak in the Colombian Amazonian forest. These communities are labeled hunter-gatherer, but Politis emphasizes their sustainable management of forest resources, resulting in "wild orchards" and small gardens under the rainforest canopy at their many campsites (Politis 2009:283). Use of some of the palms and other plants cultivated by the Nukak is documented in Amazon forest sites

as early as 7000 BCE (Politis 2009:333). Nukak practices supply year-round a nutritious diet superior to any that sedentary agriculture could provide in their environment (Politis 2009:286).

8. A 2005 PNAS paper reporting Asian origin for pre-Columbian domesticated bottle gourd in the Americas rejects the possibility of transmission across the Pacific, instead opting to postulate introduction of gourd seeds, along with dogs, into western America by Paleoindians coasting along the North Pacific Rim—"the south coast of Beringia" (Erickson et al. 2005:18319)—on down to subtropical latitudes. Carrying viable gourd seeds the enormous distance of the curved coastline from China, north and over the Aleutian area, south through Alaska and Canada to Mexico, is impossible, according to experts on bottle gourd seeds (Doijode 2001:301–303); it would have required hundreds of stopovers for food no matter how fast the boat people rowed. Erickson et al. did not consider the Japanese Current that could have carried boats from the Asian homeland to subtropical California-Mexico in months. Later, analysis of a larger sample of gourd seeds indicated Africa, not Asia, as the American gourd's origin, and argued for gourds drifting across the Atlantic and sprouting on American shores (Kistler et al. 2014).

## Chapter 10

1. In response to my inquiry, Jim Johnson from the company Seedman .com, said that gourd seed can remain viable (at a very, very low rate ) up to 5 years (pers. comm. Jim Johnson, February 18, 2015).

2. Dr. Bruhns does not accept pre-Columbian transpacific contacts.

3. As a close friend of David Kelley, I had many conversations with him about his calendar researches and saw his drafts of comparative systems, Eurasian and Mesoamerican. After his death in 2011, Jane Holden Kelley allowed me to look through her husband's manuscripts in their home, before they were sent to the University of Calgary archives. In the piles I found two undated typescript summaries of his hypothesis on the transpacific connection between India and Maya calendrics. The sections in his book with Eugene Milone are published summaries, less detailed than in the undated typescripts.

# References

Acheson, Steven. "The Thin Edge: Evidence for Precontact Use and Working of Metal on the Northwest Coast." *Emerging from the Mist: Studies in Northwest Coast Culture History.* Richard G. Matson, Gary Coupland, and Quentin Mackie, eds. Vancouver: University of British Columba Press, 2003, pp. 213–229.

Adams, Mark. *Meet Me in Atlantis.* New York: Dutton/Penguin, 2015.

Adams, R. E. W., and Richard C. Jones. 1981. "Spatial Patterns and Regional Growth Among Classic Maya Cities." *American Antiquity* 46(2):301–322.

Aguilera, Carmen. 1997. "Of Royal Mantles and Blue Turquoise: The Meaning of the Mexican Emperor's Mantle." *Latin American Antiquity* 8(1):3–19.

Aldenderfer, Mark, Nathan M. Craig, Robert J. Speakman, and Rachel Popelka-Filcoff. 2008. "Four-thousand-year-old Gold Artifacts from the Lake Titicaca Basin, Southern Peru." *Proceedings of the National Academy of Sciences* 105(13):5002–5005.

Anderson, Atholl, James H. Barrett, and Katherine V. Boyle, eds. *The Global Origins and Development of Seafaring.* Cambridge: McDonald Institute for Archaeological Research, 2010.

Anderson, Shelby L., Matthew T. Boulanger, and Michael D. Glascock. 2010. "A New Perspective on Late Holocene Social Interaction in Northwest Alaska: Results of a Preliminary Ceramic Sourcing Study." Portland State University *Anthropology Faculty Publications and Presentations*, Paper 31. http://pdxscholar.library.pdx.edu/anth_fac/31

Andrews, George F. *Comalcalco, Tabasco, Mexico.* Culver City, CA: Labyrinthos, 1989.

———.1996. "Arquitecturas Río Bec y Chenes." *Arqueología Mexicana* 3(18):16–25.

———. See also, online, his field notes from 1985 and 1986, accessed 2/13/2015:http:// repositories.lib.utexas.edu/bitstream/handle/2152/13488/txu-aaagfa00347.txt?sequence=3

Anthony, David W. 1990. "Migration in Archeology: The Baby and the Bathwater." *American Anthropologist* 92(4):895–914.

———. *The Horse, the Wheel, and Language: How Bronze-Age Riders from the Eurasian Steppes Shaped the Modern World.* Princeton: Princeton University Press, 2007.

Appleby, Joyce, Lynn Hunt, and Margaret Jacob. *Telling the Truth About History*. New York: W. W. Norton, 1994.

Arnold, Philip J., III. 2009. "Settlement and Subsistence among the Early Formative Gulf Olmec." *Journal of Anthropological Archaeology* 28(4):397–411.

Aubet, María Eugenia. *The Phoenicians and the West: Politics, Colonies and Trade*. 2nd ed. Cambridge: Cambridge University Press, 2001.

Bard, Kathryn, and Rodolfo Fattovich. "Recent Excavations at the Ancient Harbor of *Saww* (Mersa/Wadi Gawasis) on the Red Sea." *Offerings to the Discerning Eye: An Egyptological Medley in Honor of Jack A. Josephson*. Sue H. D'Auria, ed. Leiden: Brill, 2009, pp. 33–38.

Barnard, Noel, and Douglas Fraser. *Early Chinese Art and its Possible Influence in the Pacific Basin*. New York: Intercultural Arts Press, 1972.

Barnes, Ruth. "Early Indonesian Textiles: Scientific Dating in a Wider Context." *Five Centuries of Indonesian Textiles*. Ruth Barnes and Mary Hunt Kahlenberg, eds. Munich: Delmonico Books-Prestel, 2010, pp. 39–44, 250.

Barrett, James H., and Atholl Anderson. "Histories of Global Seafaring: A Discussion." *The Global Origins and Development of Seafaring*. Atholl Anderson, James H. Barrett, and Katherine V. Boyle, eds. Cambridge: McDonald Institute for Archaeological Research, University of Cambridge, 2010, pp. 305–314.

Bauer, Marta Louise. 2011. "Christopher Columbus: An Analysis of Myth Creation and Longevity in Early America." Honors thesis, Oakland University. Online pdf, accessed March, 2014.

Bednarik, Robert G. 1997. "The Earliest Evidence of Ocean Navigation. *International Journal of Nautical Archaeology* 26(3):183–191.

———. 2000. "Crossing the Timor Sea by Middle Palaeolithic Raft." *Anthropos* 95(1):37–47.

Bellina, Bérénice, and Ian C. Glover. "The Archaeology of Early Contact with India and the Mediterranean World, from the Fourth Century BC to the Fourth Century AD." *Southeast Asia, from the Prehistory to History*. Ian C. Glover and Peter Bellwood, eds. London: Routledge/Curzon Press, 2004, pp.68–89.

Bellwood, Peter. *Prehistory of the Indo-Malyasian Archipelago*. 2nd ed. Honolulu: University of Hawaii Press, 1997. The third edition, 2007, is a reprint of this, from ANU Press, Canberra.

Bhardwaj, Surinder M. "Geography and Pilgrimage: A Review." *Sacred Places, Sacred Spaces: The Geography of Pilgrimages*. Robert H. Stoddard and Alan Morinis, eds. Baton Rouge: Geosciences Publications, Louisiana State University, 1997, pp. 1–23.

Bijker, Wiebe E. 2009. "Globalization and Vulnerability." *Technology and Culture* 50(3):600–612.

Bird, Junius. 1947. "A Pre-Spanish Peruvian Ikat." *Bulletin of the Needle and Bobbin Club* 31(1–2):72–77.

Birket-Smith, Kaj. 1967, 1971. *Studies in Circumpacific Culture Relations*. Kongelige Danske Videnskabernes Selskab Historisk-filosofiske Meddelelser 42(3), 45(2).

Bischof, Henning, and Julio Viteri Gamboa. 1972. "Pre-Valdivia Occupations on the Southwest Coast of Ecuador." *American Antiquity* 37(4):548–551.

Bjerck, Hein B. 2008. "Colonizing the So-called Margins: The Development of Marine Relations and the Colonization of Coastal Northwest Europe." *Irish Naturalists' Journal* 29 (special supplement): "Mind the Gap," pp. 35–44.

Blake, Michael. "Dating the Initial Spread of Zea Mays." *Histories of Maize*. John E. Staller, Robert H. Tykot, and Bruce F. Benz, eds. Amsterdam: Elsevier, 2006, pp. 55–72.

Blench, Roger M. 1982. "Evidence for the Indonesian Origins of Certain Elements of African Culture: A Review, with Special Reference to the Arguments of A. M. Jones." *African Music* 6(2):81–93.

———. "Using Linguistics to Reconstruct African Subsistence Systems: Comparing Crop Names to Trees and Livestock." *Rethinking Agriculture: Archaeological and Ethnoarchaeology Perspectives*. Tim Denham, José Iriarte, and Luc Vrydaghs, eds. Walnut Creek, CA: Left Coast Press, 2007, pp. 408–438.

———. 2009. "Bananas and Plantains in Africa: Reinterpreting the Linguistic Evidence." *Ethnobotany Research and Applications* 7:363–380.

———. "Evidence for the Austronesian Voyages in the Indian Ocean." *The Global Origins and Development of Seafaring*. Atholl Anderson, James H. Barrett, and Katherine V. Boyle, eds. Cambridge, UK: McDonald Institute for Archaeological Research, 2010, pp. 239–248.

———. 2014a. "Using Diverse Sources of Evidence for Reconstructing the Past History of Musical Exchanges in the Indian Ocean." *African Archaeological Review* 31:675–703.

———. 2014b. *Austronesian: An Agricultural Revolution that Failed*. Pre-circulated paper for Conference on Formosan Indigenous Peoples, Taipei, Taiwan, September 15–17, 2014.

———. 2014c. *The Boiling Pot: 4000 Years Ago in the Luzon Straits*. Pre-circulated paper for Conference on Formosan Indigenous Peoples, Taipei, Taiwan, September 15–17, 2014.

———. 2014d. *Lapita Canoes and their Multiethnic Crews: Marginal Austronesian Languages are Nonaustronesian*. Workshop on the Languages of Papua 3, Manokwari, West Papua, Indonesia, January 20–24, 2014.

Blomster, Jeffrey P. 2005. "Response [to Meggers' letter, same page]." *Science* 309:556.

Boas, Franz. "The Principles of Ethnological Classification; The Aims of Ethnology." *The Shaping of American Anthropology, 1883–1911: A Franz Boas Reader*. George W. Stocking, Jr., ed. New York: Basic Books,1974 (1887, 1889).

Boehm, David A., Stephen Topping, and Cyd Smith, eds. *Guinness Book of World Records*, 1983. New York: Sterling.

Bokenkamp, Stephen R. "This Foreign Religion of Ours: Lingbao Views of Buddhist Translation." *India in the Chinese Imagination: Myth, Religion, and Thoughts*. John Kieschnick and Meir Shahar, eds. Philadelphia: University of Pennsylvania Press, 2013, pp. 182–197.

Bonnefoy, Yves, compiler. *Asian Mythologies*. Translated under direction of Wendy Doniger. Chicago: University of Chicago Press, 1993.

Boruchoff, David A. "The Three Greatest Inventions of Modern Times: An Idea and Its Public." *Entangled Knowledge: Scientific Discourses and Cultural Difference*. Klaus Hock and Gesa Mackenthun, eds. Münster: Waxmann, 2012, pp. 133–163.

Bray, Francesca. "Agriculture." *Science and Civilisation in China* vol. 6, Pt. II. Cambridge: Cambridge University Press, 1984.

Broudy, Eric. *The Book of Looms: A History of the Handloom from Ancient Times to the Present*. New York: Van Nostrand Reinhold, 1979. (Reprinted 1993, University Press of New England, Hanover, NH.)

Bruhns, Karen Olsen. "Cihuatan Project News," April 2015. Online at http://on-line.sfsu.edu/kbruhns/cihuatan/news.htm, accessed 6/1/2015, and personal communication to Kehoe, January 2013.

Burger, Pauline, Armelle Charrié-Duhaut, Jacques Connan, Michael Flecker, and Pierre Albrecht. 2009. "Archaeological Resinous Samples from Asian Wrecks: Taxonomic Characterization by GC–MS." *Analytica Chimica Acta* 648(1):85–97.

Bushman, Claudia L. *America Discovers Columbus: How an Italian Explorer Became an American Hero.* Hanover, NH: University Press of New England, 1992.

Carson, Mike T., Hsiao-chun Hung, Glenn Summerhayes, and Peter Bellwood. 2013. "The Pottery Trail From Southeast Asia to Remote Oceania." *Journal of Island and Coastal Archaeology* 8:17–36.

Chang, Kwang-Chih. *The Archaeology of Ancient China.* New Haven: Yale University Press, 1977.

Chase, Arlen F. "Time Depth or Vacuum: The 11.3.0.0.0 Correlation and the Lowland Maya Postclassic." *Late Lowland Maya Civilization: Classic to Postclassic.* Jeremy A. Sabloff and E. Wyllys Andrews V, eds. Albuquerque: University of New Mexico Press, 1986, pp. 99–140.

"China's Oldest Peanuts." China Heritage Project 2007. www.chinaheritagequar-terly.org/briefs.php?searchterm=012_HAM_Briefs.inc&issue=012, accessed 6/18/2014.

Clarke, Anne, and Ursula Frederick. "Closing the Distance: Interpreting Cross-Cultural Engagements through Indigenous Rock Art." *Archaeology of Oceania.* Ian Lilley, ed. Malden, MA: Blackwell, 2006, pp. 116–133.

Cleland, Carol E. 2002. "Methodological and Epistemic Differences between Historical Science and Experimental Science." *Philosophy of Science* 69:474–496.

Cline, Eric H. *1177 B.C., The Year Civilization Collapsed.* Princeton: Princeton University Press, 2014.

Coggins, Clemency. 2002. "Toltec." *RES: Anthropology and Aesthetics* 42:34–85.

Compton, Stephen C. *Exodus Lost.* Published on Amazon Books, 2010.

Counsell, David J. "Intoxicants in Ancient Egypt? Opium, Nymphea, Coca and Tobacco." *Egyptian Mummies and Modern Science.* A. Rosalie David, ed. Cambridge: Cambridge University Press, 2008, pp. 195–215.

Craig, O. E., H. Saul, A. Lucquin, Y. Nishida, K. Taché, L. Clarke, A. Thompson, D. T. Altoft, J. Uchiyama, M. Ajimoto, K. Gibbs, S. Isakssson, C. P. Heron, and P. Jordan. 2013. "Earliest Evidence for the Use of Pottery." *Nature* 496:351–354.

Crawford, Michael, and Benjamin Campbell, eds. *Why Do We Migrate? An Interdisciplinary Exploration of Human Migration.* Cambridge: Cambridge University Press, 2012.

Crill, Rosemary. *Indian Ikat Textiles.* London: Victoria and Albert Museum, 1998.

Crook, Paul. *Grafton Elliot Smith, Egyptology and the Diffusion of Culture: A Biographical Perspective.* Eastbourne: Sussex Academic Press, 2012.

Curtin, Philip D. *Cross-cultural Trade in World History.* Cambridge: Cambridge University Press, 1984.

Davis, Virginia. "Resist Dyeing in Mexico: Comments on Its History, Significance, and Prevalence." *Textile Traditions of Mesoamerica and the Andes: An Anthology.* Margot Blum Schevill, Janet Catherine Berlo, and Edward B. Dwyer, eds. Austin: University of Texas Press, 1991, pp. 311–336.

De Langhe, Edmond. "The Establishment of Traditional Plantain Cultivation in the African Rain Forest: A Working Hypothesis." *Rethinking Agriculture: Archaeological and Ethnoarchaeology Perspectives*. Tim Denham, José Iriarte, and Luc Vrydaghs, eds. Walnut Creek, CA: Left Coast Press, 2007, pp. 361–370.

Dickason, Olive Patricia. *The Myth of the Savage*. Edmonton: University of Alberta Press, 1984.

Diehl, Richard A., and Margaret D. Mandeville. 1987. "Tula, and Wheeled Animal Effigies in Mesoamerica." *Antiquity* 61(232):239–246.

Doijode, S. D. *Seed Storage of Horticultural Crops*. Boca Raton FL: CRC Press, 2001.

Doran, Edwin, Jr. *Nao, Junk, and Vaka: Boats and Culture History*. College Station: Texas A&M University, 1973.

Drake, Brandon L. 2012. "The Influence of Climatic Change on the Late Bronze Age Collapse and the Greek Dark Ages." *Journal of Archaeological Science* 39(6): 1862–1870.

Drögemuller, Cord, Elinor K. Karlsson, Marjo K. Hytönen, Michele Perloski, Gaudenz Dolf, Kirsi Sainio, Hannes Lohi, Kerstin Lindblad-Toh, Tosso Leeb. 2008. "A Mutation in Hairless Dogs Implicates FOXI3 in Ectodermal Development." *Science* 321(5895):1462.

Dumarçay, Jacques. *Architecture and Its Models in South-East Asia*. Bangkok: Orchid Press, 2003.

Edlin, Duncan. "The Stoned Age?" Interview with Balabanova. Online at www .hallofmaat.com/modules.php?name=Articles&file=article&sid=45, accessed June 4, 2014.

Ekholm, Gordon. 1946. "Wheeled Toys in Mexico." *American Antiquity* 11:222–228.

———.1950. "Is American Indian Culture Asiatic?" *Natural History* 59(8):344–351, 382.

———.1953. "A Possible Focus of Asiatic Influence in the Late Classic Cultures of Mesoamerica." *Memoirs of the Society for American Archaeology* 9:72–89.

Enghoff, Inge Bødker n.d. "Regionality and Biotope Exploitation in Danish Ertebølle and Adjacent Periods." Online at www.zmuc.dk/VerWeb/Stenalder-knogler/eng/index.htm. Accessed 2/3/2015.

Enghoff, Inge B., Brian R. MacKenzie, and Einer Eg Nielsen. 2007. "The Danish Fish Fauna During the Warm Atlantic Period (ca. 7000–3900 BC): Forerunner of Future Changes?" *Fisheries Research* 87:167–180.

Erickson, David L., Bruce D. Smith, Andrew C. Clarke, Daniel H. Sandweiss, and Noreen Tuross. 2005. "An Asian Origin for a 10,000-year-old Domesticated Plant in the Americas." *Proceedings of the National Academy of Sciences* 102(51):18315–18320.

Eriksson, Gunilla, and Kerstin Lidén. 2013. "Dietary Life Histories in Stone Age Northern Europe." *Journal of Anthropological Archaeology* 32(3):288–302.

Erlandson, Jon E. "Anatomically Modern Humans, Maritime Voyaging, and the Pleistocene Colonization of the Americas." *The First Americans*. Nina G. Jablonski, ed. San Francisco: California Academy of Sciences, 2002, pp. 59–92. Updated in *Prehistoric California: Archaeology and the Myth of Paradise*. L. Mark Raab and Terry L. Jones, ed. Salt Lake City: University of Utah Press, 2004, pp.108 –120.

Erlandson, Jon M., Michael H. Graham, Bruce J. Bourque, Debra Corbett, James A. Estes, and Robert J. Steneck. 2007. "The Kelp Highway Hypothesis: Marine Ecology, the Coastal Migration Theory, and the Peopling of the Americas." *Journal of Island & Coastal Archaeology* 2:161–174.

Erasmus, Charles J. 1950. "Patolli, Pachisi, and the Limitation of Possibilities." *Southwestern Journal of Anthropology* 6(4):369–387.

Estrada, Emilio, and Betty J. Meggers. 1961. "A Complex of Traits of Probable Transpacific Origin on the Coast of Ecuador." *American Anthropologist* 63(5):913–939.

Evans, Susan Toby, and David L. Webster, eds. *Archaeology of Ancient Mexico and Central America: An Encyclopedia.* New York: Taylor and Francis, 2001.

Feinberg, Richard. *Polynesian Seafaring and Navigation.* Kent OH: Kent State University Press, 1993 [1988].

Finney, Ben. 1994. "Polynesian-South America Round Trip Canoe Voyages." *Rapa Nui Journal* 8(2):33–35.

Fitzhugh, William. 1974. "Ground Slates in the Scandinavian Younger Stone Age with Reference to Circumpolar Maritime Adaptations. *Proceedings of the Prehistoric Society* 40:45–58.

———. "Arctic Cultures and Global Theory: Historical Tracks Along the Circumpolar Road." *A Circumpolar Reappraisal: The Legacy of Gutorm Gjessing.* Christer Westerdahl, ed. Oxford: BAR International Series 2154, 2010, pp. 87–109.

Forbes, Jack D. *The American Discovery of Europe.* Urbana: University of Illinois Press, 2007.

Ford, James A. *A Comparison of Formative Cultures in the Americas: Diffusion or the Psychic Unity of Man.* Smithsonian Contributions to Anthropology vol. 11. Washington, D.C: Smithsonian Institution Press, 1969.

Fornander, Elin, Gunilla Eriksson, and Kerstin Lidén. 2008. "Wild at Heart: Approaching Pitted Ware Identity, Economy and Cosmology through Stable Isotopes in Skeletal Material from the Neolithic Site Korsnäs in Eastern Central Sweden." *Journal of Anthropological Archaeology* 27:281–297.

Fowler, William R. "The Figurines of Cihuatan, El Salvador." *The New World Figurine Project,* vol. I. Terry Stocker, ed. Provo, UT: Research Press, 1991, pp. 39–53.

Fraser, Douglas. 1965. "Theoretical Issues in the Transpacific Diffusion Controversy." *Social Research* 32:(4)452–477.

Garrow, Duncan, and Fraser Sturt. 2011. "The Mesolithic-Neolithic Transition within the 'Western Seaways' of Britain, c. 5000–3500 BC." *Antiquity* 85:59–72.

Gavin, Traude. "Triangle and Tree: Austronesian Themes in the Design Interpretation of Indonesian Textiles." *Five Centuries of Indonesian Textiles.* Ruth Barnes and Mary Hunt Kahlenberg, eds. Munich: Delmonico Books-Prestel, 2010, pp. 227–239.

Gellner, David N. 2005. "The Emergence of Conversion in a Hindu-Buddhist Polytropy: The Kathmandu Valley, Nepal, c. 1600–1995." *Comparative Studies in Society and History* 47(4):755–780.

Gibbs, Kevin, and Peter Jordan. 2013. "Bridging the Boreal Forest." *Sibirica* 12(1):1–38.

Gjessing, Gutorm. 1948. "Some Problems in Northeastern Archaeology." *American Antiquity* 13(4):298–302.

———. "Maritime Adaptations in Northern Norway's Prehistory. *Prehistoric Maritime Adaptations of the Circumpolar Zone.* William Fitzhugh, ed. The Hague: Mouton, 1973, pp. 87–100.

Glover, Ian. 1977. "The Late Stone Age in Eastern Indonesia." *World Archaeology* 9:42–61.

Goldenweiser, Alexander A. 1913. "The Principle of Limited Possibilities in the Development of Culture." *Journal of American Folklore* 26:259–290.

Goldenweiser, Alexander. "The Diffusion Controversy." *Culture, the Diffusion Controversy.* New York: W. W. Norton, 1927, pp. 99–106.

Green, Roger C. 2005. "Sweet Potato Transfers in Polynesian Prehistory." *The Sweet Potato in Oceania: A Reappraisal.* Chris Ballard, Paula Brown, R. Michael Bourke, and Tracy Harwood, eds. Pittsburgh: Ethnology Monographs 19 (Oceania Monographs 56), pp. 43–62.

Guy, John S. *Oriental Trade Ceramics in South-East Asia, Ninth to Sixteenth Centuries: with a Catalogue of Chinese, Vietnamese and Thai Wares in Australian Collections.* Oxford: Oxford University Press, 1986.

———. "South Indian Buddhism and Its Southeast Asian Legacy." *Cultural Interface of India with Asia.* Anupa Pande and Parul Pandya Dhar, eds. New Delhi: National Museum Institute, Monograph Series, no. 1, 2003, pp. 155–175.

Hägerstrand, Torsten. *Innovation Diffusion as a Spatial Process.* Chicago: University of Chicago Press, 1967.

Hallgren, Fredrik. *Identitet i praktik. Lokala, regionala och överregionala sociala sammanhang inom nordlig trattbägarkultur.* (Identity in Practice. Local, Regional and Pan-Regional Aspects of the Northern Funnel Beaker Culture). Uppsala: Coast to Coast Books 17, Uppsala University, 2008. Online English summary. www .northerntrb.net/about.html, accessed 2/2/2015.

Hamdani, Abbas. 2006. "Arabic Sources for the Pre-Columbian Voyages of Discovery." *Maghreb Review* 31(3–4):203–221.

Hather, Jon G., and Patrick V. Kirch. 1991. "Prehistoric Sweet Potato (*Ipomoea batatas*) from Mangaia Island, Central Polynesia." *Antiquity* 65:887–893.

Hauser-Schäublin, Birgitta, Marie-Louise Nabholz-Kartaschoff, and Urs Ramseyer. *Balinese Textiles.* London: British Museum Press, 1991.

He, Hongyi. 2005. "Mexican Paper-cut and Chinese Culture." *China's Ethnic Groups* 3(2):116–117.

Heine-Geldern, Robert. 1950. "Cultural Connections between Asia and Pre-Columbian America." *Anthropos* 45:350–352.

———. "American Metallurgy and the Old World." *Early Chinese Art and Its Possible Influence in the Pacific Basin,* vol. 2. Noel Barnard, ed. New York: Intercultural Arts Press, 1972, pp. 787–822.

Heine-Geldern, Robert, and Gordon Ekholm. "Significant Parallels in the Symbolic Arts of Southern Asia and Middle America." *The Civilizations of Ancient America.* Selected Papers of the XXIXth International Congress of Americanists. Sol Tax, ed. Chicago: University of Chicago Press, 1951, pp. 299–309.

Herbert, Sharon. "Excavating Ethnic Strata: The Search for Hellenistic Phoenicians in the Upper Galilee of Israel." *The Politics of Archaeology and Identity in a Global Context.* Susan Kane, ed. Boston: The Archaeological Institute of America, 2003, pp. 101–115.

Higham, Charles. *The Civilization of Angkor.* Berkeley: University of California Press, 2001.

Hill, Joyce. 1983. "From Rome to Jerusalem: An Icelandic Itinerary of the Mid-Twelfth Century." *Harvard Theological Review* 76(2):175–203.

Hodgen, Margaret T. *Early Anthropology in the Sixteenth and Seventeenth Centuries.* Philadelphia, PA: University of Pennsylvania Press, 1964.

Holmes, William H. "Stone Implements of the Potomac-Chesapeake Tidewater Province." *Fifteenth Annual Report of the Bureau of American Ethnology, 1893–94.* Washington, D.C.: Government Printing Office, 1897.

Hristov, Romeo H., and Santiago Genovés T. 2001. "Reply to Peter Schaaf and Gunther A. Wagner's 'Comments on "Mesoamerican Evidence of Pre-Columbian Transoceanic Contacts."'" *Ancient Mesoamerica* 12:83–86.

Hung, Hsiao-Chun, Yoshiyuki Iizuka, Peter Bellwood, Kim Dung Nguyen, Bérénice Bellina, Praon Silapanth, Eusebio Dizon, Rey Santiago, Ipoi Datan, and Jonathan H. Manton. 2007. "Ancient Jades Map 3,000 Years of Prehistoric Exchange in Southeast Asia." *Proceedings of the National Academy of Sciences* 104(50):19745–19750.

Hurley, Patrick J. *A Concise Introduction to Logic.* Eleventh ed. Boston: Wadsworth, 2012.

Iltis, Hugh H. "Origin of Polistichy in Maize." *Histories of Maize.* John E. Staller, Robert H. Tykot, and Bruce F. Benz, eds. Amsterdam: Elsevier, 2006, pp. 21–53.

Ingstad, Anne Stine. *The Discovery of a Norse Settlement in America: Excavations at L'Anse aux Meadows, Newfoundland 1961–1968.* Oslo: Universitetsforlaget, 1977.

Ingstad, Helge. *The Norse Discovery of America: The Historical Background and the Evidence of the Norse Settlement Discovered in Newfoundland.* Vol. 2. Oslo: Norwegian University Press, 1985.

———. *The Viking Discovery of America: The Excavation of a Norse Settlement in L'Anse aux Meadows, Newfoundland.* New York: Checkmark, 2001.

Iriarte, José. "New Perspectives on Plant Domestication and the Development of Agriculture in the New World." *Rethinking Agriculture: Archaeological and Ethnoarchaeology Perspectives.* Tim Denham, José Iriarte, and Luc Vrydaghs, eds. Walnut Creek, CA: Left Coast Press, 2007, pp. 167–188.

Irwin, Geoffrey. "Pacific Voyaging and Settlement: Issues of Biogeography and Archaeology, Canoe Performance and Computer Simulation." *The Global Origins and Development of Seafaring.* Atholl Anderson, James H. Barrett, and Katherine V. Boyle, eds. Cambridge: McDonald Institute for Archaeological Research, 2010, pp. 131–142.

Jackson, L. J. 1986. "New Evidence for Early Woodland Seasonal Adaptation from Southern Ontario, Canada." *American Antiquity* 51(2):389–401.

Jarus, Owen. 2015. "Evidence of Pre-Columbus Trade Found in Alaska House." Online at Livescience at www.livescience.com/50507-artifacts-reveal-new-world-trade-photos.html, accessed 5/12/2015.

Jaynes, Edwin T. *Probability Theory: The Logic of Science.* Cambridge: Cambridge University Press, 2003. ©1995, online at www-biba.inrialpes.fr/Jaynes/cpream-bl.pdf, accessed 2/23/2015.

Jett, Stephen C. 1970. "The Development and Distribution of the Blowgun." *Annals of the Association of American Geographers* 60:662–688.

———. 1991 "Further Information on the Geography of the Blowgun and Its Implications for Early Transoceanic Contacts." *Annals of the Association of American Geographers* 81(1):89–102.

———. 2008, 2009, 2010. "Recent Works on the Hairless Culinary Dog in America and in China." *Pre-Columbiana: A Journal of Long-Distance Contacts.* 4(34)/5(1), 44–46.

———. *Ancient Ocean Crossings: The Case for Pre-Columbian Contacts Reconsidered.* Tuscaloosa, AL: University of Alabama Press, 2016.

Johannessen, Carl, and Ann Z. Parker. 1989. "Maize Ears Sculptured in 12th and 13th Century A.D. India as Indicators of Pre-Columbian Diffusion." *Economic Botany* 43:164–180.

Johnstone, Paul. *The Sea-craft of Prehistory*. Cambridge: Harvard University Press, 1980.

Jones, Terry L. "The Artifact Record from North America." *Polynesians in America: Pre-Columbian Contacts with the New World*. Terry L. Jones, Alice A. Storey, Elizabeth A. Matisoo-Smith, and José Miguel Ramírez-Aliaga, eds. Lanham, MD: AltaMira, 2011, pp. 71–93.

Jordan, Peter. "Sacred Landscapes of Siberia: Symbolic Uses of Space by Hunter-Gatherers." *Archaeology International* 2002/3:33–36. London: UCL Press, 2003.

———. *Technology as Human Social Tradition*. Berkeley: University of California Press, 2015.

Joyce, Rosemary A., and David C. Grove. "Asking New Questions About the Mesoamerican Pre-Classic." *Social Patterns in Pre-Classic Mesoamerica*. Rosemary A. Joyce and David C. Grove, eds. Washington, D.C.: Dumbarton Oaks, 1999.

Jumsai, Sumet. *Naga: Cultural Origins in Siam and the West Pacific*. Singapore: Oxford University Press, 1988.

Kahlenberg, Mary Hunt. "Close Observations and Priceless Memories." *Five Centuries of Indonesian Textiles*. Ruth Barnes and Mary Hunt Kahlenberg, eds. Munich: Delmonico Books-Prestel, 2010, pp. 11–25.

Keay, John. *The Spice Route*. Berkeley: University of California Press, 2006.

Keddie, Grant. "The Question of Asiatic Objects on the North Pacific Coast of America: Historic or Prehistoric?" *Contributions to Human History* no. 3, Royal British Columbia Museum, Victoria, 1990.

Kehoe, Alice B. 1962. "A Hypothesis on the Origin of Northeastern American Pottery." *Southwestern Journal of Anthropology* 18:20–29.

———. "Small Boats Upon the North Atlantic." *Man Across the Sea*. Carroll L. Riley, J. Charles Kelley, Campbell W. Pennington, and Robert L. Rands, eds. Austin: University of Texas Press, 1971, pp. 275–292.

———.1978. "Early Civilizations in Asia and Mesoamerica." Report of 1977 Wenner-Gren conference organized by Kehoe and David H. Kelley. *Current Anthropology* 19(1):204–205.

———. 1979. "The Sacred Heart: A Case for Stimulus Diffusion." *American Ethnologist* 6:763–771.

———. "'In Fourteen Hundred and Ninety-two, Columbus Sailed...': The Primacy of the National Myth in American Schools." *The Excluded Past*. Peter Stone and Robert MacKenzie, eds. London: Unwin Hyman, 1990, pp. 201–216.

———. *The Land of Prehistory: A Critical History of American Archaeology*. New York: Routledge, 1998.

———. "From Spirit Cave to the Blackfoot Rez: The Importance of Twined Fabric in North American Indian Societies." *Fleeting Identities*. Penelope Drooker, ed. Carbondale: Southern Illinois University Press, 2001, pp. 210–225.

———. "Deconstructing John Locke." *Postcolonial Perspectives in Archaeology*. Peter Bikouis, Dominic Lacroix, and Meaghan M. Peuramaki-Brown, eds. Calgary: University of Calgary Archaeological Association, 2009, pp. 125–132.

———. "'Prehistory's' History." *The Death of Prehistory*. Peter R. Schmidt and Stephen A. Mrozowski, eds. New York: Oxford University Press, 2013, pp. 31–46.

Kelley, David H. 1960. "Calendar Animals and Deities." *Southwestern Journal of Anthropology* 16(3):317–337.

———. 1990. "The Invention of the Mesoamerican Calendar." Unpublished ms., archived at University of Calgary.

Kelley, David H., and Eugene F. Milone. *Exploring Ancient Skies*. 2nd ed. New York: Springer, 2011.

Kipp, Darrell Robes. 2010. Opening address, Blackfoot History Symposium, Cutswood School, Browning, MT, August 20, 2010.

Kirch, Patrick V. 2010. "Peopling of the Pacific: A Holistic Anthropological Perspective." *Annual Reviews in Anthropology* 39:131–148.

Kirch, Patrick Vinton, and Roger C. Green. *Hawaiki, Ancestral Polynesia*. Cambridge: Cambridge University Press, 2001.

Kirchoff, Paul. 1964. "The Diffusion of a Great Religious System from India to Mexico." *Actas del XXV Congreso Internacional Americanistas* I:73–100.

Kistler, Logan, Álvaro Montenegro, Bruce D. Smith, John A. Gifford, Richard E. Green, Lee A. Newsom, and Beth Shapiro. 2014. "Transoceanic Drift and the Domestication of African Bottle Gourds in the Americas." *Proceedings of the National Academy of Sciences* 111(8): 2937–2941.

Klar, Kathryn A. "Words from Furthest Polynesia: North and South American Linguistic Evidence for Prehistoric Contact." *Polynesians in America: Pre-Columbian Contacts with the New World*. Terry L. Jones, Alice A. Storey, Elizabeth A. Matisoo-Smith, and José Miguel Ramírez-Aliaga, eds. Lanham, MD: AltaMira, 2011, pp. 194–207.

Klausen, Arne Martin, ed. *Kultur og Diffusjon*. University Ethnographic Museum, Oslo, Bulletin 10. Oslo: Universitetsforlaget, 1961.

Kolodny, Annette 2012 *Search of First Contact: The Vikings of Vinland, the Peoples of the Dawnland, and the Anglo-American Anxiety of Discovery*. Durham NC: Duke University Press.

Kristiansen, Kristian, and Thomas B. Larsson. *The Rise of Bronze Age Society*. Cambridge: Cambridge University Press, 2005.

Kroeber, A. L. "Stimulus Diffusion." *The Nature of Culture*. Chicago: University of Chicago Press, 1952(1940), pp. 344–357.

———. *Anthropology*. New York: Harcourt Brace, 1948.

Kuhn, Thomas. *The Structure of Scientific Revolutions*. 2nd ed. Chicago: University of Chicago Press, 1970[1962].

Kuhnt-Saptodewo, Sri. "Indian Influences." *The Art of East Asia*, vol. I. Gabriele Fahr–Becker, ed. Cologne: Könemann, 1999, pp. 312–385.

Lacan, Marie, Christine Keyser, François-Xavier Ricaut, Nicolas Brucato, Francis Duranthon, Jean Guilaine, Eric Crubézy, and Bertrand Ludes. 2011. "Ancient DNA Reveals Male Diffusion Through the Neolithic Mediterranean Route." *Proceedings of the National Academy of Sciences* 108(24):9788–9791.

Ladefoged, Thegn N., Michael W. Graves, and James H. Coil. 2005. "The Introduction of Sweet Potato in Polynesia: Early Remains in Hawai'i." *Journal of the Polynesian Society* 114(4):359–373.

La Flesche, Francis. *The Osage Tribe: Two Versions of the Child-naming Rite*. 43rd Annual Report, Bureau of American Ethnology, Smithsonian Institution. Washington, D.C.: Government Printing Office, 1928, pp. 23–164.

Lakoff, George, and Mark Johnson. *Metaphors We Live By*. Chicago: University of Chicago Press, 1980.

Larsen, Helge, and Froelich Rainey. *Ipiutak and the Arctic Whale Hunting Culture*. Anthropological Paper No. 42. New York: American Museum of Natural History, 1948.

Laskaris, N., A. Sampson, F. Mavridis, and I. Liritzis. 2011. "Late Pleistocene/Early Holocene Seafaring in the Aegean: New Obsidian Hydration Dates with the SIMS-SS Method." *Journal of Archaeological Science* 38:2475–2479.

Lathrap, Donald W. 1967. "Review of Meggers, Evans, and Estrada, 'Early Formative Period of Coastal Ecuador: The Valdivia and Machalilla Phases.'" *American Anthropologist* 69(1):96–98.

———.1973. "Summary or Model Building: How Does One Achieve a Meaningful Overview of a Continent's Prehistory. Review of Gordon R. Willey, An Introduction to American Archaeology," Vol. 2: South America. *American Anthropologist* 75(6):1755–1767.

———. "Our Father the Cayman, Our Mother the Gourd: Spinden Revisited, or a Unitary Model for the Emergence of Agriculture in the New World." *Origins of Agriculture.* Charles A. Reed, ed. The Hague: Mouton, 1977, pp. 713–751.

Laufer, Berthold. 1930. "The Early History of Felt." *American Anthropologist* n.s. 32(1):1–18.

Layton, Robert H. "Hunter-gatherers, their Neighbors and the Nation States." *Hunter-Gatherers, an Interdisciplinary Perspective.* Catherine Panter-Brick, Robert H. Layton, and Peter Rowly-Conwy, eds. Cambridge: University of Cambridge Press, 2001, pp. 292–321.

Lee, Sherman. *A History of Far Eastern Art.* Fifth ed. Naomi Noble Richard, ed. New York: Harry N. Abrams, 1994.

Leidy, Denise Patry. *The Art of Buddhism: An Introduction to Its History and Meaning.* Boston: Shambhala, 2008.

Leighly, John. 1976. "Carl Ortwin Sauer, 1889–1975." *Annals Of The Association Of American Geographers* 66(3):337–348.

Lewis, Archibald R., and Timothy J. Runyan. *European Naval and Maritime History, 300–1500.* Bloomington: Indiana University Press, 1985.

Lieberman, Victor B. *Strange Parallels: Southeast Asia in Global Context, c. 800–1830.* Cambridge: Cambridge University Press, 2003 (vol. I) and 2009 (vol. II).

Linduff, Katheryn M., and Jianjun Mei. 2008. "Metallurgy in Ancient Eastern Asia: How Is It Studied? Where Is the Field Headed?" Presented at Society of American Archaeology 73rd annual meeting, Vancouver B.C. Online at www.britishmuseum.org/pdf/Linduff%20Mei%20China.pdf, accessed 6/5/2015.

Linton, Ralph. 1931. "One hundred per cent American." *American Mercury* 40: 427–29.

Littman, Edwin R. 1958. "Ancient Mesoamerican Mortars, Plasters, and Stuccos: Comalcalco, Part II." *American Antiquity* 23(3):292–296.

Locke, John. "Two Treatises of Government." *Two Treatises of Government and A Letter Concerning Toleration.* Ian Shapiro, ed. New Haven: Yale University Press 2003[1689], pp. 3–209.

Lunenfeld, Marvin. "Columbus-Bashing: Culture Wars Over the Construction of an Anti-Hero." *Columbus: Meeting of Cultures.* Columbus Supplement, Filibrary no. 4. Mario B. Mignone, ed. Stony Brook NY: Forum Italicum, 1993, pp. 1–12.

Lyman, Stanford M. "Asian American Contacts before Columbus." *Civilization: Contents, Discontents, Malcontents, and Other Essays in Social Theory.* Fayetteville: University of Arkansas Press, 1990, pp. 46–75.

Macpherson, C. B. *The Political Theory of Possessive Individualism.* Oxford: Oxford University Press, 1962.

Mair, Victor. *Painting and Performance: Chinese Picture Recitation and Its Indian Genesis.* Honolulu: University of Hawai'i Press, 1988.

Malinowski, Bronislaw. *Argonauts of the Western Pacific.* London: Routledge and Kegan Paul, 1922.

———. "The Life of Culture." *Culture, the Diffusion Controversy.* New York: W. W. Norton, 1927, pp. 28–46.

Malmström, H., A. Linderholm, P. Skoglund, J. Storå, P. Sjödin, M. T. Gilbert, G. Holmlund, E. Willerslev, M. Jakobsson, K. Lidén, and A. Götherström. 2015. "Ancient Mitochondrial DNA from the Northern Fringe of the Neolithic Farming Expansion in Europe Sheds Light on the Dispersion Process." *Philosophical Transactions of the Royal Society of London B, Biol Sci.* 2015 Jan:370.

Martí, Samuel. *Mudrā: Manos Simbólicas en Asia y América.* Two editions. México, D. F.: Ediciones Euroamericanas, 1971, 1992.

Matisoo-Smith, Elizabeth A. "Human Biological Evidence for Polynesian Contacts with the Americas." *Polynesians in America: Pre-Columbian Contacts with the New World.* Terry L. Jones, Alice A. Storey, Elizabeth A. Matisoo-Smith, and José Miguel Ramírez-Aliaga, eds. Lanham, MD: AltaMira, 2011, pp. 208–222.

———. 2014. "Ancient DNA and the Human Settlement of the Pacific: A Review." *Journal of Human Evolution* 30:1–12.

McCartney, Allen P. "Late Prehistoric Metal Use in the New World Arctic." *The Late Prehistoric Development of Alaska's Native People.* Robert D. Shaw, Roger K. Harritt, and Don E. Dumond, eds. Aurora AK: Alaska Anthropological Association Monograph Series, 1988, pp. 57–79.

McGrail, Seán. *Studies in Maritime Archaeology.* Oxford: BAR British Series 256, 1997.

———. *Boats of the World: From the Stone Age to Medieval Times.* Oxford: Oxford University Press, 2001.

Meggers, Betty J. 1975. "The Transpacific Origin of Mesoamerican Civilization: A Preliminary Review of the Evidence and Its Theoretical Implications." *American Anthropologist* 77(1):1–27.

———. 2005. The Origins of Olmec Civilization [Letter]. *Science* 309:556.

Meggers, Betty J., Clifford Evans, and Emilio Estrada. "Early Formative Period of Coastal Ecuador: the Valdivia and Machalilla Phases." *Smithsonian Contributions to Anthropology*, Vol. 1. Washington, D.C.: Smithsonian Institution, 1965.

Merrien, Jean (real name, René Marie de la Poix de Fréminville). *Lonely Voyagers [Les Navigateurs Solitaires].* English translation 1954, by J. H. Watkins. New York: G. P. Putnam's Sons, 1954.

Merton, Robert K. *The Sociology of Science: Theoretical and Empirical Investigations.* Chicago: University of Chicago, 1973.

McMillan, Alan D. *Since the Time of the Transformers: The Ancient Heritage of the Nuuchah-nulth, Ditidaht, and Makah.* Vancouver: University of British Columbia Press, 1999.

Metropolitan Museum of Art. 2014. *Lost Kingdoms: Hindu-Buddhist Sculpture of Early Southeast Asia.* www.metmuseum.org/.../lost-kingdoms, accessed 7/22/2014.

Miller, Mary, and Karl Taube. *The Gods and Symbols of Ancient Mexico and the Maya.* New York: Thames and Hudson, 1993.

Montenegro, Alvaro, Richard T. Callaghan, and Scott M. Fitzpatrick. 2014. "From West to East: Environmental Influences on the Rate and Pathways of Polynesian Colonization." *The Holocene* 24(2):242–256.

Morgan, Lewis Henry. *Ancient Society.* Tucson: University of Arizona Press, 1985[1877] (facsimile).

Morrison, Kathleen D., and Laura L. Junker, eds. *Forager-Traders in South and Southeast Asia: Long Term Histories.* Cambridge: Cambridge University Press, 2002.

Mountjoy, Joseph. "An Archaeological Patolli from Tomatlan, Jalisco, Mexico." *Contributions to the Archaeology and Ethnohistory of Greater Mesoamerica.* William J. Folan, ed. Carbondale, IL: Southern Illinois University Press, 1985, pp. 240–262.

Müller, Romy, Charlotte A. Roberts, and Terence A. Brown. 2015. "Complications in the Study of Ancient Tuberculosis: Non-specificity of IS6110 PCRs." *Science and Technology of Archaeological Research* 1(1):1–8. STAR 2015; 1(1), STAR20141 12054892314Y.0000000002.

Nault, Lowell R., Richard C. Pratt, Patrick Finney, and Christine J. Bergman. 1995. Four Letters to Carl Johannessen. Manuscripts on file from Seminar at Ohio Agricultural Research and Development Center, Ohio State University, organized by Jeneen Beckett, Wooster, OH.

Needham, Joseph. "General Conclusions and Reflections." *Science and Civilisation in China,* vol. 7, pt. II. Kenneth Girdwood Robinson, ed. Cambridge: Cambridge University Press, 2004.

Needham, Joseph, and Lu Gwei-Djen. "Chemistry and Chemical Technology: Spagyrical Discovery and Invention: Physiological Alchemy." *Science and Civilisation in China,* vol. 5, pt. V. Cambridge: Cambridge University Press, 1983.

———. *Trans-Pacific Echoes and Resonances: Listening Once Again.* Singapore: World Scientific, 1985.

Needham, Joseph, and Wang Ling. *Science and Civilisation in China,* vol. 5, pt. II. Cambridge: Cambridge University Press, 1965.

Needham, Joseph, Wang Ling, and Lu Gwei-Djen. *Science and Civilisation in China,* vol. 4, pt. III. Cambridge: Cambridge University Press, 1971.

Neff, Hector. 2011. "Evolution of the Mesoamerican Mother Culture." *Ancient Mesoamerica* 22:107–122.

Newman, Marshall T. 1950. "The Blond Mandan: a Critical Review of an Old Problem." *Southwestern Journal of Anthropology* 6:255–272.

Nichols, Johanna. "The Eurasian Spread Zone and the Indo-European Dispersal." *Archaeology and Language I: Theoretical and Methodological Orientations.* Roger Blench and Matthew Spriggs, eds. New York: Routledge, 1997, pp. 220–266.

O'Connor, Sue, Rintaro Ono, and Chris Clarkson. 2011. "Pelagic Fishing at 42,000 Years Before the Present and the Maritime Skills of Modern Humans." *Science* 334:1117–1121.

Olalde, Iñigo, and Carles Lalueza-Fox. 2015. "Modern Humans' Paleogenomics and the New Evidences on the European Prehistory." *Science and Technology of Archaeological Research (STAR)* 1(1):1–9.

Olmos, Ileana I. 2009. "El Tajin: Preserving the Legacy of a Unique Pre-Columbian Architecture in Mesoamerica." M.A. thesis, University of Florida. Online at http://ufdcimages.uflib.ufl.edu/UF/E0/04/10/40/00001/olmossparks_i.pdf, accessed 2/7/2015.

Onians, John. *Neuroarthistory.* New Haven: Yale University Press, 2007.

O'Reilly, Dougald J. W. *Early Civilizations of Southeast Asia.* Lanham, MD: AltaMira, 2007.

Paine, Lincoln. *The Sea and Civilization: A Maritime History of the World*. New York: Knopf, 2013.

Palloni, Alberto. 1998. *Theories and Models of Diffusion in Sociology*. Center for Demography and Ecology, University of Wisconsin-Madison, CDE Working Paper No. 98–11.

Paludan, Ann. *Chinese Tomb Figurines*. Oxford: Oxford University Press, 1994.

Pande, Anupa, and Parul Pandya Dhar, eds. *Culture Interface of India with Asia*. New Delhi: D. K. Printworld and National Museum Institute, 2003.

Papmehl-Dufay, Ludvig. "Pitted Ware Culture Ceramics: Aspects of Pottery Production and Use at Ottenby Royal Manor, Öland, Sweden." *Ceramics Before Farming: The Dispersal of Pottery Among Prehistoric Eurasian Hunter-Gatherers*. Peter Jordan and Marek Zvelebil, eds. Walnut Creek, CA: Left Coast Press, 2009, pp. 421–445.

Parlett, David. *The Oxford History of Board Games*. Oxford: Oxford University Press, 1999.

Paulsen, Allison C. 1977. "Differential Survival of the Jomon-Valdivia Hypothesis." *American Anthropologist* 79(3):652–653.

Pearson, Richard. 1968. "Migration from Japan to Ecuador: The Japanese Evidence." *American Anthropologist* 70(1):85–86.

Pepper, Stephen C. *World Hypotheses*. Berkeley: University of California Press, 1942.

Perrier, Xavier, Edmond De Langhe, Mark Donohue, Carol Lentfer, Luc Vrydaghs, Frédéric Bakry, Françoise Carreel, Isabelle Hippolyte, Jean-Pierre Horry, Christophe Jenny, Vincent Lebot, Ange-Marie Risterucci, Kodjo Tomekpe, Hugues Doutrelepont, Terry Ball, Jason Manwaring, Pierre de Maret, and Tim Denham. 2011. "Multidisciplinary Perspectives on Banana (Musa spp.) Domestication." *Proceedings of the National Academy of Sciences* 108(28):11311–11318.

Philippsen, Bente, and John Meadows. 2014 "Inland Ertebølle Culture: The Importance of Aquatic Resources and the Freshwater Reservoir Effect in Radiocarbon Dates from Pottery Food Crusts." *Internet Archaeology* 37, http://intarch
.ac.uk/journal/issue37/9/toc.html.

Phillips, Kelly M. 2014. "Solutrean Seal Hunters? Modeling Transatlantic Migration Parameters Fundamental to the Solutrean Hypothesis for the Peopling of North America." *Journal of Anthropological Research* 70(4):573–600.

Piperno, Dolores R. *Phytoliths: A Comprehensive Guide for Archaeologists and Paleoecologists*. Lanham, MD: AltaMira, 2006.

Politis, Gustavo G. *Nukak: Ethnoarchaeology of an Amazonian People*. Translated by Benjamin Alberti. Paperback edition. Walnut Creek, CA: Left Coast Press, 2009[2007].

Pomeranz, Kenneth, and Steven Topik. *The World That Trade Created*. Armonk, NY: M. E. Sharpe, 2013.

Pringle, Heather. 2012. "Vikings and Native Americans." *National Geographic* online at http://ngm.nationalgeographic.com/2012/11/vikings-and-indians/pringle-text, accessed 1/27/2015.

Proskouriakoff, Tatiana. *An Album of Maya Architecture*. Norman: University of Oklahoma Press, 1963.

Pryce, Thomas Oliver, Sandrine Baron, Bérénice H.M. Bellina, Peter S. Bell-
wood, Nigel Chang, Pranab Chattopadhyay, Eusebio Dizon, Ian C. Glover,
Elizabeth Hamilton, Charles F.W. Higham, Aung Aung Kyaw, Vin Laychour,
Surapol Natapintu, Viet Nguyen, Jean-Pierre Pautreau, Ernst Pernicka, Vin-
cent C. Pigott, Mark Pollard, Christophe Pottier, Andreas Reinecke, Thongsa
Sayavongkhamdy, Viengkeo Souksavatdy, Joyce White. 2014. "More Ques-
tions Than Answers: The Southeast Asian Lead Isotope Project 2009–2012."
*Journal of Archaeological Science* 42:273–294.

Quinn, David Beers. *England and the Discovery of America, 1481–1620*. London:
Allen and Unwin, 1974.

Rainey, Froelich. *Reflections of a Digger: Fifty Years of World Archaeology*. Philadelphia: University Museum of Archaeology and Anthropology, University of
Pennsylvania, 1992.

Relethford, John H. 2008. "Genetic Evidence and the Modern Human Origins
Debate." *Heredity* 100:555–563.

Ribeiro, Nuno, Anabela Joaqunito, and Sérgio Pereira. 2012. "New Unknown
Archaeological Data in Azores: The Hipogea of the Brazil Mount, Terceira
Island (Portugal) and its Parallels with the Cultures of the Mediterranean."
SOMA Mediterranean Archaeology Congress 2012. Serra Tomar, Portugal:
APIA [Portuguese Association of Archaeological Research].

Rogers, Everett M. *The Diffusion of Innovations*. New York: The Free Press, 1962.
Revised editions in 1973, 1983, 1988, 1995, 2003.

Roberts, Charlotte A., and Jane E. Buikstra. *The Bioarchaeology of Tuberculosis*.
Gainesville: University Press of Florida, 2003.

Roullier, Caroline, Laure Benoit, Doyle B. McKey, and Vincent Lebot. 2013. "Historical Collections Reveal Patterns of Diffusion of Sweet Potato in Oceania
Obscured by Modern Plant Movements and Cecombination." *Proceedings of
the National Academy of Sciences* 110(6):2205–2210.

Runnels, Curtis. 2014. "Early Paleolithic on the Greek Islands?" *Journal of Mediterranean Archaeology* 27(2):211–230.

Russell, Jeffrey Burton. *Inventing the Flat Earth: Columbus and Modern Historians*.
New York: Praeger, 1991.

Sandstrom, Alan R., and Pamela Effrein Sandstrom. *Traditional Papermaking and
Paper Cult Figures of Mexico*. Norman: University of Oklahoma Press, 1986.

Sandweiss, Daniel H. 2007. "Small is Big: The Microfossil Perspective on Hu-
man-Plant Interactions." *Proceedings of the National Academy of Sciences*
104(9): 3021–3022.

Sauer, Carl O. "Cultivated Plants of South and Central America." *Handbook of
South American Indians*, vol.6. Julian H. Steward, ed. Smithsonian Institution, Bureau of American Ethnology Bulletin 143. Washington, D.C.: Government Printing Office, 1950, pp. 487–543.

———. *Agricultural Origins and Dispersals*. New York: American Geographical
Society. Cambridge, MA: M.I.T. Press, 1952 (2nd ed. 1969).

———. "Maize into Europe." *Proceedings of the 34th International Congress of
Americanists* (Vienna, 1960). Horn-Vienna, Austria: Verlag Ferdinand Berger,
1962, pp. 777–788.

———. "Observations on Trade and Gold in the Early Spanish Main." *Carl O.
Sauer: A Tribute*. Martin S. Kenzer, ed. Corvallis: Oregon State University
Press, 1987, pp. 164–174.

Sauer, Jonathan D. *Historical Geography of Crop Plants: A Select Roster.* Boca Raton, FL: CRC Press, 1993.

Scaglio, Richard, and María-Auxiliadora Cordero. "Did Ancient Polynesians Reach the New World? Evaluating Evidence from the Ecuadorian Gulf of Guayaquil." *Polynesians in America: Pre-Columbian Contacts with the New World.* Terry L. Jones, Alice A. Storey, Elizabeth A. Matisoo-Smith, and José Miguel Ramírez-Aliaga, eds. Lanham, MD: AltaMira, 2011, pp. 171–193.

Schele, Linda, and Mary Ellen Miller. *The Blood of Kings.* New York: George Braziller, 1986.

Schledermann, Peter. 1980. "Notes on Norse Finds from the East Coast of Ellesmere Island, N. W. T." *Arctic* 33:454–463.

Schmidt, Peter R., and Stephen A. Mrozowski, eds. *Death of Prehistory.* New York: Oxford University Press, 2013.

Seaver, Kirsten A. *The Frozen Echo: Greenland and the Exploration of North America, Ca. A. D. 1000–1500.* Stanford: Stanford University Press, 1996.

Severin, Tim. *The Brendan Voyage.* New York: Avon, 1978.

Sedyawati, Edi. "From Kāvya Alaṁkāra to the Javanese Kagunan Basa." *Cultural Interface of India with Asia.* Anupa Pande and Parul Pandya Dhar, eds. New Delhi: National Museum Institute, Monograph Series no. 1, 2003, pp. 185–189.

Shaffer, Lynda Norene. *Maritime Southeast Asia to 1500.* Armonk, NY: M. E. Sharpe, 1996.

Shao, Paul. *Asiatic Influences in Pre-Columbian American Art.* Ames: Iowa State University Press, 1976.

———. *The Origin of Ancient American Cultures.* Ames: Iowa State University Press, 1983.

Sharrock, Peter D. "The Mystery of the Face Towers." *Bayon, New Perspectives.* Joyce Clark, ed. Bangkok: River Books, 2007, pp. 230–281. Cited pp. from online dated 07/29/2013, pages 1–54.

Shi, Zhiru. "From Bodily Relic to Dharma Relic Stūpa: Chinese Materialization of the Aśoka Legend in the Wuyue Period." *India in the Chinese Imagination.* John Kieschnick and Meir Shahar, eds. Philadelphia: University of Pennsylvania Press, 2014, pp. 83–109.

Simmons, Alan H. *Stone Age Sailors.* Walnut Creek CA: Left Coast Press, 2014.

Simpson, George Gaylord. "Uniformitarianism. An Inquiry into Principle, Theory, and Method in Geohistory and Biohistory." *Essays in Evolution and Genetics in Honor of Theodosius Dobzhansky.* Max K. Hecht and William C. Steere, eds. New York: Appleton-Century-Crofts, 1970, pp. 43–96.

Smith, Grafton Elliot. "The Diffusion of Culture." *Culture, the Diffusion Controversy.*[*] New York: W. W. Norton, 1927, pp. 9–25.

Smith, Joshua D. *Egypt and the Origin of Civilization: The British School of Culture Diffusion, 1890s–1940s.* Vindication Press (no place given), 2011. [Note that Joshua D. Smith is not the same person as Joshua James Smith, who works on the Boas Papers Project.]

[*] WorldCat and other bibliographic sources list the book as: Smith, Grafton Elliot, Bronislaw Malinowski, Herbert J. Spinden, and Alexander Goldenweiser. Culture, the Diffusion Controversy. New York: W. W. Norton, 1927.

Smith, Michael E. 2003. "Postclassic Urbanism at Calixtlahuaca: Reconstructing the Unpublished Excavations of José García Payón. FAMSI online www.famsi .org/reports/01024/01024Smith01.pdf, accessed 2/7/2015.

Solheim, Wilhelm G. II. *Archaeology and Culture in Southeast Asia: Unraveling the Nusantao.* Quezon City: The University of the Philippines Press, 2006.

Sorenson, John L., and Carl L. Johannessen. "Biological Evidence for Pre-Columbian Transoceanic Voyages." *Contact and Exchange in the Ancient World.* Victor H. Mair, ed. Honolulu: University of Hawai'i Press, 2006, pp. 238–297.

———. 2013. *World Trade and Biological Exchanges Before 1492 C.E.* Revised and Expanded Edition, published through Amazon.

Solyom, Garrett. "Heirloom Ceremonial Cloth (*bidak*)." *Five Centuries of Indonesian Textiles.* Ruth Barnes and Mary Hunt Kahlenberg, eds. Munich: Delmonico Books-Prestel, 2010, p. 49.

Specht, Jim, Tim Denham, James Goff, and John Edward Terrell. 2014. "Deconstructing the Lapita Cultural Complex in the Bismarck Archipelago." *Journal of Archaeological Research* 22:889–140.

Starr, S. Frederick. *Lost Enlightenment: Central Asia's Golden Age from the Arab Conquest to Tamerlane.* Princeton: Princeton University Press, 2013.

Steffy, J. Richard. 1985. "The Kyrenia Ship: an Interim Report on its Hull Construction." *American Journal of Archaeology* 89:71–101.

Stillborg, Ole, and Lena Holm. "Ceramics as a Novelty in Northern and Southern Sweden." *Ceramics Before Farming: The Dispersal of Pottery Among Prehistoric Eurasian Hunter-Gatherers.* Peter Jordan and Marek Zvelebil, eds. Walnut Creek, CA: Left Coast Press, 2009, pp. 319–345.

Storey, Alice A., J. M. Ramirez, D. Quiroz, D. V. Burley, D. J. Addison, R. Walter, A. J. Anderson, T. L. Hunt, J. S. Athens, L. Huynen, and E. A. Matisoo-Smith. 2007. "Radiocarbon and DNA Evidence for a pre-Columbian Introduction of Polynesian Chickens to Chile." *Proceedings of the National Academy of Science* 104:10335–10339.

Storey, Alice A., and Terry L. Jones. "Diffusionism in Archaeological Theory." *Polynesians in America: Pre-Columbian Contacts with the New World.* Terry L. Jones, Alice A. Storey, Elizabeth A. Matisoo-Smith, and José Miguel Ramírez-Aliaga, eds. Lanham, MD: AltaMira, 2011, pp. 7–24.

Straus, Lawrence Guy. 2000. "Solutrean Settlement of North America? A Review of Reality." *American Antiquity* 65(2):219–226.

Straus, Lawrence Guy, David J. Meltzer, and Ted Goebel. 2005. "Ice Age Atlantis? Exploring the Solutrean-Clovis 'Connection.'" *World Archaeology* 37(4): 507–532.

Summerhill, Stephen J., and John Alexander Williams. *Sinking Columbus: Contested History, Cultural Politics, and Mythmaking during the Quincentenary.* Gainesville: University Press of Florida, 2000.

Sutherland, Patricia D. "The Norse and Native North Americans." *Vikings: The North Atlantic Saga.* William W. Fitzhugh and Elisabeth I. Ward, eds. Washington, D.C.: Smithsonian Institution Press, 2000, pp. 238–247.

———. 2015. "Dorset-Norse Interactions in the Canadian Eastern Arctic." Revised online version of paper published 2000, at www.historymuseum.ca/ research-and-collections/research/resources-for- scholars/essays-1/archaeology-1/patricia-sutherland/dorset-norse-interactions-in-the-canadian-eastern-arctic/, accessed 1/27/2015.

Sawatzky, H. L., and W. H. Lehn. 1976. "The Arctic Mirage and the Early North Atlantic." *Science* 192:1300–1305.

Taché, Karine. 2004. "Explaining Vinette I Pottery Variability: The View from the Batiscan Site, Québec." *Canadian Journal of Archaeology* 29:165–233.

Taché, Karine, and Oliver E. Craig. 2015. "Cooperative Harvesting of Aquatic Resources and the Beginning of Pottery Production in North-eastern North America." *Antiquity* 89:177–190.doi:10.15184/aqy.2014.36

Terrell, John Edward, John P. Hart, Sibel Barut, Nicoletta Cellinese, Antonio Curet, Tim Denham, Chapurukha M. Kusimba, Kyle Latinis, Rahul Oka, Joel Palka, Mary E. D. Pohl, Kevin O. Pope, Patrick Ryan Williams, Helen Haines, and John E. Staller. 2003. "Domesticated Landscapes: The Subsistence Ecology of Plant and Animal Domestication." *Journal of Archaeological Method and Theory* 10(4):323–368.

Theunissen, Robert, Peter Grave, and Grahame Bailey. 2000. "Doubts on Diffusion: Challenging the Assumed Indian Origin of Iron Age Agate and Carnelian Beads in Southeast Asia." *World Archaeology* 32(1):84–105.

Thomas, David Hurst. *Refiguring Anthropology: First Principles of Probability and Statistics.* Prospect Heights, IL: Waveland, 1986.

Tolstoy, Paul. 1963. "Cultural Parallels Between Southeast Asia and Mesoamerica in the Manufacture of Bark Cloth." *Transactions of the New York Academy of Sciences* ser. II, vol. 25, no. 6:646–662.

———. 1991. "Paper Route: Were the Manufacture and Use of Bark Paper Introduced to Mesoamerica from Asia?" *Natural History* 100(6):6–14.

———. 2008. "Barkcloth, Polynesia and Cladistics: An Update." *Journal of the Polynesian Society* 117(1):15–57.

Tomasi, Luigi. "*Homo Viator*: From Pilgrimage to Religious Tourism via the Journey." *From Medieval Pilgrimage to Religious Tourism: the Social and Economic Economics of Piety.* William A. Swatos, Jr., and Luigi Tomasi, eds. Westport, CT: Praeger, 2002, pp. 1–24.

Tsien, Tsuen-Hsuin. *Paper and Printing. Science and Civilisation in China,* vol. 5, pt I. Cambridge: Cambridge University Press, 1985.

Turner, Derek. *Making Prehistory: Historical Science and the Scientific Realism Debate.* Cambridge: Cambridge University Press, 2007.

Uchida, Etsuo, Kojiro Tsuda, and Ichita Shimoda. 2014. "Construction Sequence of the Koh Ker Monuments in Cambodia Deduced from the Chemical Composition and Magnetic Susceptibility of its Laterites." *Heritage Science* 2:10 (unpaged online). Online at www.heritagesciencejournal.com/content/2/1/10, accessed 2/7/2015.

Usner, Daniel H. 2013. "'A Savage Feast They Made of It:' John Adams and the Paradoxical Origins of Federal Indian Policy." *Journal of the Early Republic* 33:607–641.

Van de Noort, Robert. *North Sea Archaeologies.* Oxford: Oxford University Press, 2011.

van Dijk, Toos. "Ritual Weaving, Tampan Pasisir." *Five Centuries of Indonesian Textiles.* Ruth Barnes and Mary Hunt Kahlenberg, eds. Munich: Delmonico Books-Prestel, 2010, p. 74.

VanStan, Ina. 1957. "A Peruvian Ikat from Pachacamac." *American Antiquity* 23(2):150–159.

Ward, Gerald W. R., ed. *The Grove Encyclopedia of Materials and Techniques in Art.* Oxford: Oxford University Press, 2008.

Wear, Gregory Douglas. 2012 "The Commodities Race: Greeks and Phoenicians in the North Atlantic, Beyond the Pillars Of Herakles and Melqart Respectively: Can Archaeology Help Resolve the Question Whether Greeks, Phoenicians, or Carthaginians Explored the North Atlantic Coast as Far as the British Isles Before the Age of Pytheas?" M.A. thesis, University of Leicester, UK

Weinberg, Albert K. *Manifest Destiny: A Study of Nationalist Expansionism in American History.* Baltimore: Johns Hopkins University Press, 1935.

Wen, Bo, Hui Li, Daru Lu, Xiufeng Song, Feng Zhang, Yungang He, Feng Li, Yang Gao, Xianyun Mao, Liang Zhang, Ji Qian, Jingze Tan, Jianzhong Jin, Wei Huang, Ranjan Deka, Bing Su, Ranajit Chakraborty, and Li Jin. 2004. "Genetic Evidence Supports Demic Diffusion of Han Culture." *Nature* 431:302–305.

Whiten, Andrew, and Alex Mesoudi. 2008. "Establishing an Experimental Science of Culture: Animal Social Diffusion Experiments." *Philosophical Transactions of the Royal Society of London B, Biological Sciences* 383(1509):3477–3488.

Wicke, Charles R. 1984. "The Mesoamerican Rabbit in the Moon: An Influence from Han China?" *Archaeoastronomy* 7(1–4):46–55.

Williams, Gwyn A. *Madoc: The Making of a Myth.* New York: Methuen, 1980.

Wilmshurst, Janet M., Terry L. Hunt, Carl P. Lipo, and Atholl J. Anderson. 2011. "High-precision Radiocarbon Dating Shows Recent and Rapid Initial Human Colonization of East Polynesia." *Proceedings of the National Academy of Sciences* 108(5):1815–1820.

Wylie, Alison. 2012. "Feminist Philosophy of Science: Standpoint Matters." *Proceedings and Addresses of the American Philosophical Association* 86(2):47–76.

———. 2013. "A Plurality of Pluralisms: Collaborative Practice in Archaeology." Online, accessed 6/28/2014. Lecture first presented Nov. 18, 2011, Rotman Institute of Philosophy, Western University, London, ON.

Ziegler, Martin, Margit H. Simon, Ian R. Hall, Stephen Barker, Chris Stringer, and Rainer Zahn. 2013. "Development of Middle Stone Age Innovation Linked to Rapid Climate Change." *Nature Communications* 4:1905 doi: 10.1038/ncomms.2897 (2013).

Zimmerman, Mario, Carlos Matos, Lilia Fernandez, and Rafael Cobos. 2015. "Games and Foodstuffs at Chichén Itzá: Relating Patolli and Starch Grains at Structure 2D6." Paper presented at Society for American Archaeology 80th annual meeting, San Francisco, CA, April 16, 2015.

# Index

**Alice Beck Kehoe** is emeritus professor of anthropology from Marquette University and Honorary Fellow at the University of Wisconsin–Milwaukee. A specialist on Native America, the history of archaeology, and archaeology of gender, she is the author of numerous articles and more than a dozen books on those subjects. Unafraid of controversial topics, she has participated in numerous debates in her fields, among them, the role of shamanism and the authenticity of the Kensington Runestone.

Made in the USA
Monee, IL
04 May 2024